KAMAL AL-SOLAYLEE

RETURN

Why We Go Back to Where We Come From

HarperCollins*Publishers*Ltd

Published by HarperCollins Publishers Ltd.

First edition

Portions of the introduction and coda were previously published,
in slightly different form, in 2019 in *Sharp* magazine.

HarperCollins books may be purchased for educational, business or
sales promotional use through our Special Markets Department.

HarperCollins Publishers Ltd
Bay Adelaide Centre, East Tower
22 Adelaide Street West, 41st Floor
Toronto, Ontario, Canada
M5H 4E3

www.harpercollins.ca

Library and Archives Canada Cataloguing in Publication

Title: Return : why we go back to where we come from / Kamal Al-Solaylee.
Names: Al-Solaylee, Kamal, author.
Description: First edition. | Includes bibliographical references.
Identifiers: Canadiana (print) 20210226951 | Canadiana (ebook) 20210228644
ISBN 9781443456159 (hardcover) | ISBN 9781443456166 (ebook)
Subjects: LCSH: Reverse culture shock. | LCSH: Return migration.
LCSH: Return migration—Psychological aspects. | LCSH: Return migrants.
LCSH: Return migrants—Psychology. LCSH: Cross-cultural orientation.
LCSH: Social adjustment. | LCSH: Repatriation. | LCSH: Al-Solaylee, Kamal.
Classification: LCC GN517 .A47 2021 | DDC 303.48/2—dc23

Printed and bound in the United States of America
LSC/H 9 8 7 6 5 4 3 2 1

To my niece Yousra in Sana'a
and my friend Dorene in Toronto,
for being my homelands

CONTENTS

Introduction

THE LANGUAGE OF HOME

W here do you want to be buried?"

Since my date and I were walking alongside Mount Pleasant Cemetery in midtown Toronto, the question didn't come as a complete surprise. Its morbidity threw me off, nonetheless. I had planned this to be a romantic post-dinner summer stroll. My dream list of questions included, but was not limited to, "Do you want to move in together?" and "Where would you like to go for our honeymoon?" He and I had just braved the crowds at a nearby ice cream shop and devoured double servings of pistachio and chocolate gelato in a scene worthy of a rom-com.

"Toronto," I replied.

Although I was born in Yemen, raised in Lebanon and Egypt, and educated in England, I had come to see Toronto (and Canada) as my homeland. I revelled in the kindness the city had shown me and the career opportunities it had afforded me. I dedicated my first book to it, for giving me what I'd been looking for: a home. In my second, I called it my "sanctuary," a good place to be brown. My love affair with Toronto started the moment I landed at its international airport, on April 20, 1996. Like many immigrants who have left oppressive regimes or escaped civil wars, I think of that arrival date as a second birthday, a parallel timeline in which life began just as I was about to turn thirty-two. I no longer entertained thoughts of a secret "unled life" because I finally had the one I wanted.

"I want to be buried in Sana'a, next to my grandparents," countered my date, who was born near Detroit to a Yemeni family and had spent most of his adult life in the United States. Although he was a natural-born citizen, he didn't think that America deserved his remains because he'd never felt connected to it as a country of birth or of residence.

I remember thinking how fortunate I was to claim a dot on the world map as mine—one place for my body to play, love, work, grow old and, when the time came, be put to rest. My date's words suggested an inner turmoil and un-belonging to which I was immune.

That exchange took place in August 2012. Barack Obama was three months away from winning his second term as president of the United States. I knew Donald Trump mostly as a C-list reality TV star who'd had cameos in *Home Alone* and on *Sex and the City*, and as the gauche multimillionaire behind the racist birther movement. Back then, very few journalists and university professors were willing to defend with a straight face the free speech rights of bigots or adopt a "both sides" approach to one race-based conflict after another—at least not publicly. American democracy had exhibited signs of weakness before, but it was yet to receive the near-fatal blow of the Trump White House. Canada, meanwhile, was in the advanced stages of a rigid conservative ideology known as Harperism, and Toronto's then mayor, Rob Ford, had emerged as a prototype of the populist standard-bearers to come. But these signs of an approaching right-wing backlash didn't strike me as significant then—or more likely, I chose to ignore them. Toronto was too much of a dream come true for me to see beyond my privileged place within it.

If I were asked the same question today, almost a decade later, I wouldn't know how to respond. I suspect I wouldn't be as definitive about Toronto as I once was. My date's remark, which seemed irrational and troubling then, strikes me now as reasonable and in a way prescient. Our relationship has ended, but the question lingers. So much has happened to recalibrate my affinities that I've been forced to rethink my resting place and where I call home. There's something broken in my sense of belonging, that "necessary mediation between an individual and society" that Adrienne Clarkson explores in her book *Belonging: The Paradox of Citizenship*. In belonging to ourselves and our societies, "we have the greatest possibility to live full lives," she writes. And yet, the longer I live in this city, the further I drift away from it and the less it feels like my place in the world.

I can't stop thinking about what it would be like to just go home—to return to the Arab world in general and Yemen in particular, and put my current life behind me.

Maybe I'm at a stage when a return to roots is natural and inevitable. Or perhaps the world that has sheltered me from the vagaries of the Middle East for three decades is becoming less hospitable and more vicious to people of darker skin tones and different religions. The idea that Western liberal democracies are declining in popularity among voters frightens me. That never bodes well for racial and religious minorities. In the past five years, I've experienced more incidents of racism on the streets of Toronto, at work, in interactions with friends and on mainstream and social media than I had in the previous twenty.

Every time I call my family in Yemen to check in on them, they in turn express concerns about my safety. Their local news programs feature a constant rotation of stories about attacks against Muslims in the West. "That's in America, not here," I lie to them. When a gunman stormed into an Islamic cultural centre in Quebec City in 2017, killing six and injuring nineteen, I all but fabricated a history of racism in English Canada and French Canada to set their minds at ease. "This sort of thing doesn't happen in English Canada, where I live," I said, fake news-ing my way through the rest of the call.

I knew then and I know now that I'm lying only to myself.

I draw a straight line between the insecurities and fears that animate my return thoughts and the United States during the Trump administration, where nationhood hinged on deporting and barring those people (Hispanics and Muslims, respectively) whom the president's base continues to regard as a threat to the majority status of whites. "You will not replace us," chanted neo-Nazis on the streets of Charlottesville, Virginia, during the infamous Unite the Right rally in 2017. With its roots in age-old antisemitism and the Great Replacement (*grand remplacement*) theory of French writer Renaud Camus—who believes

4

that white Europeans are being "reverse-colonized by black and brown immigrants" in an "extinction-level" event—that phrase has become a rallying cry for the right in North America.

The Great Replacement theory provides context for the rise of far-right Western European politicians who advocate closing borders and repatriating immigrants and refugees. Unofficially, it defined Trump's immigration policies and views on race. Although Trump himself is now firmly in history's dustbin as a president, the "legacy" of Trumpism will take years—decades, perhaps—to undo. You can hear and see its echoes in this country in popular Conservative slogans such as "Take Back Canada" and in the outsized influence of far-right strategists on provincial politics in Ontario and Alberta.

The pandemic revealed what I had known all along: even in a place like Toronto, which projects equality and racial tolerance as its brand, people of colour are often seen as lesser than, expendable. In the first wave of the pandemic, studies suggest, 83 percent of COVID cases were among racialized people, who are more likely to be employed as essential or frontline health workers and in precarious positions with no paid sick days. I strongly believe that the response to the pandemic, on both the municipal and the provincial level, would have been different had its victims not been mostly minorities and the elderly.

For now, and in one hell of a silver lining, the expression "go back to where you come from" no longer sounds to me like a racist chant or a threat. It's something that millions of people have done and will continue to do, by choice or as a last resort. I feel an urge to join them and to be part of an ongoing, multi-destination, multi-ethnic narrative about return to roots.

Return encompasses and transcends race, geography and history.

Ultimately, it was a humanitarian crisis—described by the United Nations as the world's largest—that crystallized the pull of homeland for me. This book wouldn't exist had I not been preoccupied with the tragedy unfolding in Yemen, a country I couldn't wait to leave in my twenties and now fantasize about returning to in my fifties. Since March 2015, a Saudi Arabia–led coalition has waged a war to restore Yemen's legitimate, internationally recognized government, which was deposed by Iran-supported Houthi rebels in the fall of 2014. It's a quagmire of foreign intervention on a level with Iraq and Afghanistan. According to a 2020 report from the United Nations, an estimated 233,000 Yemenis have died since 2015, including 131,000 from indirect causes (lack of food, health services and infrastructure). Nearly twenty-four million of a population of just under thirty million are considered people in need.

Yemen is where I was born (the port city of Aden), and where most of my siblings and extended family still live (the capital, Sana'a). Cholera, famine, water and electricity shortages, floods and more than a year of COVID-19—in addition to and exacerbated by the war—have left Yemenis reeling as the world watched, helplessly, indifferently.

I hear stories from family and friends about life in Yemen, and I wonder how any nation can cope with so many problems simultaneously. In some years, the inflation rate has surpassed 30 percent, putting food and shelter beyond the reach of millions. I watch news reports of dying and starving children on social media. The images crush my spirit, but I can't look away. I'm outraged and sad in ways that go beyond humanitarianism or a sense of duty to help the less fortunate. Among those suffering are members of my immediate family and people with whom I share blood, a language and a faith.

The biggest connection, however, remains our shared homeland—soil, seas, streets, structures, mountains, trees, smells and sounds—even if I've been away from the country for decades.

A house on a hill has been fuelling my own return fantasy for several years now.

* * *

Ever since I was a child, my exiled family has talked about a dilapidated old house on the outskirts of Aden. My father built *beit el gabal*, or the mountain house, for his parents in the early 1950s to save his marriage. My grandparents lived with their first-born son, as was the custom then, but they tormented my mother with their nagging and their interference in how she raised her children. By sending his parents to live in the new house, my father, ever the dutiful son, could keep them nearby but away from my mother.

The two-bedroom house and the mostly arid land around it have been in my family's possession ever since, despite a few decades of communism, when the government of what was then South Yemen confiscated private properties, all but destroying my father's real estate business. My surviving nine siblings and I now own it jointly.

I've never set foot in that house, but I recall seeing it from a distance when I last visited Aden, in the spring of 1992, after four years of living in England. "Who would want to live there?" the twenty-seven-year-old me asked my uncle, who had taken me on a guided tour of my birthplace. I felt the sting of his disappointment as he lectured me on my indifference to family history and our homeland. "Millions dream of a house like this," he chided. I wasn't sold on his argument back then. I just wanted to go back to my student residence in leafy Nottingham.

Over the past decade, my brothers and sisters have been restoring the house and decorating it with old furniture from various households. Because of its elevation, it provides a reprieve from Aden's punishing heat in the spring and summer. It's not connected to the local sewage system, such as that is, but it's the closest we come to owning a summer home. The mountain house conjures Aden—the city where I was born, where my late mother and father got married and lived for twenty-two years before we all fled the post-independence turbulence of 1967. It's Aden, it's always Aden, that I dream of returning to. It's not Sana'a, where I lived as an adult for two years in the 1980s. It's not Cairo, my home for fifteen years and my reference point for the Arab world. It's Aden, the former British colony where my family's story began, that keeps calling me back.

When I met up with my sister Raga'a in Cairo in 2019, while working on this book, I drove her to distraction with my non-stop questions about the mountain house. I stared at pictures on her mobile phone and mentally redecorated the space with furniture I'd bought specially for it. No more mismatched sofas and chairs. Raga'a couldn't understand why someone who lives in Toronto—a place as materially far from her Sana'a base as Earth is from Saturn—would want to revisit such a rundown spot. Let alone live in it. "You will not be able to handle the heat in the summer," she warned me, "or the smell of garbage that stays uncollected for days."

I take her point but offer my own.

I have an uncontrollable desire to "return" to the house, to live in it for however long I can. The logistics, I'll deal with later. I want to feel close to my beginnings; to my great-grandmothers, who died before I was born; to the memory of aunts and uncles, now all gone, whose faces stare at me from family photos. And closer still to my late mother, who was grateful to see her in-laws banished there from her domestic kingdom. I wonder what she would have made of her favourite son living there.

The mountain house was the place I longed to escape to when the pandemic hit in the spring of 2020 and thoughts of dying and burial places became more than passing morbidity. The unnamed heroine of Daphne du Maurier's *Rebecca* dreamed of going back to Manderley; I dreamed of a mountain house in Aden.

When I was a theatre critic, I often poked fun at the return stories so beloved by Black, brown and East Asian artists in Toronto. These torn-between-two-cultures stories were popular with theatre companies, and arts councils eagerly funded them as part of a push for diversity and inclusion. I owe *some* of them an apology. (Many were spectacularly awful.) I get it now, even if my experience, so late in life, differs from that of the characters in these stories. Fiction repeats the pattern. In *Curry: Eating, Reading, and Race*, Naben Ruthnum calls the South Asian "I miss the homeland" novels "currybooks." These narratives, he writes, "typically detail a wrenching sense of being in two worlds at once, torn between the traditions of the East and the liberating, if often unrewarding, freedoms of the West . . . Most often we're looking at a displaced South Asian character in the U.K., North America, or Western Europe, searching for place, belonging, and an outer and inner shape to her identity."

I keep thinking of a scene from the film *Bittersweet*, a 2010 Egyptian social comedy in which Masry, the lead character, returns to Cairo to reconnect with his past after more than two decades in the United States. Masry tells an old family friend that his father's last wish was to spend his final days in the city. The friend responds with what I suspect millions of Egyptians think of when they encounter someone like Masry (or me): "These people are strange. They migrate, waste their lives abroad, and at the end of the day, they say, 'I want to go home and be buried there.' As if the country is a big cemetery."

Have I become the cultural cliché that I so often dismissed, and that Egyptian filmmakers view as "strange"? I don't know why it has taken me so long to think of my own return, and I don't know if these thoughts represent a natural progression, a delusion—or a midlife crisis. All I know is that for the past five years or so, I've been thinking of return, my own and other people's.

As I write these words in late 2020, there seems to be no end to the fighting and suffering in Yemen. Is my own homeland return just a dream, or worse, an inconvenience, given what the country is going through? Yemen and my family do not need the return of this native—now a Canadian citizen whose adopted country is selling armoured vehicles and other weapons to the Saudis with one face and donating (negligible) aid with the other. And if I do return, how do I make sense of my privileges, from money to the simple fact that I can leave the country whenever I want? I just have to wave my Canadian passport. How will I express what I feel to the people I want to share this homeland with when my Arabic has atrophied over the years? I've become so conscious of the effort it takes to sustain any serious conversation in Arabic that I often feel like a stranger—and a tongue-tied one at that—in my own community.

Arabic was my birthright. How did I squander it?

This decline had been happening for a number of years, but a short visit to Muscat in 2014 confirmed it, and Ameen, the taxi driver I'd hired, forced me to do something about it.

* * *

Ameen's English was too limited for someone whose job was to ferry tourists and visiting businesspeople to landmarks or government buildings. By then, my Arabic had deteriorated to the point where simple instructions like "Take me to the night market" or "Pick me up in an hour" required feats of word-scouting. I tried to recall moments from childhood when I might have heard my parents say something similar. As my frustration rose, I asked Ameen point-blank, in English, why on earth he'd chosen to work in tourism. He didn't respond and probably didn't understand, but my outburst helped me realize that I was trying to blame him for something I had brought on myself.

I had flown into Muscat, capital of the Sultanate of Oman, for a break after interviewing South Asian construction workers in Dubai for about ten days, during which I barely uttered a word of Arabic. The workers I'd encountered were mostly foreign labourers who spoke other languages (Urdu, Hindi, Tagalog) and used English as a lingua franca. I'd assumed Oman would be the same. But in restaurants, street markets and even some parts of the international airport in Muscat, locals spoke poor English or none at all, forcing me to resort to my dwindling Arabic.

I could tell that what came out of my mouth must have sounded like broken Arabic to Ameen and others who often looked a lot like me. I was asked if I were an Arab Israeli or a Pakistani—the former with suspicion, the latter dismissively. I felt like a stranger, an interloper among my tribe. I dared not tell anyone I was born in Yemen, the country that shares a western border with Oman. When asked, I said I was of Egyptian "background," since that country's Arabic was (and still is) the dialect I understand and speak best.

My dereliction of Arabic was a conscious move and part of a journey of reinvention I embarked on in my late teens. The Quran, the holy book of the Muslim faith, is written in Arabic. As I was coming out as a gay man in the early 1980s and reading up on sexual liberation, I needed distance from both the religion and its official text, which, I felt, vilified my desires. English became more than a second language; it drew a personalized road map to freedom, dignity and sex.

I didn't see being gay as an experience that could unfold in Arabic. The language lacked the vocabulary and the textual resources to help me find out who I was, who I chose to love or sleep with. If anything, it mobilized hate and discrimination against homosexuality, which was portrayed in literature and popular arts as a sin or a Western affliction. The only Arabic words for it while I was growing up were *shaz*, which meant abnormal, and *looty*, a reference to Abraham's nephew Lot, of Sodom and Gomorrah.

English, on the other hand, had it all figured out. What could be lovelier than the word "gay" to describe how I felt about myself? Happiness and a *joie de vivre* lie at its roots. And what was more aspirational than the gay liberation movement, by then more than a decade in progress? Not even the emergence of AIDS at around the same time could dull my interest in English as a gay language. As journalists began to write about the connection between gay men and what was then a deadly disease, I gained access to more reading material about homosexuality than I ever could have dreamed of in Cairo of the early to mid-1980s. A decade later, several LGBTQ rights activists in the Middle East would point out that their work in AIDS prevention had given them an opportunity to broach issues like sexual rights and support for the queer community. The more neutral-sounding word *methly*, meaning "same" and used to refer to gay men in particular, grew out of this new health-focused context.

When I was about nineteen, I made it a point to stop reading or listening to Arabic, to speak it only when necessary and to upgrade English from second to first language—a process that became more immersive when I moved to England at twenty-four to study literature and eventually earn a PhD in Victorian fiction. Such was my complete adoption of English that I turned down suggestions from potential doctoral supervisors that I work on "colonial" fiction—Richard Burton's translation of *Arabian Nights* or Lawrence Durrell's *Alexandria Quartet*, among others—and instead pursued such authors as Charles Dickens and Wilkie Collins, who, I thought, were more "purely" English. Arabic words and settings meant contamination, a corruption of my resolve to exile myself from my native tongue and homeland.

All along, I picked up, quite naturally and through exposure to mostly native speakers, a refined English accent, which made me sound if not posh, then at least educated and middle class in a country defined by class politics and resentments. (I still don't know what to think of the comparison a former professor once made to Eliza Doolittle's transformation from a cockney flower girl to a refined society lady.) With each graduate seminar, dinner party or visit to a gay club, I drifted further away from the world of my mother, an illiterate shepherdess, and my father, a self-made businessman and Anglophile whose own command of English had deteriorated once he stopped using it for work. His fate would not be mine.

I rewired my brain to think, speak and write in English, burying Arabic deep in the recesses of my brain. I thought of my plans not as an artifice or a makeover, but as a means of countervailing my birth identity and establishing a real, new self. This was the me I deserved. There could be no sexual liberation if the language that oppressed me still lived within me and came out of my mouth. I took classes in German and Spanish to further suppress my native tongue. "Languages become a home," Canadian author Jessica J. Lee writes in *Two Trees Make a Forest*, a memoir of her own return journey to Taiwan. My home was English.

Two more decades in Canada followed, and before I realized it, my Arabic had deteriorated to the point where talking to my own siblings about anything beyond their general welfare became a trial. Before every call, I'd brace myself for the awkwardness that inevitably followed. I tried—I always do— but my vocabulary couldn't sustain a deep conversation about their emotional well-being, their frustrations, dreams, sorrows. I never shared any of mine.

When the war in Yemen began in 2015—forcing us to discuss such subjects as staying alive, claiming refugee status in Egypt, sheltering from airstrikes or selling family assets to survive financially—my damaged Arabic probably made things worse. Who needs a tortured phone conversation with a sibling living in Canada when there's so much suffering in their immediate world?

I abandoned my family physically by studying in England and then immigrating to Canada, and psychologically by willing away the native tongue that once bound us. When they speak of it, my siblings view my transition into English as a combination of self-loathing and a rebellion that has outlasted my younger years. My sister Hoda reads the Quran several times a year, a ritual she has maintained for almost two decades now. Imagine her disappointment when I told her I didn't have a copy in my Toronto apartment and probably couldn't read it even if I did. (She said she'd pray for me.)

Linguists refer to the phenomenon of losing native tongues as first language attrition (FLA). It's a process that happens when people are isolated from other speakers of their native language or when another language dominates. The term "mother tongue" has always implied an umbilical connection to the language you first learn at home—a fixed identity based on what you heard the most as an infant. In a world where nearly 272 million people do not live in their country of birth and mostly function in a second language, studies of FLA are testing what we know about how we acquire, use and lose what is most native to us.

This body of research offers a valuable frame of reference for those of us experiencing FLA. There's a sense of relief in learning that our "condition" has a name—that what I'd come to regard as a personal and private shift is being studied by linguists and psychologists. But it offers little comfort to my troubled soul and does little to diminish my sense of loss. In my mind, my language dilemma has always been a drama in which I was a leading man and my siblings the supporting cast. But it feels more and more like a one-person show, a one-sided expression of longing and memory. For me, there can be no physical return without a linguistic one.

* * *

For the past four years, I've been working toward an understanding of what return—to a homeland, to a native tongue, to one's roots—means, to me and to others.

The following pages represent my attempt to locate my longing for home in the context of return stories taking place around the world. My goal is to witness, record and demystify this desire. The stories are set in the present but draw on decades—centuries, even—of migration, mobility and dislocation. Every place I visited revealed a return narrative uniquely influenced by larger historical movements such as imperialism, slavery, fascism, sectarian violence and ethno-nationalism. Sometimes a return spans continents; at others it traverses a much shorter distance.

The people I talked to made me feel nostalgic, envious, relieved and conflicted about what a return can or should be. I asked questions. I looked for signs. I waited for a revelation. I wanted to know what it felt like not just to return home, but to leave behind a place that had been a safe haven for so long. I kept thinking about my own attachment to Toronto and Canada, strained as it may be at times. How much will I miss these places? Will my longing for my life in Canada undermine my homeward-bound dreams? I craved words of encouragement to guide me, even when I knew that as a gay man returning to the Arab world, I might have to confront a legacy of violence and homophobia—and even the prospect of death. There's something deeply rational *and* inherently irrational about returns, and their essence lies in that friction between the two.

I wanted to know what's it like to "go home," or as the late cultural critic Stuart Hall put it, to experience "the endless desire to return to 'lost origins,' to be one again with the mother, to go back to the beginning." That desire burned within me even when the people and places I visited suggested that a homeland return marked not the end of a journey but the start of a new and complex one.

In Jamaica, deportees face a stigma when they are sent back to their homeland from the United Kingdom or the United States, whether for visa violations or more serious crimes. To be sent home means they haven't been financially successful in their adopted countries. At the same time, voluntary returnees from the same places who dream of retirement on the island after decades of work are often targeted, and sometimes killed, for the very wealth they're perceived to bring with them.

A generation of Taiwanese born or raised in the United States and Canada are leaving behind their relatively sheltered family homes in suburban Montreal or Minneapolis to return to the land their parents left behind, always with the express goal of creating a better life for their offspring. Young men in particular see Taipei as a land of opportunity, a wild, wild East in a world that was still recovering from the Great Recession when it started to feel the economic rupture of the COVID-19 pandemic. This coming-home story unfolds even as mainland China continues to regard the entire island (officially known as the Republic of China) as a breakaway province that will be returned to the motherland, by force if necessary.

Businesses, politicians and government bodies in Belfast work hard to facilitate a physical and emotional connection between millions of Irish Americans and a city that not long ago was the setting of massacres and bloody confrontations over the fate of Northern Ireland. The businesspeople are arriving, but will peace depart? Brexit brought its share of troubles to Belfast homeland returns, as the possibility of a hard border between the Republic of Ireland and Northern Ireland threatened to derail more than two decades of peaceful crossings and the free flow of people and goods.

In the Basque region of Spain, the terrorist organization ETA may have given up its arms and campaigns of violence, but the centuries-long dream of an independent homeland remains both alive and elusive. Fuelled by the return of people with ancestral ties and threatened by the arrival of thousands of immigrants from North Africa and beyond (and the inevitable ethnonationalist backlash), this dream offers overlapping insights into the return of diasporic communities and the exclusion of newer racialized ones.

In Ghana, return is part marketing scheme, part continuation of a postcolonial, pan-African vision. The successful Year of Return campaign in 2019 marked the four hundredth anniversary of the first slave ship to reach North America by encouraging global Black citizens to "return" to Africa through Ghana. Some of the Canadian and American Black men and women I spoke to returned to Ghana because they had direct ancestral ties to the country. Others saw Africa at large as their long-lost motherland, and Ghana as a gateway to a deeper exploration of their roots—a "back to Africa" dream that has been kept alive for more than two centuries through the stories of returning freed slaves and then as part of the civil rights movement of the 1960s.

In the Middle East, Palestinian refugees' right of return to their home villages and towns clashes with what Israel now sees mostly as the homeland of the Jewish people. Official policies such as the Israeli Law of Return and the religious duty to make aliyah, or immigrate to Israel from the diaspora, are the foundations on which the country is built. Israelis and Palestinians share the same land but two competing notions of return.

The forced and voluntary returns of people and lands, the repatriation and resettlement of the young and old, the erasure and resurgence of languages—all charted different courses but often offered one startling point of departure: for some to feel at home, others have to return to theirs. Returns reveal the realities of the homelands we go back to *and* the countries we leave behind.

Tucked among all these stories, you'll find fragments of mine. My story can't live apart from them. It lives naturally next to some and in opposition to others. But it's just one of the many return journeys taking place in the world today.

PART I

Chapter 1

THE AGE OF RETURN. MAYBE

In February 2020, Global Affairs Canada warned Canadians living or vacationing abroad that flight cancellations and local restrictions might leave them stranded for longer than they had initially anticipated or budgeted for. When the World Health Organization declared the coronavirus outbreak a pandemic on March 11, Canadians received a more urgent message from Global Affairs: "Find out what commercial options are still available to return to Canada. Consider returning to Canada earlier than planned if these options are becoming more limited."

And so began the largest repatriation effort in modern Canadian history. Between March 14 and 20, about 959,000 Canadian citizens and 43,890 permanent residents returned to Canada after Prime Minister Justin Trudeau "made a public plea for their quick return," the *Toronto Star* reported, citing figures provided by the Canada Border Services Agency. Of those, an estimated

449,000 crossed the Canada–US border by land and about 553,000 flew home.

Almost every employee of Global Affairs Canada turned into a travel agent with one task in mind: bring Canadians home. "Staffers who used to write ministerial briefing notes are now booking hotels, buses and flights," a CBC report from March suggested. Global Affairs doesn't break down travellers by category, but a look at news reports and social media posts from the period paints a picture of those who found themselves stranded. Some were stuck abroad while on vacation or visiting family. Snowbirds were spending the winter in sunny climates and holiday spots. Many had been working abroad, while others divided their time between two homelands.

The largest number of repatriated Canadians came from India, which shut down its airspace on March 22. Stories of Canadians trying to come home from South Korea, Lebanon, Somalia and the Philippines, among other places, also made headlines. Many others gave up trying to catch one of the government's repatriation flights and decided to wait for travel restrictions to lift in host countries. In a statement in late March, a Global Affairs spokesperson acknowledged that "it will not be possible to ensure the return of all Canadians who wish to come home." Some countries offered Canadians seats on their national carriers, while Qatar Airways and Ethiopian Airlines shuttled Canadians from different airports in South Asia and Africa, respectively.

To its credit, the Liberal government made no distinction between racialized Canadians who had returned to their home countries and their compatriots who were temporarily working or living abroad (think of the mostly white English teachers in South Korea, Taiwan or the United Arab Emirates, for example). Contrast this with the grudging effort of Stephen Harper's Conservative government to repatriate Canadians of Lebanese origin following the conflict between Israel and Hezbollah in the summer of 2006. At an estimated cost of $85 million, the operation brought home about fifteen thousand Lebanese Canadians out of roughly fifty thousand citizens living in the country. The operation gave rise to the term "Canadians of convenience," coined by Conservative MP Garth Turner, and even some Liberal MPs talked about the burden to taxpayers.

While many other countries called their citizens back in early 2020, perhaps the most dramatic illustration of a mass homecoming took place not across international borders but within a single country. When India announced its lockdown on March 24, thousands of daily-wage migrant workers who had left their villages to seek opportunities in the country's booming urban economies found themselves abandoned by their employers and the country at large. The lockdown affected factories, offices, schools and domestic and international travel routes. Work dried up instantly. Trains and buses were cancelled. The World Bank estimates that at least 40 million of India's 130 million migrant labourers experienced the worst of the pandemic's economic impact in its first few weeks.

The vast majority of those workers began the long walk home, covering hundreds and thousands of miles—many with children and spouses in tow. Some died on the road. Others arrived at their destinations traumatized, only to discover that remote villages aren't immune to the coronavirus. Thousands more travelled on emergency trains provided by the government. Dubbed the Shramik Specials (after the Indian word for "labourers"), these trains became contagion zones and spread the virus to different parts of the country. Despite government promises to screen passengers before boarding, few were tested. According to a report in the *New York Times* in late 2020, the trains "disgorged passengers into distant villages, in regions that before had few if any coronavirus cases." India is, as I write this, home to the second-largest number of coronavirus cases after the United States.

This home-return journey became the biggest mass movement in India probably since Partition in 1947, when the former jewel in the British Crown was divided into a Hindu-majority India and a Muslim-majority Pakistan. More than one in ten of the country's 1.3 billion people are believed to be migrant workers earning, on average, just six US dollars a day. Those who survive the virus may opt to stay away from Delhi or Mumbai, putting their own livelihoods and India's economic recovery on the line.

The pandemic has left a mark on every aspect of modern life, but it shone a light and galvanized thinking on what homeland returns look like and what they mean in global and regional contexts.

* * *

Immigrants, no matter our origins and skin tones, share a common delusion: we think we take pieces of our homelands with us and leave parts of ourselves behind whenever we choose or are forced to resettle elsewhere. The truth is that those homelands, lodged in our memories, in our brains and in our DNA, have been loosening and tightening their grip on us at will. Homelands dictate when we leave and predict when we return. Author Elif Shafak, a Turk by birth and a Brit by citizenship, describes homelands as castles made of glass. "It is easy to forget they are there . . . and go on with your life, your little ambitions and important plans, but at the slightest contact the shards will remind you of their presence. They will cut you deep."

History, politics, critical theory, literature and social sciences have given us multiple, even definitive, narratives and theories about why people leave their homelands. Returns, however, remain underexplored.

In an influential study of diasporas, globalization scholar Robin Cohen identifies a return movement as an essential step in establishing international communities organized around a shared national or ethnic origin. There's no migration without return. Still, it's the outward journey that takes precedence when researchers document global movements. Within the burgeoning field of diaspora and migration studies, return is a *relatively* new addition.

In *Return Migration: Journey of Hope or Despair?*, immigration researcher Russell King called return "the great unwritten chapter in the history of migration." In the essay collection *Homecomings: Unsettling Paths of Return*, anthropologist Anders H. Stefansson writes that for the better part of the twentieth century, "returns of immigrants, refugees, and exiles were hardly noticed by scholars, or at least not seen as phenomena of much academic interest." Terms like "understudied," "conspicuously absent" and "little understood" regularly appeared whenever researchers broached the subject of return migration at the dawn of the twenty-first century. (For the most part, I followed the more inclusive use of "migration" and "migrant" in this literature to refer to the numerous acts of leaving, and returning to, the homeland.)

In early 2020, at a symposium in Toronto hosted by Anna Triandafyllidou, Ryerson University's Canada Excellence Research Chair (CERC) in Migration and Integration, I asserted that returns suggest defeat, failure and exhaustion, while migrations reinforce agency, action and resilience. Perhaps this explains why the latter receives so much attention from scholars. Journalists, I explained, basing my viewpoint on personal experience, get all excited (or panicked) when refugees arrive but drop the story when host governments give the displaced incentives to return home. In 2020, for example, the European Union unveiled a voluntary return program designed to reduce the number of migrants in overcrowded Greek refugee camps. Each migrant who agreed to go back to his or her home country would receive €2,000 (or about C$3,000). I've always felt that these stories receive little coverage compared to ones about the dangers of living in those same camps.

I realize now, having spent more than a year reading and re-reading studies of return migration and another year reporting on the ground, that I may have assigned a simplistic designation to what Stefansson refers to as the "complex and contested" nature of returns. Perhaps I've put too much emphasis on individual choices and not enough on the geopolitical forces undergirding most returns. Returns span continents, civilizations, races and conflicts. Each return story belongs to the person making the homeward journey, but it's rarely detached from its historical moment.

Returns, I've come to realize, are complicated because they challenge much of what we think we know about migration patterns and our entrenched notions of identity, home, hybridity, globalization and multiculturalism, among other Big Subjects. They upend and show the cracks in many popular stories that migrants and governments like to tell about themselves.

Many liberals in the Western world think of immigration as a uni-directional process. Individuals or families leave their country of birth or an intermediate setting to find a permanent home in the United States, Canada, Australia or New Zealand, to name four of the most popular destinations for global migration. The host country benefits materially from the newcomers' labour and brain power, and reputationally as a land of opportunities and new beginnings.

The safe-harbour narrative gains additional power when the new arrivals are refugees fleeing intolerable conditions, as suggested by the non-stop shoulder-patting that Canada engaged in when it opened its doors to thousands of Syrian refugees. Total number admitted to Canada between 2015 to 2017? Just over forty thousand refugees. By comparison, Germany had taken in more than five hundred thousand by 2018. When some of these same people later decide to go back to where they came from, migration observers begin to question the benevolent role of the host country. Suddenly, the country that opened its doors is perceived as hostile, literally and emotionally cold. Whenever I've asked Canadians who returned to their homelands what they remembered most about their time in this country, they cited racism, followed closely by inhospitable winters.

By their very nature, returnees seek a reconnection to a past life, a former identity marked more often than not by a single language or a single cultural frame of reference. We go back to what we know, including our native tongues. This process of reclaiming a homogenous existence runs counter to multiculturalism on a societal level and hybridity on an individual level. Aren't we supposed to be complex, hybrid creatures containing multitudes? What about the concept of multiple belongings promoted by such internationally successful authors as Elif Shafak and Zadie Smith? On paper, where it mostly lives, this concept sounds ideal. "Multiple belongings are nurtured by cultural encounters but they are not only the preserve of people who travel," writes Shafak. "It is an attitude, a way of thinking, rather than the number of stamps on your passport. It is about thinking of yourself, and your fellow human beings, in more fluid terms than solid categories."

I wouldn't go as far as to suggest that returns imply a repudiation of a complex view of identity or of globalization—it's globalization that has allowed the many people you'll meet in this book, me included, to come and go, to cross borders and cultures—but they force us to think of movement in multi-directional ways. Some returnees find that the life they thought they would have back home is a fantasy, so they make their way back to the host country. Homeland returns remain unpredictable, in part because despite their historical contexts, they don't have the clear road maps and narratives that outward migrations enjoy.

Above all, returns question what we think we know about

homes and homelands, and the connections between the two. Indeed, some researchers assert that returns have proven thorny because of the contested nature of homelands themselves. I suggest as much in the chapters about Northern Ireland, the Basque region, Taiwan, and Israel and the Palestinian territories (the mother of all motherland battles). A return gives people licence to redraw boundaries and reclaim spaces that were once denied or lost to them. A home, a physical structure that literally stands for their presence, is an essential part of their plan to turn a homecoming fantasy into a reality. The mountain house in Aden is a physical manifestation of desires, emotions and dreams that I've been harbouring for years now.

As anthropologist Fran Markowitz writes in her essay *Homecomings*, "a home, a homeland, and a home in the homeland" remain salient cultural imperatives. Home is "security, comfort, certainty, the people who 'have to take you in' while understanding that the 'have to' is not a matter of externally imposed law but an automatic response to similitude." It's not so much the return that baffles some of us as the land, or the piece of property, on which it plays out. Although the idealization of a homeland feeds into some dangerously nationalist notions about sovereignty and borders—the Nazi slogan *Blut und Boden*, or "blood and soil," connects racial purity with the land in essentialist ways—return helps soften the hard edges of nationalism because the people engaged in it slip in and out of state-sanctioned definitions of citizenship and residence. It brings dual consciousness to states where a single story has dominated for too long.

So yes, I was wrong in once thinking that returns suggest

defeat or weakness. I certainly don't think of my own story in such terms. In her essay, Markowitz cites migration scholar R. Radhakrishnan, who stresses that return is a "matter of political choice by people on behalf of their own authenticity." There is nothing "regressive or atavistic about people revisiting the past with the intention of reclaiming it." I'm convinced that my ideas of return stem from a desire to reclaim the Arabic language and my cultural fluency. Return makes it possible to regain a language and a lost sense of place.

While the desire to reconnect with one's roots is elemental and for the most part universal—people who lack a homeland founding myth, such as the Roma and various nomadic tribes, are notable exceptions—the frequency and intensity of that desire have been aided by technological advances in the first two decades of this century. (Perhaps this explains why studies of return picked up speed around the same time.)

The internet and social media have given people around the world the means to research family trees and locate long-lost relatives. Even in Yemen, where internet access is spotty and costly, my nephews and nieces have become experts at establishing contact with people around the world who share our relatively rare last name. Sometimes they even find a blood relation going back to our great-great-grandparents.

The physical distance between the homeland and the adopted home also seems to vanish with easy access to news, music, TV programs, films and other cultural traditions that were left behind. The "nost" in "nostalgia" derives from the Greek word for homecoming while the "algia" means "pain" or "ache" and comes from the New Latin. Swiss physician Johannes Hofer coined the term in the late seventeenth century to refer to patients, mostly soldiers, who suffered from a homesickness so acute, he prescribed a return trip to their place of origin. The internet has turned nostalgia into a way of life for many members of diasporic communities. Is there a song that you danced to in the 1950s or 1960s in Sri Lanka or Argentina or Poland or Senegal and thought you'd never hear again? Well, someone, somewhere has just uploaded it to YouTube. If you can't travel back physically, you can at least travel back in time. YouTube has turned into a global warehouse of homeland and diasporic memories.

In *Rites of Return: Diaspora Poetics and the Politics of Memory*, Marianne Hirsch and Nancy K. Miller suggest that advances in genetic testing and the decoding of the human genome in 2000 "seemed to offer a reliable way to decipher difference through the language of genes." Both genetic ancestry tests (GATs) and digital communications, they add, "enable, and underwrite, the quest and feed nostalgic fantasies about homecoming."

For a small fee, companies will run a DNA test that, they claim, will uncover your ethnic mix and connect you with your ancestry. For some participants, this is a bit of harmless fun—part of a natural human instinct to discover what makes us unique. Genealogy has turned into an entertainment cottage industry with such programs as *Who Do You Think You Are?* on TLC and *Finding Your Roots* on PBS, proving that watching celebrities discover their roots has both low- and high-brow appeal.

But for a rising number of white supremacists in the United States, genetic ancestry tests have become a way of demonstrating racial purity (defined as being of non-Jewish, white, wholly

European descent). Prospective members of the online forum Stormfront who posted genetic analyses showing traces of African, Native American or Middle Eastern blood were sometimes shamed by older posters, but they were also told by others not to put too much credence into what they believe to be faulty science. In a 2019 analysis of six hundred posts on the forum, published in the *Social Studies of Science* journal, researchers Aaron Panofsky and Joan Donovan found that to refute evidence of non-white ancestry, most posters engage in so-called repair strategies—including anti-scientific, counter-knowledge attacks on GATs.

What fascinates me about this episode is how science continues to be used extremely selectively in matters of racial identity and origins. As Panofsky and Donovan suggest, white nationalism's rejection of GATs is a "citizen science movement" that challenges any positive views of the democratization of science.

* * *

The twentieth century, marked as it was by the upheavals of two world wars and the political divisions that followed the emergence of the United States and the former Soviet Union as the two superpowers, was the age of great migration. Will the twenty-first century turn into the age of return, especially if advances in technology and genomic testing continue at their current pace?

I believe so, but with some caveats.

The return path may be getting clearer, or at least more accessible, thanks to technology, but it faces serious challenges from climate change and, if epidemiologists' readings of COVID-19 are accurate, the possibility of more pandemics. In many ways, the two are related.

Climate change will likely force more people from the Global South to seek refuge in the northern hemisphere to escape rising water levels and scorching temperatures. The most conservative studies put the probable number of climate refugees at eighty to one hundred million by the end of the century. The house in the homelands that many returnees dream of—including the mountain house in Aden—may not survive the floods, heat or fires that are now the new normal. People born in the Middle East or South Asia may learn to be grateful for Canadian winters after all. (Complaining about winter is my personal brand.)

We also face the possibility that global pandemics will become a once-in-a-decade instead of once-in-a-century event. As deforestation continues and humans encroach on spaces that were once the habitat of wild animals, we'll face more zoonotic viruses to which we have no immunity, resulting in more infections. While some may be contained at a local level, others likely will spread to create pandemics like the current one. If and when that happens, we can't always assume that governments will mount as robust a repatriation effort as the one in 2020. I know I'm re-examining my own return plan in light of COVID-19. Countries like Canada with universal healthcare and capable public health may see fewer people leaving for their homelands.

The previous two paragraphs come from my own reading of current and future threats to humanity, and while based on current research and trends, they are still speculative. Return, as a phenomenon, encompasses more than just people, however.

In the natural world, natal homing refers to the process by which certain marine animals make their way home to reproduce and, inevitably, end their life cycles. The list includes certain species of bluefin tuna, sea turtles and, of course, salmon, whose return is a highly anticipated annual event and even a tourist attraction, particularly in British Columbia.

According to the US Geological Survey, marine animals that return to their natal homes by and large rely on geomagnetic maps that are imprinted onto their brains. Bluefin tuna spend much of their lives in the ocean. However, data shows that almost 96 percent of electronically tagged yearlings return to the Mediterranean to spawn. For tagged bluefin tuna that return to their natal shores in the Gulf of Mexico, the number is a staggering 99.3 percent.

Young salmon spend the early parts of their life cycle (which lasts from five to seven years) in the streams where they hatched. They then move to salt water and spend four or five years in the oceans. When they've reached sexual maturity, they return to the streams where they were born to spawn. Marine biologists suggest that salmon navigate their return voyage by using the Earth's magnetic field, the same way humans rely on a compass. Another theory posits that salmon build a "smell-memory bank" when they migrate to facilitate their eventual homeward-bound trip. Those that make it back to their natal streams begin laying eggs, and when "they're spent," as a Vancouver Island website explains it, "their carcasses lie rotting along the riverbanks, providing food for scavenging birds and mammals, and cycling nutrients back into the ecosystem." Once the eggs hatch, the cycle starts over.

The most divisive manifestation of the return concept, though, has been taking place not within migration and diaspora studies and not among marine biologists. It's happening in real time between museums and their curators on one side, and on the other, activists and artists from the developing world who are demanding the repatriation of looted and dubiously acquired artifacts and even human remains. This is not a new conversation, and it has been especially vigorous around restoring artworks stolen by the Nazis to their rightful (mostly Jewish) owners and heirs.

The debate on returning cultural artifacts currently held in Western collections took a dramatic turn in 2017, when French president Emmanuel Macron, speaking at Ouagadougou University in Burkina Faso, announced that over the following five years, he'd create "conditions" for the "temporary or permanent" restitution of what he described as African patrimony. "I am from a generation of the French people for whom the crimes of European colonialism are undeniable and make up part of our history," he told the crowd, much to the consternation of the art establishment and museum officials in France.

A year after that speech, Senegalese economist Felwine Sarr and French art historian Bénédicte Savoy published a 252-page report, commissioned by Macron, which recommended granting restitution to African countries requesting or demanding the return of objects removed to France in the late nineteenth and first half of the twentieth century. (The majority of items eligible for repatriation, Savoy told the *Guardian* newspaper, arrived in Europe between 1885 and 1930. France holds an estimated ninety thousand objects from Africa alone.)

The report reset the terms of the debate by giving it the imprimatur of a sitting president and a major art historian. Encyclopedic museums—the Louvre in Paris, the British Museum in London and the Metropolitan Museum of Art in New York City, among them—mounted a stern defence, reiterating their importance as custodians of world heritage and citing their record of preservation and documentation as support for keeping their collections intact. They also pointed out that because they're located in global cities, it's possible for more people around the world to experience the best that human civilization has produced. As journalist Tari Ngangura writes in the "Unthinkable Ideas" issue of *Vice* magazine, a mass repatriation of stolen art and objects requires an "intentional refusal to bask in colonial triumph" and "poses the possibility of a different kind of return for African nations and once-pillaged countries." This return would reject standard Western ideals of collecting and safeguarding art and make space for "local ways of showcasing culture," which, among other things, would honour the oral traditions of Africa. Exhibition catalogues and placards that "explain" collections, Ngangura argues, are at odds with the history and origins of the artifacts.

But even when the provenance suggests a legitimate transaction or a reasonable exchange between archaeologists or explorers and the people from whom the work was extracted, the return of such objects taps into a nationalist agenda that continues to reveal the long shadows of colonialism and imperialism. In *A World Beneath the Sands*, a thorough exploration of the golden age of Egyptology, historian Toby Wilkinson shows how the collections in the Louvre and the British Museum tell a parallel story of a race between France and Britain to gain control of Egypt's past and present. Egyptology emerged as the handmaiden of imperialism in the nineteenth and twentieth centuries.

For more than a hundred years, Egypt has been arguing for the repatriation of a long list of artifacts held in European and American museums. As Wilkinson suggests, the 1912 discovery and removal to Berlin of the legendary limestone bust of Nefertiti gave rise to Egyptian nationalism, which, four decades later, led to the country's independence. Among the artifacts on Egypt's return wish list is the 2,200-year-old bust of Ankhhaf, currently in the collection of the Museum of Fine Arts, Boston, and the Rosetta Stone, which has been in the possession of the British Museum since 1802. Without such objects, the country's Grand Egyptian Museum, which was scheduled to open in the summer of 2021, falls short of its proposed name.

There are too many other examples, of course—from the Greek government's call to repatriate the Parthenon Marbles, taken by Lord Elgin in the nineteenth century, to Nigeria's request to return the Benin Bronzes, seized by British troops in 1897 during a raid on the capital city of what was then the Benin Kingdom. The British Museum, where many of the Benin Bronzes are on display, refuses to return them and has instead offered to loan them to Nigeria when work on the Edo Museum of West African Art is completed in 2023. Writing for the *New York Times* in 2020, Nigerian artist Victor Ehikhamenor made a passionate plea for their return. "Generations of Africans have already lost incalculable history and cultural reference points because of the absence of some of the best artworks created on the continent," he wrote. "We shouldn't have to ask, over and over, to get back what is ours."

People, lands, animals and cultural artifacts—they all recount distinct stories of return as a global phenomenon. This book focuses on the return stories and aspirations of people as they play out on contested lands. While my first two locations—the Basque Country in Spain and Jamaica—differ culturally and geographically, they both offer a highly romanticized vision of what a homeland should be and how it changes with wave after wave of returning citizens.

Chapter 2

THE BASQUE COUNTRY

A Homeland for the Basques. A Homeland for Everyone?

Iñigo Larrinaga sports a look so classically handsome—angular face, olive skin, trimmed but wavy hair—it comes as no surprise that this fifty-year-old schoolteacher in Durango, near Bilbao, Spain, once starred in *Goenkale* (*High Street*), the most celebrated soap opera in the history of Basque-language television.

On and off over a fifteen-year stretch, Iñigo played Koldo, an ambitious, nationalist Basque politician and mayor of the fictional coastal village of Arralde, where the show was set. He and his character became so synonymous in the Basque Country that to this day (he left the show in 2009), fans call him Koldo when they run into him in Durango, where he lives with his wife and two children. His elementary school pupils, many of whom were born around the time he quit the show, know him only as Mr. Larrinaga, the teacher who drills into them the value of Basque language and history. It's possible that some parents have revealed his past to their children, but Iñigo doesn't know for sure or care much about it.

The transition from soap star to chalk-stained teacher captures more than Iñigo's career choices or his desire to move into stable, pensionable earnings; it's the story of what an attachment to an ancestral homeland and native language means in emotional and practical terms. In Iñigo's case, that homeland is the Basque Country, a region of Spain bordered by the Bay of Biscay and the western Pyrenees and encompassing just over 10,000 square kilometres (3,900 square miles). It's divided into seven regions grouped under three political entities: the Basque Autonomous Community (Álava, Biscay, Guipúzcoa); Navarre; and three provinces (Labourd, Lower Navarre and Soule) that fall under France's jurisdiction and are referred to as the French Basque Country. The language, spoken by about a third of the region's nearly three million residents, is known as Euskara and is believed to be one of the oldest on the continent, predating and having no connection to any Indo-European languages.

Iñigo and his character had little in common, but they shared one defining trait: a devotion to Basque nationalism. While Koldo may have schemed and plotted his way into politics, as many soap opera characters do, Iñigo came by his naturally, he tells me when we sit down for a chat on the balcony of his Durango apartment.

Born in Etxebarria, a small Basque village of around eight hundred people, Iñigo doesn't recall having specific conversations with his parents about their heritage. "My mother and father gave me my mother tongue," he says. "I was living all the time in a very Basque context. Everyone talked in Basque in my village. My parents didn't tell me being Basque means this or that. The context gave me my identity."

Only when he commuted to the more culturally diverse Bilbao to study journalism, in Spanish, did Iñigo begin to notice the relationship between his homeland and the nation-state of which it remains a part, despite enjoying an incredible degree of autonomy. After graduation, he kept a side gig as a spokesperson for a group that lobbied for small businesses, but he also enrolled in clown classes and dabbled in local stage and television work. He was always a performer, he recalls, having taken part in school and amateur shows in his home village. Casting directors took notice of his talent and his looks, and it wasn't long before he joined *Goenkale* as a series regular. The show sounds Seinfeldian, in that it was about "nothing in particular," Iñigo explains. "It tried to describe the Basque society. Everyday life."

After seven years, he took a leave from *Goenkale* to work on film and TV projects in the bigger pond of Spanish-language entertainment in Madrid. Doors opened, even if the roles in made-for-TV movies and the Spanish drama *Central Hospital* were usually small or supporting in nature. He may have been too clean-cut for Pedro Almodóvar movies, but judging by some clips on YouTube, he plays doctors, lawyers and detectives effortlessly. (Think Thomas Gibson from *Dharma & Greg* and *Criminal Minds*.)

Yet as glamorous as it was to be a heartthrob in Madrid, Iñigo felt restless. And there was more to this restlessness than the standard thespian anxieties about the grind of auditioning or the pain of rejection. "I wanted to live here," he says as he points to the view from his balcony overlooking a row of residential low-rises. "I didn't want to travel to Madrid to work as an actor." As our meeting has fallen on a perfectly warm fall evening, with the distant sounds of Durango's outdoor restaurants underscoring our chat, I know instantly what he means. Life is good in Durango: a lower crime rate than anywhere else in Spain, temperate weather, excellent public transport and a good social safety net, among other privileges.

Iñigo returned to the Basque Country and to the role of Koldo, but he also enrolled in a teacher-training program on a part-time basis. He had no problem landing a teaching job, even if there were a few raised eyebrows at interviews from those who recognized him from his soap opera role. The trade-off—a lower but more steady income—seems to be working for him, for the most part. "I could live better. But I'm fighting to get that," he says, gesturing to the inside of an apartment that, to me, looks tastefully but humbly furnished. "I live very close to my friends, my family, the people I love. I have more or less a good job, a good salary. Where else can I have this life?" He still takes on the odd public-speaking or modelling gig, he says, cashing in on his history with *Goenkale*, but transforming himself into a schoolteacher in Durango validates the role he wants to play for the rest of his life: the Basque nationalist citizen and father.

Iñigo works in a school where both Basque and Spanish are taught, but he encourages his children to speak only in Basque. His teenage son was five when the family relocated to Durango from Madrid, so Iñigo cuts him slack and allows him some Spanish words at home. No such leniency with his younger daughter. "I have to tell her, 'In Basque, not in Spanish. With me, in

Basque.'" I ask Iñigo why such a strict language code with his children, and he gives me that "Do I really need to explain this?" look that he's been sporting for much of our interview. He seems so steadfast in his devotion to his homeland and native tongue that my ambivalence about both concepts strikes him as heretical. "It's very important to defend your language . . . The best present I'm going to give them is the language. It's the best present that my mother gave me. She [his daughter] has to take care of it." He says he'll be bitterly disappointed if she becomes more fluent in Spanish than Basque. His words land like a punch to the gut for me, the man who lost command of his mother tongue.

Like many Basque nationalists, Iñigo sees Euskara as a heritage to be claimed and protected from the intrusion of Spanish—the language and the culture. This sense of being under siege from a larger, more imperial force runs throughout many of the communities I've spoken to for this book, but it feels more urgent and more politicized here. "When I sit in my dining room and watch TV and see Spanish society, I'm not identifying myself with that world," Iñigo says. "It's another planet. It's not my universe." He doesn't seek political isolation, he insists, but he wants a realignment of the Basque Country inside the European Union and outside Spain.

He recognizes this may be a long shot and suspects that his society is too segregated politically for a Basque homeland to happen in his lifetime. Several polls confirm his suspicions. One conducted by the University of Deusto in Bilbao in December 2017 showed that the number of Basque people who want independence from Spain has fallen to 14 percent, a record low. A year later, another poll revealed that the number of Basques who oppose independence has risen to 37 percent, the highest level in twenty years.

And yet the dream of a Basque homeland remains alive—and so does the politicking for people like Iñigo and our mutual friend, Guillermo, a university teacher I first met when we were both in our twenties and living in Nottingham, England. It was Guillermo's enthusiasm for the Basque Country on social media that convinced me to pay it a visit and see for myself why this homeland has been contested, mythologized, raided and terrorized—and still remains popular with tourists and a return destination for many living in the Americas and beyond. Why does this particular homeland call its people, and why do many of them heed the call?

* * *

Although the Basque Country encompasses territories in both France and Spain, any discussion of the struggle for autonomy mainly revolves around the latter. The three Basque provinces in France have been absorbed by the French government's department of the Atlantic Pyrenees. By and large, the French have relegated Euskara to the private domain and promoted a centralized state where the Basque think of themselves as French first and foremost. By contrast, the four Basque provinces in Spain currently enjoy the highest level of self-governance among non-states within the European Union. Such autonomous status has been enshrined in the Spanish Constitution since 1978 and is supported by a unique tax system that allows local authorities in the Basque Autonomous Community and Navarre to agree on how much they send Madrid every year. As Jan Mansvelt Beck notes in *Territory and Terror: Conflicting Nationalisms in the Basque Country*, "France would [seem to] be a perfect breeding ground for mobilizing Basque grievances, whereas in Spain democratic decentralization and the official promotion of Basque culture ought conversely to reduce the potential for conflict." Why, then, have the majority of Basques in France "evolved" into Frenchmen and -women, but their counterparts in Spain have remained mostly Basque?

The answer lies in the complicated and contested histories of the Basque region and its peoples, and in the political culture of Spain itself. To ask who is, or what makes, a Basque, particularly in Spain, is to enter into an arena where myth and folklore collide with genetic testing and archaeology; where fascism meets liberationist movements; and where the utopian narratives of a homeland are upended by the reality of the longest-running violent conflict in modern western Europe.

Basque nationalists' version of their story begins in prehistoric times, as many believe themselves to be descendants of the earliest human inhabitants of Europe. One theory that held sway among some archaeologists and anthropologists in the twentieth century was that the Basques trace their lineage to the Cro-Magnon people who settled in Europe forty thousand years ago, supplanting the Neanderthals. In his cultural history of the region, Irish journalist Paddy Woodworth doesn't dispute that the Basques are probably the continent's oldest people, or that they have lived in what they believe to be their homeland longer than any other ethnic group. But he dismisses Basque claims to be "Europe's aboriginals" as part of a carefully constructed narrative designed to make them as distinct as possible from the Spanish and the French. "Archaeology is politics in this corner of the world," he writes. The tenuous link between Stone Age inhabitants and modern-day Basques, Woodworth continues, "was seized upon by the Basque nationalists as proof that the Basque 'race' had evolved *in situ* from the Cro-Magnon period."

A 2015 study from Uppsala University in Sweden analyzed the genomes of people who lived in northern Spain around the time when southwest Europe transitioned to farming. These early Iberians, researchers suggest, are more likely the direct ancestors of modern-day Basques. After a period in which the farmers mixed with the hunter-gatherers, they retreated and became isolated from other groups for reasons that probably have to do with the geography of the Pyrenees (or perhaps for unknown cultural reasons). Such isolation explains why the Basques show no traces of the early migrations (of Stone Age pastoralists, for example) that have altered the genetic makeup in other parts of Europe.

Equally as pervasive—but now mostly underplayed—was the belief that being Basque was in the blood. Basque people exhibit the highest concentration of type Rh-negative blood in the world. This blood theory circulated heavily in the early twentieth century to support the "purity" of the Basques, who, unlike the Spanish, didn't mix with Muslim Moors during their seven-century reign over Spain. The theory persisted in popular histories of the Basques even after a 2001 genetic study suggested that the Y chromosomes of Celtic people "do not differ statistically from the Basques'," implying a link between the two ethnic groups. You can still find examples of the blood theory circulating among older Basques or online (where you're also likely to see suggestions that Basques are descended from an alien race in another galaxy). But in contemporary Basque political culture, the fixation with blood purity goes against local governments' efforts to defuse the nativism and extremism that have marred nationalist demands for an independent state over the centuries.

"Nationalists can't speak of race. They can't say that our DNA or blood is very different," says Joseba Abaitua, a professor at the University of Deusto who specializes in Basque linguistics and culture, during a chat in his office. Instead, he tells me, the conversation has shifted to language as the line that separates Basques from other ethnic groups in Spain. If you speak Euskara, you're Basque; if you don't, you're not. (Arabic has served a similar purpose in identifying those who belong in the Arab world, which is itself a mixture of cultures, ethnicities and tongues.) But even this emphasis on language strikes the professor as wrong-headed, since Spanish has been spoken in the Basque Country for centuries, and many local writers and thinkers use it in their creative and political work. "The big mistake is to make Basque [language] the definition of who is," says Abaitua, the father of four children who speak both languages. "We have to preserve and promote it, but not think that everything else is the enemy."

My friend Guillermo and I had got into an argument about our relationships with our respective mother tongues just before I met Abaitua. We are both gay men of the same vintage. His family accepted his sexuality; mine wouldn't. He was able to live and love in his native tongue; I wasn't and couldn't even if

I'd tried. I had one advantage over him, however: the number of Arabic speakers is on the rise, while Euskara speakers are a vanishing breed. Intellectually and politically, I could afford to lose Arabic because I knew the language wouldn't die with me.

For a minority, any minority, the loss of language equals a loss of a way of life, of its very existence. Extinction begins when a language disappears. I take comfort in knowing that Arabic will not disappear as a language just because I've lost my command of it. Egypt's population alone more than doubled between the time I left it (in 1986) and my last visit (2019): from 50.5 million to nearly 103 million. For every person who abandons Arabic, hundreds of thousands more are born into it.

It may prove challenging to separate efforts to protect the language from the Basque struggle for an independent state (or at least demands for increased autonomy). When Francisco Franco took power after defeating the Republicans in the Spanish Civil War (1936–39), he ushered in his dictatorship by promoting Castilian-only language policies that targeted and banned minority languages, including Euskara and Catalan. In her definitive study *Reclaiming Basque: Language, Nation, and Cultural Activism*, anthropologist Jacqueline Urla writes that during the Franco regime, people who used or taught Basque in a context other than folklore were seen as "anti-Spanish." This explains why ethnographic studies of the Basques in the 1930s and 1940s tended to reduce them to stock characters in a whimsical travel guide—variations of Victor Hugo's description of them, a century earlier, as "the people who sing and dance at the foot of the Pyrenees." Eventually, Basque nationalists turned folklore into an act of ethnic and cultural resistance. Abaitua's interest in Basque linguistics stemmed, in part, from his fascination with local folklore.

Franco's persecution drove thousands of Basques out of the country and into North and South America, and furthered the region's transformation from fishing and farming to industrialization. (Basque iron mines had already jump-started the Spanish industrial revolution in the nineteenth century.) In the 1950s and 1960s, immigration from more economically depressed parts of Spain to Biscay and Guipúzcoa further eroded Euskara's dominance.

Credit for preserving the language, and by extension Basque nationalism, goes to the Basque Nationalist Party (Partido Nacionalista Vasco, or PNV), founded in 1895 on Christian democratic principles—and an intense dislike for immigrants from other parts of Spain (who were seen as undermining the territory's ethnic and linguistic purity). As a result, Franco declared the PNV a criminal conspiracy and named Biscay and Guipúzcoa, which had enjoyed some degree of self-governance before his win, "traitor provinces." Many party leaders and government officials went into exile.

The birth of the terrorist group Euskadi Ta Askatasuna (Basque Homeland and Freedom)—better known as ETA—as a socialist, liberationist organization, with armed struggle as a strategy harks back to that oppressive period in Spain's history. ETA started in 1959 as a splinter group of students who were dissatisfied with the PNV's moderate approach to independence, but members quickly adopted a radical Marxist alternative to what they saw as the political centre's collaboration, intentional and otherwise, with the Franco regime. Again, language protection figured as largely in ETA's manifestos as the liberation of the Basque people. In an early issue of its magazine *Zutik!* (Arise!), ETA wrote that the "day that Basque ceases to be a spoken language, the Basque nation will have died and, in a few years, the descendants of today's Basque will be simply Spanish or French." (An official at PNV headquarters in 2018 told me more or less the same. "If our language disappears," he said, "maybe the Basque people will.")

Between its first killing, of a notorious San Sebastián police chief in 1968, until 2018, when it disbanded—a year after it surrendered its cache of weapons and explosives—ETA came to define Basque nationalist aspirations within Spain and beyond.

Growing up in the Middle East in the 1970s and 1980s, I had little knowledge of the Basque region beyond news coverage of ETA's terror attacks and the obligatory comparisons to the Palestinian Liberation Organization (PLO). It would be unfair to say that parts of the Arab world showed sympathy for ETA, but I recall a certain understanding of its motivation and methods expressed in local media and among the left-leaning commentariat. In some ways, Spain was to the Basques as Israel was to the Palestinians. Like both the PLO and ETA, the Front de libération du Québec (FLQ) used violence and terrorism as a strategy, although it was more influenced by the anti-colonial and communist movements in Algeria and Cuba, respectively, among others. Its campaign to liberate the people of Quebec from the influence of English and capitalism between 1963 and 1971 may have been relatively short, but it left an indelible mark on the way Quebec (and the rest of Canada) sees itself. I knew almost nothing about the FLQ when I first arrived in Toronto, but the frequency with which older friends mentioned the October Crisis and Prime Minister Pierre Elliott Trudeau's invocation of the War Measures Act in 1970 was my introduction to Quebec's history of political violence.

ETA's most violent years in the late 1970s and early 1980s coincided with the 1979 statute of autonomy, which recognized Basque identity as separate from Spanish identity and enhanced the region's level of self-government. In 1978, Herri Batasuna, a left-leaning party, was established and served as ETA's political front, much in the way Sinn Féin represented the IRA in Northern Ireland. A 2015 report commissioned by the Basque government to analyze ETA's decades of violence found that the terror group committed the majority of its attacks during the consolidation of democracy following Franco's death in 1975. Between 1976 and 1994, ETA caused the deaths of 771 people. In the following fifteen years (1995 to 2010), that number was down to 98.

From a total victim list of 869 deaths (or 952, when unresolved cases are added) in its fifty years of operation, two stand out as turning points in ETA's history. In December 1973, the group assassinated Prime Minister Luis Carrero Blanco, a confidant of and heir apparent to Franco. The elaborate attack in Madrid, more than five months in planning, involved tunnels (ETA members posed as student sculptors to justify the excavation noise) and enough explosives to send Carrero Blanco's car four to five storeys into the air. The operation solidified ETA's reputation as an armed resistance group, and many consider its actions that day key to ending dictatorship in Spain. Even nationalists who didn't agree with its methods had to concede that ETA had dealt fascism a fatal blow.

Another killing of a different Blanco in the summer of 1997 turned the tide against ETA, wiping out most of its support among hardline Basque nationalists. (In 1995, ETA could still count on the support of 20 percent of Basques. That figure had dropped to 3 percent by 2007.) This one involved Miguel Ángel Blanco, a twenty-nine-year-old Basque councillor from the village of Ermua who represented the conservative Partido Popular (Popular Party). ETA kidnapped Blanco from a local train station and gave Spanish authorities forty-eight hours to transfer their prisoners to Basque-based penitentiaries. Less than an hour after the deadline expired, Blanco was shot dead and his body dumped in the town of Lasarte. Six million Spaniards, including Basques, are reported to have demonstrated against ETA shortly after the news broke, with "Nationalism = Terrorism" one of the more popular banners and sentiments on display. (Another: "Yes to Basque, No to ETA.") By the end of 1997, twenty-three leaders of Herri Batasuna had been sentenced to seven years in prison for their collaboration with ETA. The Basque conflict turned from an ethnic to an ideological one: ETA versus the state.

Among those rethinking their position was Joseba Abaitua, the University of Deusto linguist, who said he was a Basque nationalist until "the day ETA killed Blanco." Until then, he believed that "the survival of Basque culture, the Basque society, could only be guaranteed, preserved by means of the Basque nationalist movement." But a conversation with one of his philosophy colleagues changed his mind. "He convinced me that the seed of ETA was nationalism. ETA was doing what it was because in many ways they were getting protection and support from society in general. I could no longer be involved in nationalism, to be"—he pauses as he searches online for the right English word to describe his rationale for severing ties with his past—"an accomplice."

While ETA continued its attacks into the twenty-first century—including bombing tourist resorts in 2002 as Spain hosted an EU summit—by 2011 it was politically, emotionally and legally isolated enough to declare a ceasefire. To date, about three hundred ETA members are prisoners in France, Spain and Portugal. Another one hundred are believed to be on the run. The one issue that still generates *some* public support for what's left of ETA is its demand that jailed members be repatriated to prisons in the Basque region. I witnessed two such public protests in San Sebastián and Bilbao during my visit. Supporters believe that there's no reason political prisoners should be denied the right to serve the remainder of their time in their homeland, among their people.

At the time of ETA's ceasefire in 2011, a new left-leaning coalition party called Euskal Herria Bildu, or EH Bildu (Basque Country Unite), was formed to represent progressive voices in the region. Urko Aiartza, one of its first elected officials and now a political consultant, tells me during a meeting in his San Sebastián home office that the party is reluctant to call itself nationalist, even though its main objective is the creation of a Basque homeland. "We prefer patriots," he explains. "The concept of nationalism is bias. [Nationalists] consider themselves better than anyone else. We think of ourselves as equal to everyone else—in Spain and anywhere in the world."

For EH Bildu, which holds the most seats in the Basque Parliament after the PNV, the region is at a political crossroads.

"It's clear that ETA wasn't able to force the Spanish government into negotiations to recognize self-determination," Aiartza says, describing the terror group as part of "twentieth-century politics" and a child of the 1950s and 1960s. "But it's also true that the process of autonomy [favoured by the PNV] is not moving fast enough because after forty years, there are powers that should devolve but they have not." The way forward, Aiartza believes, is to confront Madrid not as a party but as a people. And to confront it *peacefully*. But first, the Basques need to agree on a framework that states they are "a very diverse nation" and insist on having a say in their future. "Once we agree to this framework in the Basque Country, we should go to Madrid and say, 'This is our point of view and you should respect it.'"

Judging from Spain's response to the Catalan independence referendum in 2017—Madrid dissolved the Catalan parliament and sacked the region's party leaders—this path to nationhood sounds improbable at the moment. Nonetheless, Aiartza sees what happened in Catalonia as an "opening" that must be acted on, at least for Spain's own peace of mind. "The question is not who are the Basque or who are the Catalan—they have very consolidated identities—but who are the Spanish?" Can Spain survive its own identity crisis with seventeen autonomous and increasingly restless territories within its borders? Does a smaller homeland depend on the fragmentation of a larger one?

I met up with Urko on my final full day in the Basque region, and when we were finished talking, I took advantage of the hot fall day to walk around San Sebastián and accompany my friend Guillermo to the beach. This part of the Basque Country is stunningly beautiful and surprisingly peaceful for a place that witnessed so much bloodshed not that long ago. I can see why the Basques want it to themselves, and why Spain continues to oversee it and at times calls it the heart of the nation. I also understand why the many Basque people who left the region when young or have lived their whole lives elsewhere yearn to return to it. But how realistic is the PNV's promise of "A homeland for the Basques, a homeland for everyone" when mass immigration, globalization and popular revolts continue to reshape this once-isolated territory?

* * *

If you lived in a country where food and medication were in short supply, prices doubled every nineteen days, and the annual inflation rate had soared to 1.3 million percent, wouldn't you do whatever possible to get away? For the nearly six million people who've left Venezuela since the drop in oil prices triggered a financial crisis in 2014, this is not a rhetorical question. And yet, as the country descended into turmoil, the disputed and beleaguered government of Nicolás Maduro responded by raising the minimum wage and printing more money—solutions that exacerbated the problem. In January 2019, Canada, the United States and several European and South American countries sided with opposition leader Juan Guaidó in an attempt to oust Maduro, which led to even more political uncertainty and street-level chaos.

Neighbouring Colombia has so far received nearly two million Venezuelans in what some experts describe as the largest mass migration in Latin America since the transatlantic slave trade. Peru, Ecuador, Argentina and Brazil have absorbed hundreds of thousands as well. But from 2016 to 2018, Spain topped the list of Venezuelans' asylum requests. This is the point of departure, the original homeland of their ancestors. Spanish authorities estimate that just over 255,000 Venezuelans have fled to their country. It's one of the biggest international examples of homeland return in the twenty-first century.

And the return journeys continue, even though only 40,000 of the relocated Venezuelans are registered to work and just 15 out of 12,875 applicants were given asylum status by early 2019. Some enter Spain on tourist visas, overstay and work in the black market, but the majority (60 percent) come in armed with Spanish passports that they or their parents maintained for sentimental reasons or in case of emergency. Since Venezuela has traditionally been one of the top-ten destinations for Basque migrants worldwide, it's inevitable that their descendants are choosing to return to what they view as their true homeland.

Mikel Burzako, a high-ranking foreign affairs official with the PNV, notes that Basques went through a dress rehearsal of this with Argentina when that country's financial crisis started in 1998. But the volume and the level of desperation have changed. "We've had a lot of demands from third- or fourth-generation Basques: 'I can't live here. I want to go back to my homeland' . . . We say, 'You helped Basque people decades ago. We try to help you.'" This help ranges from providing financial aid to connecting Venezuelans with families they may have been cut off from for generations.

What the PNV can't assist with is the gap between what the new immigrants imagined the Basque Country to be and its reality. "They idealize the homeland," José Mari Etxebarria, a member of the PNV foreign affairs committee, tells me. They think of the rural landscape that their grandparents often mythologized (or that they saw in watercolours bought from flea markets), or of the villages where they spent their childhoods before escaping to Venezuela. But then "they come here and see a modern country, very different races of people."

While Aitzbea Ramos says she moved to Bilbao for romantic reasons—she met a man during a visit in 2011 and fell in love—the fifty-year-old graphic designer from Caracas, capital of Venezuela, shares a similar history of affinity for and return to an ancestral homeland with the thousands of her compatriots who have settled in the Basque Country since 2014. She describes herself as a "typical Venezuelan girl" who is also very Basque. Ultimately, she had to make a choice between the two.

Her grandparents moved from Bilbao to Caracas in 1947, when her father was seven years old. An anti-Franco Basque nationalist who fought in the Spanish Civil War on the side of the defeated Republicans, Aitzbea's grandfather had no choice but to leave when the Franco regime began to persecute its political enemies. She remembers hearing stories about his underground radio broadcasts, in which he urged the Basque people to rise and fight for their homeland. In 1950, three years after the family moved to Venezuela, the Basque Center of Caracas (Euskal Etxea, or Basque Home) was opened to serve the six hundred families that had settled in the prosperous country. It was there in the 1960s that Aitzbea's father met her mother, another child of Basque immigrants.

The Euskal Etxea is equal parts community centre and cultural hub, but it's also an instrument of the Basque government's global "ethnicity-maintenance" efforts, in the words of Gloria Pilar Totoricagüena, who analyzes the phenomenon in her book *Identity, Culture, and Politics in the Basque Diaspora*. With more Basques living outside the territory's borders in Spain and France than inside them, nationalists, especially in the PNV, invested in these centres with the express goal of establishing communication channels between the diaspora and those at home. This strategy, Totoricagüena suggests, explains why fourth- and fifth-generation Basques generally exhibit fewer characteristics of their adopted countries than, say, German or Italian immigrants. This process of sustaining cultural ties to the homeland, says the PNV's Burzako, trumps any explicit political or activist agenda. It keeps the homeland as a desire to be fulfilled, a dream to be realized.

For most of her childhood and teenage years, Aitzbea spent weekends playing cards or swimming at the Caracas Euskal Etxea, where she absorbed many lessons about being Basque from the older people who frequented the club. If this all sounds idyllic, it's because Aitzbea's coming of age coincided with Venezuela's oil-rich golden years, when it was the wealthiest country in South America. Even in the midst of the current economic crisis, oil accounts for 25 percent of the country's GDP and up to 95 percent of its export earnings.

Aitzbea recalls a very comfortable standard of living that continued even after 1999, when Hugo Chávez took over and began implementing his socialist agenda, which was designed in part to address the economic shocks of the 1980s and to hurt (or level the playing field with) the country's elite. Aitzbea's graphic design business thrived, and her client roster included a major

pharmaceutical company in Caracas. But in the 2000s, misman-
agement of the state-owned oil company, widespread corruption
and government control of exchange rates added up to an economic meltdown and a disruption of social norms. Aitzbea, an
only child, recalls inviting friends to hang out with her at home
because it was too dangerous to go outside.

She began to think about leaving Caracas and starting over
somewhere else, perhaps in Europe. Although she had lived in
Paris, it was Bilbao that kept calling her. Her father, who was
born there, also dreamed of returning one day, so he encouraged
her. Her mother, born in Caracas, was less enthusiastic. Still, a
certain gut feeling convinced her to go back to the homeland of
her parents. "I think there's a connection," she tells me as she
tries to explain her attachment to a place she hardly knew. "I
don't know. It's in my skin. When I [came] to Bilbao seven years
ago, I was in a bar outside, a terrace, and suddenly I see the
buildings, the skies . . . I never felt like that. In that afternoon, I
felt I wanted to live here."

Although her income from her graphic design business has
plummeted since her move, Aitzbea says that many other quality-
of-life factors mitigate the career loss. "You can walk the street
at eleven at night. No problem. You can live alone. You can
leave your bag and phone to get a Coca-Cola. I have a social
life here." There's the boyfriend, who owns a deli shop and has
made her return easier, of course, but there's also the less romantic and more frightening thought that the country where she was
born and raised is experiencing a humanitarian crisis and a total
collapse of civil society that goes beyond unsafe streets.

Almost 87 percent of people in Venezuela lack money to buy

basic food or toiletries. The infant mortality rate has reached 30 percent, and maternal mortality is double that. By 2016, the homicide rate had jumped to 91.9 per 100,000 residents. (In Canada in the same year, it was 1.68 per 100,000.) For Aitzbea, there may never be a return to the Venezuela of Basque cultural centres or family ties, since both her parents have now died (of natural causes). "The society is destroyed," she says. It sounds like a civil war, I tell her, drawing comparisons between Venezuela and Yemen. "It's not a civil war because the weapons are all on one side: his," she responds, referring to Maduro. I show Aitzbea an opinion piece in the *New York Times* that suggests some in Venezuela believe Maduro is deliberately hollowing out the country and driving its citizens—in particular, its elites—out of their homeland. I then read her part of what Javier Corrales, a professor of political science, has written: "An extremist government like his prefers economic devastation to economic recovery because misery destroys civil society, and with it the potential challenges to tyranny." She has suspected that all along.

Aitzbea keeps herself busy by volunteering for a local organization that helps the people of Venezuela, regardless of their ethnic origins. Recently she designed a new logo featuring a bird from Venezuela and two human hands that act as its nest. The symbolism may be a bit on the nose, but the message comes from the heart and captures one aspect of the return of Basque Venezuelans: the exhausting flight path of this homeward journey.

José Ramón Cengotitabengoa represents a different side of the same journey: a voluntary return after almost fifty years abroad, including thirty-five prosperous ones in the United States. He left the Basque Country at eighteen to study engineering in Belgium and—with the exception of a few years in the early 1970s—stayed away until 2006, when he returned at almost sixty-eight to retire. As he tells me over lunch in the fall of 2018 in Vitoria-Gasteiz, capital of the Basque Autonomous Community, this is also where he wants to be buried, next to his wife (she died three years earlier). When I ask why returning to the Basque Country mattered so much to him, he seems perplexed by my question. "It was a priority for me," he says, adding that he didn't even discuss his return with his three adult children. (I met José Ramón through a mutual friend of his son Sam, who lives in Washington.) I explain to him that to many people like me and the millions of migrants from war-ravaged countries, returning to the homeland is an elusive dream. "Yemen may be different," he concedes. "In Yemen, the situation has changed. There will be peaceful days." I took his words as a sign from an older and wiser man that my own return, in some form, remained a possibility.

Like many Basques of his generation, José Ramón maintained a strong connection with this territory throughout his travels. He went to university in Belgium to escape Franco's persecution of the Basques—and, he admits, to avoid getting conscripted into the Spanish army. From there, he moved to England, where he worked for almost a decade casting engines in various car-manufacturing plants, including Rolls-Royce in Nottingham. He returned to Spain only when he was too old to be drafted. ("We're not very patriotic, the Basques," he tells me.) In 1970—or "something like that"—he met his wife, Gema, and by 1975, they had their three children, Sam, Beatrice and

Ana, and decided to leave again, this time for the United States. After two years in Scarsdale, New York, the family relocated to suburban Chicago. He continued to work in the steel industry, representing European mills.

By any measure, financial or emotional, José Ramón lived the dream that many immigrants and baby boomers in the 1970s aspired to—the big house in the suburbs, the well-educated children, the steady job with pension that allowed a one-income family to thrive, etc. Yet what gave his life in America its purpose was the life he left behind. For most of his thirty-five years there, José Ramón acted as an unofficial ambassador for the Basque Country. As a member and then president of the Society of Basque Studies in America, he dedicated much of his free time to promoting his homeland's language, culture and history, using his work-related travel to connect with the many Basque centres in the United States.

At home, he insisted that his children learn Euskara and pass it on to their own children, which they have, the grandfather of six tells me. "It's very important for us. For Jews, to keep Israel is very important. For us, to keep our language, a minority language, that we the Basque speak." (In an interview with a Basque online magazine in 2009, he described the language as his "religion.") José Ramón laments the fact that many Basques who moved to Argentina, Chile and Uruguay in the twentieth century have lost their native tongue. His mastery of Euskara helped make his return to Vitoria-Gasteiz smoother, especially since he had never lived in this more industrialized and somewhat drab part of the Basque Country before. He chose it because an old friend from school had retired there. This is an example of something the Basques refer to as the *cuadrilla*, a kind of second family made up of close friends from childhood. The decades-long bond between my friend Guillermo and Iñigo, the actor-turned-teacher, is another.

I ask José Ramón if he misses life in the US. "I wouldn't say that. I respect the US." You lived there for so long and you have children and grandchildren there, I respond, but he fires back. "I like how business works. Compared to Europe, there's much less corruption . . . But I would not defend the United States in a war." Would he defend the Basque Country, then? "In my heart, I would. All the wars we had, we lost. We're a small group."

In some ways, José Ramón never left the Basque Country. His return to it seems to have been predestined. No level of success or deep family roots in Illinois could have stopped it. I've often wondered what that tells us, not about the homeland but about the places that have taken in immigrants in large numbers: Canada, the United States, Australia, Argentina. The so-called New World. If our hearts and minds remain in the places we left behind, does that turn our lives in our adopted countries into phases or mere stops on a travel itinerary—granted, a very long one—that ends back where we came from? Does the return to one homeland mean the abandonment of the place that welcomed or at least sheltered us?

* * *

For many people in art and photography, Erika Ede is better known as "Courtesy Guggenheim Museum Bilbao." The fifty-seven-year-old Basque native has been the official photographer of the deservedly iconic Frank Gehry–designed institution since its inauguration in 1997. The museum hired her a year earlier to document the final stages of constructing what one architecture critic has described as a "convulsive, majestic, climactic assembly of titanium and stone." It's difficult to think of Bilbao today without the museum, even if the town has been around since the fourteenth century. When urban planners and theorists talk about the "Guggenheim effect," they mean the transformation of an industrial city into a cultural and digital hub, in part owing to a bold architectural project. For Erika, this connection resonates on an even deeper level: her father, she says, is a descendant of Diego López de Haro, generally accepted as the founder of Bilbao.

When Erika and I meet at the terrace café of the Guggenheim, she points out the very building where she was born: "That black one close to the tall white one." But neither her family history nor her current occupation has proven seductive enough to turn her into a Basque nationalist. The fact that she left Bilbao when she was three-and-a-half years old and didn't return to it until she was almost thirty-six has a lot to do with her anti-nationalist views—"I don't feel this homeland thing," she insists—but a bigger factor is nationalism's xenophobic undercurrents. "Since nations were born . . . that was really the beginning of 'us' and the 'other,'" she notes. "The beginning of all the conflicts all over the world." With an American husband and three children who have American, Spanish and even Latvian ancestry, Erika feels more like a global citizen than a local one. Many people in the Basque Country, however, still wrestle with their homeland's history of cultural and linguistic purity on one hand, and on the other a globalization that endures, despite the rise in populism and renewed calls for borders and trade protections.

Erika's first move out of Bilbao came when her father relocated the family to Madrid in search of a drier climate to manage his bronchitis. Since he didn't identify strongly as a Basque person and her mother didn't speak the language, Erika never learned what was technically her native tongue. (She still hasn't, even after working in the Basque region for more than two decades.) She studied history and art in Madrid, focusing on contemporary art and restoration, before launching a career in culture, photography and public broadcasting that took her to France, Romania, the United States, Germany and various cities in Spain. Until she landed the Guggenheim position—"a very nice job," she concedes—she never thought she'd return to her city of birth.

I don't use the word "homeland" much in our conversation because she's signalled her discomfort with it. But it was her birthplace that helped her get the job. In Spain—unlike Canada and the United States—job applicants list their place of birth on their resumes. "I know I would have never got this position . . . had I not been from the Basque," Erika acknowledges. She says that almost all her colleagues also come from the region—a fact that she describes as "completely nationalistic on a high level." (For the record, she spoke to me as an individual and not an employee of the museum.) But if this kind of nationalism got her the job, what does she hold against it? A lot, it seems.

"When I was living and studying and working for the state, at the cultural ministry [in Madrid] for three years, nobody asked me where I came from," she says. "What was really important was what I did. Could I perform my job? In France, exactly the same. In Germany, the same. I come here and I realize that there's nobody who comes from outside. I don't like this . . . exclusion of the others . . . I'm from here, but I'm also the other." Erika reminds me that when she moved back to Bilbao in 1996, ETA was still active. Months before the Guggenheim opened its doors, Spanish police foiled an ETA plan to place explosives inside Jeff Koons's giant flower puppy installation, one of several international public art projects that stand on the museum's grounds along the Nervión River, connecting the city with the art and the art with the city. "People in Madrid thought I was crazy coming here," Erika recalls. But a good quality of life—an easy, clean city with a strong public transportation system and easy access to beaches—keeps her content, even "happy." That is, until she's drawn into local politics, and in particular, debates on immigration from North Africa and the Middle East.

In 2012, a government survey found that while more than half of local Basques have had interactions with Muslims, 49 percent oppose the construction of mosques to cater to the fifty thousand or so Muslims who live in the region. The years leading up to that survey saw several confrontations between Muslims and local authorities (mayors, councils) over proposed mosques or Islamic centres. In late 2018, former Basque parliamentarian Santiago Abascal, a Spanish nationalist, led the far-right Vox party, formed in 2013, into a marginal victory in the local elections in Andalucía. Vox's twelve seats were enough to make it the kingmaker in a right-leaning alliance between the conservative Popular Party and the centrist Citizens—after it dropped a campaign promise to send home fifty-two thousand North African immigrants it deemed "illegal."

"Nobody ever in history can stop people from moving to a better place," Erika says when I ask about the traditional definition of Basque identity and the reality of demographic changes. "I know I'm paying my taxes, and I have to pay for the new people. I don't mind." The centrist PNV prefers to see the Basque Country as a "host culture" into which people, especially from North and sub-Saharan Africa, integrate quickly. "We try to give them the primary needs," Etxebarria, of the party's foreign affairs committee, told me. "We're a patriotic party, but we're not populists. Never, ever. We're not using people to gain votes."

I remind Erika of the PNV's "A homeland for the Basques, a homeland for everyone" slogan, and she shakes her head—more annoyed than angry. This whole homeland talk, she says, is based on a misunderstanding of the history of Spain, and particularly, Basque dreams of independence. "The Basque Country has never been free," she says. "They had their autonomy, freedom. Then Franco came. They couldn't speak Basque. So what's the point? It's not like they've been there [and want it back]. Most of the people who live here come from Andalucía, Barcelona, Madrid."

* * *

It's late on a Saturday afternoon, and the town of Guernica in Biscay province feels deserted. Stores have closed for the day, and restaurants are yet to open their doors for the supper rush.

Dozens of tourists, East European by the looks and sounds of them, have flocked to a mural that faithfully reproduces Pablo Picasso's 1937 painting bearing the town's name. It's one of the artist's and the twentieth century's most recognized paintings, perfectly capturing the "pity and terror"—to borrow the title of an exhibition commemorating its seventieth anniversary at the Reina Sofía museum in Madrid—of the bombing of this Basque town. At the request of Franco, German and Italian planes carried out a three-hour aerial attack on Guernica (Gernika in Basque), a forerunner of the Blitzkriegs of the Second World War. The number of victims remains disputed, but at a conservative count, 250 civilians died and thousands were injured. Guernica's reputation as a Republican stronghold and its significance to Basque independence as the home of the Assembly House and the Tree of Gernika (both national symbols) made it a strategic choice for Franco.

I had caught glimpses of the original Picasso painting in Madrid during a visit to a packed Reina Sofía more than a decade earlier. Its cast of four anguished women, a child and a dismembered soldier—and a bull and a horse—was more familiar, and made less meaningful, to me from numerous reproductions I'd seen in books or articles about the Spanish artist. Seeing the mural in the actual town where the bombing took place warmed me to it somewhat. But what surprised me was the impact it had on my friend Guillermo, a proud Basque who had seen this reproduction and been to this town many times, as a child and an adult. As he tried to explain the painting's many possible meanings, his emotions switched from uncontrollable sobbing to intense anger at the persecution of his people before, during and after the Spanish Civil War and the almost forty years of Franco's dictatorship.

Months later, I'm still not entirely sure what to make of this outburst. Is it the weight of history? A trauma passed through generations of Basque people? The power of art, even in replica? Or was it simply an emotional response to his recently finalized divorce from his husband of many years? Why am I trying to find psychological or subliminal reasons when the simplest one, per Occam's razor, is the most likely? This is how many people express love for their homeland: an emotional, vulnerable attachment to an actual or imagined place. Minutes after the mural experience, Guillermo struck up a conversation with a Catalan tourist—his "Free Catalonia" T-shirt was the giveaway—in the courtyard separating the Assembly House and the Tree of Gernika. The bearded, stocky Catalan was teary by the end of it. Each wished the other good luck, Guillermo later told me, with his people's struggle to decide the future of their homelands within the European Union without the unilateral imposition of an EU member state.

As genuine and loving as that exchange might have been, my visit to the Basque Country also confirmed why some homeland longings contain a hateful streak of ardent nationalism. I subscribe more to Erika's theory of "them" and "us" as the root of nationalism than to the pure love of Guillermo and his friends. Rewind some of Franco's nationalist diatribes against Republicans and you'll hear the same ideas now promoted by Vox's Abascal and several other far-right leaders in Europe: a strong central government that attacks religious and sexual minorities, pushes conspiracy theories and doesn't tolerate dissent or a free press. Abascal is the Spanish politician with the highest number of followers on Instagram, and he knows how to use social media (especially unedited images and personal content) to promote his policies.

Basque nationalism may have evolved over the centuries to become less dependent on blood purity, creation myths and even typography, and in the more centrist and leftist circles of the PNV and EH Bildu, it's nobly inclusive. At least in theory and at least for now. But will this benign nationalism survive the influx of immigrants from Africa and the Middle East and Venezuela? Something tells me the Venezuelans will do better than people from the other two groups. They are simply returning to their homeland, while the others will likely continue to be seen as a threat to it. Nationalists never let a chance to bash outsiders go to waste. It's how they sustain homeland fervour in the minds and hearts of their people.

If Muslim and North African immigrants and refugees hit a nerve in Spain, it's because their movement is seen by some—including the Vox party—as a return to the land from which they were expelled during the Reconquista, or Reconquest, the many wars that ended in 1492. In one inflammatory speech, in which he stressed his party's relationship to Europe, Abascal crowed, "After all, we saved Europe from the Muslim onslaught during our 700-year Reconquest!" (No wonder American white nationalist Steve Bannon has endorsed his party.) A homeland is a place where one culture must dominate in order to stop the return of an earlier one.

Even if that return is simply the manifestation of religious and ethnic paranoia.

Chapter 3

JAMAICA

Come from Foreign

The developers behind the Gates of Edgehill, a proposed community in the Parish of St. Mary, Jamaica, know how to draw crowds to their showcase event at the Toronto Botanical Garden. Host Oliver Samuels, the Caribbean King of Comedy, provides star power to a night that has already promised a guest appearance from well-known hockey dad Karl Subban, whose book *How We Did It* is one of the evening's giveaways.

Anyone interested in buying a "piece of the rock" in a gated community on Jamaica's north coast can take a slick virtual-reality (VR) tour of the two main types of homes for sale. The more affordable and smaller Diana model, at 1,658 square feet, comes with a price tag of just under $240,000 (US); the Elizabeth is a steal at $299,000 and 1,904 square feet. Both homes have three bedrooms, two bathrooms and cathedral ceilings, but the basement in the Elizabeth accounts for the extra $60,000. And for one night only, all prices are slashed by 10 percent.

If VR induces headaches or nausea, patrons can instead watch a traditional video or browse brochures promising "sunshine, swimming and socializing" and highlighting the golf course and spa. The island is poised for great things, a representative from the Jamaica Tourist Board tells the audience, and this new community offers a "great opportunity to be shining with us."

What's for sale tonight is not merely a home but the next phase in the lives of the exclusively Black Jamaican audience members. (Many Europeans, South Asians and Chinese call Jamaica home, but there was no sign of any other ethnic groups at this event.) The people I chat with have already reached retirement or are beginning to think about it. Even on this mild late-October night, some fantasize about a getaway from Toronto's winters. "The sun—I miss the sunshine," a woman who has lived in Ontario for almost forty years tells me, before also mentioning the warmth of the people and the vibe of the place. This will become a refrain when I visit the island later the same week. A younger woman speaks of ties to her family and roots that took her back to the island for a year-long visit to lay the groundwork for an eventual permanent return.

I'm not Jamaican, but even I start to crunch some numbers in my head during a monotone presentation from a mortgage broker. If I borrow against the equity in my place, maybe I can get myself a Diana and spend as much of the Canadian winter away from icy sidewalks and bone-chilling weather as my job and commitments will allow. The Caribbean setting aside, my longing for the mountain house in Aden and what's on sale this evening stem from the same emotional place of returning to where we come from.

Investors in the Gates of Edgehill and other purpose-built communities in Jamaica understand that human desire to spend the final chapter of life closer to the land that shaped its earlier stages. Tonight, the free flow of Jamaican patties, rice pilaf and non-alcoholic beverages that you find only in "ethnic" supermarkets package that desire into nostalgia-driven bite sizes and sips.

What almost everyone in the room seems to avoid talking about is what happens to some elderly returnees when they make it back to the homeland. According to a 2018 report in the *Guardian*, around eighty-five returnees holding Canadian, American or British passports have been murdered in Jamaica since 2012. That number is small, given that the island takes in roughly thirty thousand returnees a year—a figure that includes those who are deported or repatriated—but the stories have acquired a certain poignancy. In most cases, the victims had returned with their life savings after working thirty or more years in the West. One British woman was killed within six days of her return. In 2017, Jamaican police recorded 1,616 murders (an average of 31 a week, according to the *Guardian*). Window grilles, CCTV cameras and twenty-four-hour security patrols are common—at least in the more exclusive gated communities—but they don't eliminate the risk of being murdered in your own home. Add break-ins and assaults that don't end in death, and you may well wonder why anyone wants to return.

And yet here they are at the Gates of Edgehill showcase in Toronto, some window shopping—in it for the free food and the star power—while others are negotiating upgrades and signing on dotted lines. "I think that's something very Jamaican," says

Yvonne Grant, the director of a homeless shelter in Kingston and a returnee from England. "We still have space around us. That's what the culture says: Have a nice house, a nice garden, a nice place around you." This may explain why Jamaicans sometimes refer to their island by the colloquial term "the yard." It connects the country as a political entity and the land it sits on with the dream of home ownership (elusive as the latter is to its poor, who make up roughly 20 percent of the population). The island's 2.9 million people share 10,991 square kilometres (4,244 square miles) of richly varied topography. The largest island in the Caribbean Commonwealth, Jamaica feels even bigger because of the concentration of its population in towns, leaving rural areas underpopulated, isolated and impoverished.

Percival LaTouche shakes his head in recognition and in despair when I tell him about the sales pitch in Toronto. The chair and co-founder of the Kingston-based Jamaica Association for the Resettlement of Returning Residents (JARRR), LaTouche has watched his compatriots make their way home, only to deal with the reality of a violent society and what he believes to be a corrupt police force that may have colluded in some of the recent killings. We're sitting in his office, surrounded by hundreds of files stuffed with news clippings and photocopies of birth certificates and land deeds. Not every item is related to a murder case, but almost every sentence from LaTouche's mouth betrays his belief that Jamaicans should think very carefully before deciding to come home.

"It's not hype in the media," he scolds me when I say that the sensationalist, tabloid nature of some recent murder cases may be tainting the whole country. "Returnees will be targeted because our politicians don't give a damn." Politicians want the diaspora to stay overseas and keep sending remittances, he says. The World Bank estimates that between 1976 and 2017, those remittances accounted for 9.45 percent of the country's GDP, reaching a record 17.31 percent in 2016.

Jamaicans, LaTouche says, helped rebuild the United Kingdom after the Second World War as part of a wave of immigration from then-British colonies. (Jamaica was a British colony until August 1962, when it gained independence—or as the Jamaica Independence Act refers to it, gained "fully responsible status within the Commonwealth.") At the same time, the money they sent back to their families on the island sustained the local economy. "Had it not been for us who went away in those rough days, I don't know where Jamaica would be."

LaTouche knows all of this first-hand. He left Jamaica for Britain in 1958, at seventeen, to become a mechanic. He married at nineteen, and a string of children and grandchildren followed over the course of thirty years spent living in Birmingham and London. He moved up from working as a mechanic to owning a gas station, which he sold when he began shuttling between the two countries. He returned to Jamaica for a few months in 1975 and for good in 1989. "I thought that the Jamaica I left is the Jamaica I came home for. Once I've been invested in the country, I realized I blundered. I should never have come back." He co-founded JARRR with seven colleagues as a way to help others navigate the complex system of the customs department and, he writes in the organization's brochure, to protect fellow Jamaicans from "unscrupulous lawyers, building and electrical contractors, etc."

A month after we met in November 2018, LaTouche appeared on Jamaican TV, urging the diaspora not to come home. "It makes no sense," he told Loop News. "You spend twenty, thirty or forty years overseas working hard, only to return home for people to kill you." His comments were in reaction to the murder of another British returnee, whose body was found in a shallow grave on her property in the community of Boscobel in the Parish of St. Mary. This is where the Gates of Edgehill has covered the costs of building a kindergarten as a gesture of goodwill to the mostly impoverished community and as an investment in the area's economy.

LaTouche believes that Jamaicans who return of their own choice still have it easier than the involuntary returning residents, which is his preferred term for deportees from mostly North America and Europe. The Jamaican homeland return story can be divided along these voluntary and involuntary lines. Jamaicans refer to both groups of people as "come from foreign," but the stigma that deportees (the term I and most of my subjects and commentators use) face has more to do with class than national pride. Francis Madden, a retired social worker who volunteers for a number of organizations that help deportees and the poor in Kingston, says that even though more Jamaicans travel for work or leisure than, say, two decades ago, going to foreign countries remains a big deal. And so is returning home after violating visa terms or as a result of a court order. "You're in a worse place. You've failed. You have no ambition," she says, explaining what some communities in Jamaica think of deportees.

Exact figures vary, but according to statistics from the island's national security ministry and obtained by the *Jamaica Observer* newspaper, 9,425 people were deported over a four-year period ending in September 2016. The US (which sends a monthly charter flight of deportees to Kingston) returned 4,153, the UK 1,345 and Canada 931. The rest were deported from other parts of Europe and the Caribbean. This is the highest ratio of deportees to general population in the world.

Unlike returnees, who use their savings to shield themselves as much as possible from violence, deportees often return with little money and no family to speak off. And as I found out during my visit to Kingston, many soon find themselves counted among the homeless. Their return stories confirm a larger narrative about economic disparities that run along racial, political, class and rural-versus-town lines. And yet, friends and contacts from the island tell me that perception is worse than reality, and that they take the right precautions and have rarely experienced any issues. Against this context, returns feed into facts and misconceptions about the island's history of violence, which has existed side by side with its reputation as the slice of paradise that property developers and holiday resorts promote.

In writing this chapter, I've become aware of the binary of "paradise" on one side and "violent place" on the other when it comes to telling stories about the island. As someone from the Arab Muslim world, I know the damage that reductive narratives can have on communities, both at home and in the diaspora. The people in the following pages have shared stories of lives touched by violence and joy, rejections and warm welcomes. While the truth is always somewhere in between, it would be irresponsible for me to underplay the role guns, drugs and murders play in the return experiences of Jamaicans. Blame me and not Jamaica if the stories dwell too much on the island's darker side. It's a reading of the situation that reflects my own anxieties around violence.

***

In 1962, the year Jamaica became independent after more than three centuries of colonization, the homicide rate stood at 3.9 per 100,000—among the lowest in the world. This fact and not nostalgia explains why older returnees recall a generally peaceful country. In 2018, the rate reached 47 per 100,000, which was actually a drop of 21.9 percent from the record-setting previous year. By comparison, Canada had a homicide rate of just under 1.5 per 100,000 in 1962 and 1.8 in 2018. In taking credit for the 2018 decrease, Jamaica's prime minister, Andrew Holness, promised to bring the rate down to 16 per 100,000 over a ten-year period.

Security and crime experts may differ on some of the causes of modern Jamaica's history of violence, but they (and political analysts) agree on a quartet of factors: politics, drugs, gangs and poverty. Each intersects with and reinforces the others but has also acted independently of them. Police ineffectiveness and alleged corruption shadow all four.

The three decades leading up to independence laid the groundwork for contemporary Jamaica's struggles with violence. The formation of the island's first trade union in 1938 effectively launched its two political parties and the decades-long rivalry between them: Alexander Bustamante founded the Jamaica

Labour Party (JLP), while Norman Manley led the People's National Party (PNP). (The men shared a personal history as cousins born to mixed-race parents.) A system of patronage, or "clientism," emerged in which politicians (patrons) from both parties bestowed money, job opportunities and perks such as housing on their supporters (clients) in exchange for votes. In a city already divided along uptown (white, mixed-race and affluent Blacks) and downtown (working poor and migrants from rural areas), urban fragmentation intensified.

What became known as garrison communities evolved along political lines, and supporters of one party faced harassment, physical violence and even death when caught on the other's turf. In 1966, the JLP created the community of Tivoli Gardens, which became one of its strongholds in Kingston. The PNP claimed Hannah Town and Jungle, among other areas. Politically motivated violence, researchers suggest, became endemic.

In his report *Confronting the Don: The Political Economy of Gang Violence in Jamaica*, researcher Glaister Leslie notes that by the 1960s, politicians were arming groups with guns instead of sticks and stones. A group of men defended an area and answered to a don (leader), who in turn reported to the political directorate. Both parties gave free rein to the dons within their locales, "enabling them, in effect, to become the rule of law in some instances." Several dons and their gangs continued to corral votes for their political allies, but thanks to the drug trade, they also operated outside the patronage system. Many gang members began as political goons before organizing themselves into groups that controlled territory and operated their own patronage system, a de facto government within the local government. Some of these groups have even crossed borders, becoming part of transnational crime syndicates.

In addition to being the largest exporter of cannabis in the Caribbean, Jamaica has for decades been a transit point for South American cocaine destined for North America and Europe. This has increased the power and reach of its gangs. As trade routes shifted to Central America and Mexico in the 2010s, competition among gangs for the reduced business led to several turf wars. The spike in the homicide rate between 2014 and 2017 reflects the social cost of heroin's scarcity as a resource, according to a study by A2 Global Risk, a security risk management consultancy. Other shifts in the criminal underworld reflect the US kingpin strategy, which focuses on targeting gang leaders and letting the ensuing jockeying for position among lower-ranked members consume their lives and weaken their influence.

Gang culture and police incompetence—and some say helplessness—collide in a world where indifference to the latter's authority adds to a "perceived sense of lawlessness," according to a report from the US State Department's Bureau of Diplomatic Security. The police make arrests in only 44 percent of homicides and convict just 29 percent of perpetrators. In *Confronting the Don*, Leslie suggests that most firearms seized on the island can be traced to three counties in Florida with large Jamaican populations, while ammunition enters the country through legitimate channels (for policing purposes) but makes its way to the underground market, better known as the informal economy of drug and gun cultures.

This shadow economy lies at the heart of Jamaica's struggles to eradicate poverty. Young men gravitate to gangs when they are twelve to fifteen years old. Some reports estimate that men fifteen to twenty-nine commit 85 percent of all homicides in the country. (The same age group, inevitably, tops the victim lists.) Although youth unemployment decreased in 2018, it averaged almost 30 percent between 2012 and 2017. These figures cover both urban and rural areas, but the latter's experience of poverty connects to the former in different ways. Commentators describe Jamaica as the most resource-rich poor nation on earth because of its varied agricultural output, fisheries and livestock. But growing local produce is one thing; selling it in a market where cheap imports dominate has left farmers accepting a loss and has driven younger workers into populated urban centres, where they're more likely to be recruited by gangs.

Deportees enter this mix of political war, drugs, gangs and poverty at a huge disadvantage. The police and the ministry of national security attribute much of the high homicide rate to the return of Jamaican gang members from the United States and elsewhere. A 2001 analysis by the ministry put the number of involuntary returnees who resumed criminal activities within the structures of existing gangs at 20 percent. The charter flights that bring US-based deportees to Jamaica have come to be known as "convict planes." Scholars of violence and crime don't dispute the fact that gangs sent many members to the US in the 1980s as operatives, but they believe the role of deportees in current crime statistics is much lower. A comprehensive 2008 study in the *Journal of Ethnicity in Criminal Justice* suggests that deportees commit only around 4 percent of all murders in Jamaica each year.

"It's a matter of who you were here before you left Jamaica," says Damian Hutchinson, the director of Peace Management Initiative (PMI), a non-profit organization that uses alternative dispute-resolution methods to curb community-based violence. Men who were involved with gang activity can't expect their years in the US or the UK to wipe the slate clean. The memory of what a deportee might have done before "going to foreign" persists. "He could have hurt someone. He still has that reputation, and someone wants revenge." But even Hutchinson sees the stigma against deportees as mainly social: "Someone getting deported doesn't go telling people that because they don't want to be judged." Deportees don't get voter IDs, he says, so this creates challenges in integrating them back into society. If their deportation after years or decades of living in the United States, Canada or Britain calls into question who's American, Canadian or British, then their return also raises doubts about their Jamaicanness. When it comes to Britain, deported Jamaicans talk about a particular kind of betrayal: the "motherland" has turned them away and the "homeland" of Jamaica is also rejecting them.

The deportation and repatriation of people of Caribbean origin has been a fact of British life for decades, but it took the Windrush scandal of 2017–18 to thrust it into the national conversation. The name refers to the ship HMT *Empire Windrush*, which arrived at England's south coast in 1948 with five hundred Jamaicans aboard. They came at the request of the British government, as the country was facing labour shortages after the Second World War. The term "Windrush generation" has become a catch-all for Jamaican and other Caribbean nationals who moved to the United Kingdom throughout the 1950s and 1960s and were given indefinite leave to remain.

In 2012, Theresa May, then Home Office secretary, became the public face of former prime minister David Cameron's hostile environment policy, which aimed to make life for illegal immigrants so inhospitable that they would choose to leave. In the summer of 2013, Operation Vaken, a campaign to enforce the hostile environment policy, hit the streets and community centres of London with a simple message: "In the UK illegally? Go home or face arrest." Members of the Windrush generation became entangled in May's anti-immigration scheme even though many of those who were deported—or are fighting deportation through legal channels to this day—had lived in Britain for fifty or sixty years. Most had never applied for citizenship because they believed that as colonial subjects, they were already British, or that the Jamaican passports they'd used to enter the country as invited guest workers gave them the right of abode. Some had lost older passports with the coveted ILR stamp: indefinite leave to remain. Testimonials from their UK-born children and grandchildren didn't count toward the near-impossible burden of proof of their official status that the Home Office required of them. As many Black Jamaicans have noted, deportation completes a cycle of exploitation that began with enslavement, peaked with colonization and continues with forced repatriation.

War mobilization also created an opportunity for citizens of Mexico, Jamaica and other Caribbean nations to travel to the United States under a guest-worker arrangement billed as the Emergency Labor Importation Program, better known as the H2 visa. In 1943, the British Colonial Office approved a request from the United States to recruit thousands of Jamaican men. As historian Cindy Hahamovitch notes in her book *No Man's Land*, for about a forty-year period (from 1943 to the early 1980s), H2 "was essentially a Jamaican program." The bulk of those recruited were directed to farm work, in particular cane-cutting in Florida. The program gave employers the powers to repatriate those they deemed too lazy or too troublesome if and when they asked for better working conditions.

Crime dons often played favourites with community members when selecting who to send to the US as guest workers. Although stories of the horrid living and working conditions were spread among the different garrison communities by deportees, many islanders still jumped at the opportunity to work abroad and earn double what they made in Jamaica. Deportability made these workers more vulnerable in the United States, but the program gave the island's poor a chance to travel when only those with economic resources or families in the diaspora could afford it—families like Angela's.

* * *

Angela was a few weeks short of her sixteenth birthday when she left Jamaica in 1966 to join her stepfather, who had started his PhD in Strasbourg, France, the year before. In the five decades that followed, she worked, studied and raised four children from multiple marriages in Canada, the United States, the Bahamas and St. Lucia, but she always returned to the land of her birth, whose love, she says, is in her DNA.

While I've heard variations of the same story—the same deep but hard to define sense of belonging to the homeland—in several places and from different people, Angela's experience stands out because it illustrates something about Jamaica that I haven't been able to reconcile: How can you love a place where violence has become part of everyday life? Of Angela's five husbands, two were shot dead at home or work following a break-in or an armed robbery. She herself became a target and lived under police protection for two years.

"I refuse to allow any criminal to overpower my mind," Angela tells me over an after-dinner coffee in Kingston. "I don't feel fear." Given that I hired a car and a driver to get me to and from interviews and booked a room in a hotel in part based on its security protocol, I'm not sure I relate to her sentiments, but I admire them. My friend Julie from the University of the West Indies had mentioned Angela's story as we drove past her apartment building a few days earlier, and she managed to connect us on my last night on the island. I'd desperately wanted to meet her. The way Angela talks about being in Jamaica—"The smells of the place, the people, the culture"—sounds more like a love affair, a longing that only a physical contact with the land can satisfy.

Although light-skinned enough to almost pass for white, Angela recalls many racist encounters that amplified her sense of alienation during several phases of living in North America. In 1973–74 she lived in Winnipeg with her first husband, Jerome, in what was supposed to be a long-term arrangement. One day, some white kids threw sand on her daughter in a playground and tried to intimidate her with a large dog while a priest looked on and did nothing. Angela knew then that she couldn't make a home for her family in Canada. "I didn't want her to grow up with any feelings of insecurity," she says of her daughter. When the marriage came to an end, Angela joined her parents, who were living in the Bahamas at the time.

In 1980, she married for the second time, to Christopher, a "sandy-blond, green-eyed" Jamaican she had first met at the University of Miami when both were undergraduates. At thirty, Angela went to live in Jamaica for the first time in fourteen years, but this return was harder than she'd anticipated. "I cried every day even though I was happy. Because when I opened my mouth, I was Jamaican, but I didn't know any of the major streets. I hardly knew anybody because I lived away for so long," she says. "It was shocking because coming from one island to another, I thought it wouldn't be that much of an adjustment." It took the intervention of a close friend and Christopher, "a man who loved me very much," for Angela to feel at home in Kingston. At least until a certain night in 1982.

By then, Christopher, Angela and Angela's daughter from her first marriage were living in what she describes as the "most grilled" and secure place in Kingston. One night, she got up to use the bathroom and was confronted by a burglar at the foot of her bed. He tried to rape her, but she fought him off. Christopher got into a fight with the intruder, but the man pulled a gun and shot him dead. "I was in shock. When the man ran, I ran after him in my pajamas. When I got to the landing of the stairs, my daughter called me. I realized, 'What the hell am I doing?' I went back to the room and there was Christopher on the floor, covered in blood. I didn't have a phone because they were hard to get in those days, so I screamed and screamed."

Because Angela was already in the public eye for her work

building shelters for women escaping domestic violence, the case attracted media attention. To protect her from the killer—"I was a witness to a murder, and usually in Jamaica, if you're a witness, you get murdered," she explains—she lived in a hotel and under police security for two years. She eventually went back to her parents' home in the Bahamas, but after nearly two years, she decided to return to Jamaica to continue her advocacy work. It couldn't have been an easy decision, especially as a mother, I suggest to Angela, but she disagrees. "I feel a lot of love and acceptance here, and she [her daughter] felt the same."

Five years later, Angela met Richard, a retired engineer who was from Bristol, England, and grew up in South Africa. He looked a lot like Christopher and shared many of his dreams, and he had just opened a restaurant and hotel on the water. "I was always so afraid something would happen because I was so happy. Everybody told me, 'Don't worry. Lightning doesn't strike in the same place twice.'" On December 22, 1988, one month to the day after Angela gave birth to her second child, a son, she heard some loud noises while she was nursing in her private quarters on the hotel premises. Because the island had experienced a minor earthquake and an explosion earlier that year, she didn't think much of it at first, but her intuition told her to check just in case.

Richard was hosting a private Christmas party at the restaurant for a friend's company and had hired a plainclothes policeman to help with the security because he'd gone through a violent but not fatal robbery once before. After the guests left, Richard and the policeman were set upon by a gunman as they were closing the place. The policeman fired some shots, and the gunman responded with one that hit Richard. He died on the spot. "My whole body went into shock. My milk dried up—it was traumatic," recalls Angela.

At this point I suggest a break, but she insists on carrying on. She's had thirty years to process what happened, she assures me. I find myself asking how she felt about Jamaica at that point. I don't know why, but I want her to say that she never wanted to live there again. "I still loved Jamaica, and I was never afraid," she replies. How is that possible? "Because I think it's in my DNA. I feel totally accepted here . . . There's something about this place that calls me. As soon as I land here, I feel the mountains embrace me. That makes me feel secure." She did move temporarily to St. Lucia and continued her work as a consultant there, but she says she was miserable and lonely.

It took a fourth marriage to pry her out of the Caribbean and back to the United States. Her new husband, Michael, came from Jamaica and was a successful doctor and therapist in Fort Lauderdale, Florida, where he and Angela eventually settled. The couple had two boys. The marriage to the "very controlling" Michael was Angela's longest (it lasted almost fifteen years), but also her unhappiest. She yearned to return to Jamaica, but he refused categorically. She stayed for the children, something she often told the women in her shelters never to do. Therapy and faith—"I was a sometimey Christian"—helped her survive. And running a very Jamaican household kept her sanity and satisfied her hunger for the homeland.

While immigrants are often encouraged to integrate and become part of the mainstream, Angela wanted her children to feel like minorities so they could appreciate their homeland. She didn't win that battle. The boys (two from Michael and one from Christopher) were American through and through, even as Angela became more Jamaican than ever. "When I'd meet a Jamaican, I'd ask, 'How long have you been here?'" she says. Then she'd ask if they liked living abroad. "Not one of them ever said they liked it. They all wanted to go home. That really disturbed me. That you'd live in a country for twenty, thirty years and still don't feel at home in it and yearn for your yard."

In 2009, four years after they divorced, Michael died from an aneurysm. Angela sold their big house and bought a three-bedroom condo, also in Fort Lauderdale. The next year, she closed its doors and moved to Kingston with one of her sons. "I thought I'd be sensible and ease my way into it. From the day I arrived until today, I have not regretted being here, not one day." She and husband number five—Wayne, who works in advertising and marketing—divide their time between her Kingston apartment and his studio on the beach in Negril, on the island's west coast.

No more explaining where she comes from and why she's so light-skinned for a Jamaican. She's home. Her return has a happy ending at last. But what about her American-born children, who still live in Florida? She admits that's the difficult part, but "that's another story."

* * *

The membership of the Clarendon Association of Returning Residents (CARR) is dwindling, Mrs. Elliott, its secretary and public face, tells me. In its heyday last decade, the association, in the Four Path community of the Clarendon Parish in southern

Jamaica, had seventy-five members. She counts fifty on the books today. A few have died from old age, and some simply don't feel like leaving their homes unattended to play dominoes or shoot darts every Monday and Wednesday with fellow returnees from the United Kingdom (and the odd one from Canada or the US). The association also hosts social events on the weekends, including guest lectures from experts in retirement or resettlement in Jamaica. But the membership is declining because Jamaicans in England have become more cautious about making the move home ever since British tabloids began covering stories of murdered returnees down to the goriest detail.

This Monday afternoon, I'm a guest of Percival LaTouche of JARRR. He suggested I talk to a group of returning residents (many of whom are also members of his national association and view him as their champion) to get a sense of what it's like to make the journey home. Mrs. Elliott had already told me that she would give "a firm no" if any of her Jamaican friends in Britain asked for her honest opinion about returning. Her house had been broken into twice in the past few years. "A lot of violence scares me," she says, knowing that's probably not good PR for the association or the right attitude to drum up membership. "I still have to say it's not worth coming back."

The men in the association strike me as more positive. They're certainly more vocal when it comes to their feelings about Jamaica, and more skeptical about yet another writer "from foreign" snooping around their yard. I explain my interest in homelands and say something about the war in Yemen and why I envy those who at least have the option to go home. This softens some of them up, and they agree to stop their competitive round of dominoes to talk as long as I don't use their names. (Some fear retribution from local gangs if they say the wrong thing.) One man, who eventually identifies himself as "Mr. Lawrence," dominates the conversation, but his experience seems representative of those of the thirty or so other men and one woman. (Other women played cards in a shaded outdoor spot and listened in.)

"I left Jamaica as a youth, but my only intention when I went away was to return to my homeland someday," says Mr. Lawrence, pointing out that he lived in England for almost fifty years. "Fortunately, I had enough health and strength to work for a number of years in England. I got to the state where I was able to return to my homeland, and that's what I've done. I'm sorry you can't go back to your homeland, but I wish you could because I'm enjoying it." He acknowledges that the crime worries him, but he says he still wouldn't return to England. He misses the National Health Service and his children and grand-children, though.

Another man bemoans the crime situation but sees it as part of the "home is home" philosophy of Jamaicans. "I spent like thirty years out there working, but I never found a place—Canada, America—where I felt like home. I love what I went out there to do—" He's interrupted by another man who shouts "Achieve!" because the thousands of Jamaicans who left for England or the United States in the 1950s and 1960s contrib-uted to the economy, raised families and bought homes in which they took pride of ownership. The return narrative of Jamaican retirees revolves around home ownership in a way that I haven't witnessed elsewhere in reporting this book. The promoters of the Gates of Edgehill understood this, and their sales pitch made more sense to me after my visit to the island. "This is what we know," says Mr. Lawrence. "Even if it's a shack, it's ours."

But if buying, building or living in a home increases your risk of getting murdered, how can it remain such a big force in the return fantasy of some Jamaicans? When I ask this, I know I've lost the room. The mood turns defensive. "I was in London. Had a nice home," says a man who has been quiet until now. "There's no country in the world that has more cameras than the UK. They track you from the moment you leave home to work and back again, twenty-four seven. And the crime and violence are still there. It's just a part of life. It's what we have to live with."

The men return to their games, and LaTouche and I head back to Kingston. His criticism of the Jamaican government and its law enforcement agencies may be unwavering, but so is his adoration of the country's landscape, which he proudly points out to me throughout the drive. I'm too distracted and conflicted to pay much attention, though. Something about the mountains and the rural roads triggers memories of Yemen. What Mr. Lawrence said about me not being able to go home rankled. I suspect he meant it in sympathy, but I can't help feeling envious of and mad at him at the same time. I also need to weigh his positive sentiments against the story of a couple I met the previous week. Their homeland return and home-buying experience turned into a disaster.

Carl and Angela (not the Angela from earlier in the chapter) had moved to New Jersey from the Caribbean separately but at around the same time (1996–97). They succeeded in their different professions—she as a nurse at the JFK Medical Center, he as a landlord and gas station owner—and both became American citizens, but they eventually left the US to start anew in the old country.

A family tragedy triggered Carl's return. In 2010, his eight-year-old daughter from a previous relationship drowned in a local swimming pool. The loss was incalculable, and Carl dealt with it by flying back and forth to Jamaica to clear his head. "My mind was going like crazy," he tells me when we meet at LaTouche's office. "It was a hard hit. What place to go back to but the homeland?" Despite the particular nature of his loss, he wanted to be near water, ideally an ocean.

In 2015, he and Angela, then his new wife, made the decision to retire in Jamaica, even though both were still in their early forties. They had left the island for good, they thought, when he was seventeen and she was in her twenties. Angela tells me that coming home wasn't a goal at that stage of her life, but she relented to support Carl and to see where his dream of a return would lead them. They came from different parishes and family backgrounds, and she doubted if her strict upbringing would align with his more haphazard one (Carl's mother left him out on the streets to fend for himself, Angela says). Whenever they returned for a visit, they'd spend time in Angela's family's more affluent and safer surroundings in Saint Thomas Parish, in the southeast corner of the island. But because of Carl's need to be closer to the ocean, they bought farmland in a different part of Saint Thomas and opted to build a house from scratch.

The reality of being home hit Carl shortly after they purchased the land. "You stop in a store to buy something, and they overcharge you because of your accent," he says. "You hire someone to do a job, they take your money and run. If they do it, they're sloppy." The contractors, the plumbers, the masons—almost everyone he hired to build his dream home overcharged and underdelivered. Did the fact that he's an American have something to do with it? I ask. "Because I'm a foreigner," he replies. "Not just because I'm an American. They don't discriminate . . . Once you come from anywhere different than Jamaica, you're seen as rich." It's a familiar story.

Coming Home to Jamaica, a booklet prepared with input from the island's NGOs, the Ministry of National Security and the British High Commission, advises returnees to "try to be 'Jamaican'" by using local accents and dialects, as overseas ones "attract unwanted attention." This one line in an otherwise comprehensive and practical guide drew criticism from anti-deportation activists for its cultural insensitivity and its impracticality. How can you expect people who spent most of their lives in Britain or the United States to suddenly act and sound Jamaican as if it were a party trick?

After many delays and arguments with workers, Carl and Angela moved to their new home, which they equipped with a state-of-the-art security system. At first it seemed like they could finally leave their troubles, in both New Jersey and Jamaica, behind and focus on their new lives. The farm kept Carl busy, buying tractors and livestock and trying to match unemployed young men and women from the parish with odd jobs on the land. The couple had two children back to back (they were two and one when we met in 2018). "Everything was going fine for us here," Angela recalls. Until one day in early 2018, when the house was broken into while the family was in Kingston. Break-ins had become such routine events in Saint Thomas that the most any homeowner could hope for was for the police to show up and take note of what was stolen for insurance purposes. Very few burglars get arrested, and according to Percival LaTouche, the police are often complicit or at least turn a blind eye.

Knowing this, Carl decided to play detective and investigate the break-in himself. His questioning led to a young man from the community, so he went to the boy's house to talk to his parents. The plan was not to threaten the kid but to help him get out of his life of crime. Carl cast himself as an older brother who could help a younger one. He bitterly regrets his naivety. The young man instead accused Carl of beating him up, and he now faces assault charges and has become a target of local gangs seeking retribution. With support from LaTouche and JARRR, Carl has been dealing with the legal ramifications of the assault case and police intimidation. (The actual burglar revealed the name of a policeman who was involved in covering up the break-in.) After hooking him up with a lawyer, LaTouche suggested going public: "I call names. That's why I've survived forty years now. You have to be tough."

But the real damage has been to Carl's homeland fantasy—he's willing to walk away from it all. Life is more important, he says. "I can try selling my house, but maybe I'll get next to nothing for it. And then there's the farmland." But where to next? Carl can't face the thought of going back to New Jersey, and despite everything that happened in Jamaica, he still wants to live near the ocean. For the time being, he and Angela feel imprisoned in their own home(land), having ramped up security around the property. "We didn't come up here to lock ourselves in. We tried to help the situation, and we became the bad guys," Carl says, pointing out that his story should be a cautionary tale to all Jamaicans who dream of going home.

"I wouldn't advise them to buy anything," Angela adds. "The government has to do something about its culture. They need to clear up the corruption in the [police] force. If the people can't trust the police, then you can't live because who's going to take care of you?"

* * *

The hustle came easy to Courtney. As a child in Kingston in the early 1970s, he kept an eye on dance parties and snuck out in the early hours of the morning to collect the empty beer bottles and sell them to the drink truck. He learned to dance so he could perform outside bars, collecting a shilling here or threepence there. "That was good-quality money. You can spend it and get some change," he says as he explains the old currency units.

When he turned nine and joined his mother and seven of his older siblings (all female) in the Bronx, he brought that hustling spirit (or entrepreneurialism, depending on your point of view) with him as he waited outside checkout lines at the local supermarket to return trolleys or carry bags. He offered a winning smile and the right attitude, and in return received tips that ranged from a quarter to, in one case, twenty-two dollars, an instance he recalls vividly, alongside many other details of his life in New York City. He received that tip in 1976, but before the decade was over, he'd spent time in a juvenile correction facility for attempted robbery—and the next twenty years taking his hustling to a whole new level. He was deported to Jamaica in 2001.

Courtney and I agreed to chat in the coffee shop of my Kingston hotel on a Saturday afternoon, but we had been introduced earlier in the week at Peace Management Initiative. Its executive director, Damian Hutchinson, had arranged for me to meet Courtney, now fifty-three, and a host of other male deportees who not only have rebuilt their lives after their return but are now giving back by volunteering in communities ravaged by gun and political violence. Some of the older men (those in their late sixties and early seventies) entered the US on tourist visas and then overstayed. They were deported for such criminal offences as possessing or dealing marijuana. The men of Courtney's age travelled to the United States as children, either with their parents or to join family already established there. They came of age in America, as their stories of high school and pop culture references attest. They *are* Americans. They too were deported for drug offences or more serious convictions.

But something about Courtney's memories of Kingston and New York City set him apart from his cohort and made me want to chat with him in more depth. As I transcribed our interview a few weeks later, I realized why: Courtney knows how to tell a story, or at least *his* story. Hutchinson told me that his quiet voice and gentle demeanour are genuine but belie a violent past in America.

"I was happy to leave Jamaica," Courtney begins that Saturday in the hotel coffee shop, recounting his many reasons. By the time he was eight, he had witnessed his first murder—a man opened fire and killed an activist from a rival political party in broad daylight. His father had a "tendency to loosen his belt," Courtney recalls, before clarifying that he was a caring man who provided for him, his only brother and a sister. (The three siblings were the last to join their mother in the Bronx.) The last time they saw each other was when the father dropped off his New York–bound son at the airport in 1974. "He told me, 'I owe you a beating.'" As a child with "black-pepper-grain hair" and dark skin, Courtney saw through the island's colourism, whereby lighter-skinned Jamaicans fared better and were seen as more desirable. A hierarchy based on skin tones prevailed both before and after Jamaican independence. At times, the census included such categories as White, Black, Brown, Coloured and Near Whites. "That was something that really stuck to me. We have to classify people when all I see around me is Black people."

Courtney remembers hearing that money falls from trees in America, but his mother's experience as a full-time nanny to a white family disabused him of that immigrant fantasy shortly after his arrival in the Bronx. When she got sick and faced mounting hospital bills, Courtney knew he had to chip in. First came the supermarket work, but before he turned fifteen, he'd started to deal weed. He'd buy four bags for twenty dollars, roll the joints and sell enough to earn about eighty bucks in a single day. By the time his family moved from the more genteel north end of the Bronx to an apartment in the projects in the South Bronx, Courtney had joined the junior ranks of the Black Spades gang and graduated to selling bags of weed before moving on to pills and then to mescaline and acid.

"The gang became like family," he says. "They showed me how to survive on the street." He dealt out of his school and around his high-rise. His initiation into the gang by robbing a strip club, however, landed him his first arrest. Despite her straitened circumstances, his mother raised the $7,500 bail. Courtney's first stint in a juvenile correctional facility, at the notorious Spofford Detention Center in the Bronx, lasted two months. Once released, he returned to school, where he picked up his grades. While he continued to deal marijuana before and after class, he generally kept a low profile.

That all changed one day in late 1980, when he saw a man in a neighbourhood apartment sitting at a table with a scale and a "whole lot of white stuff" that meant a "whole lot of money." He knew the profit margins of the cocaine business were higher than what he made on weed on his best days, but so were the risks in dealing it. So why would he put himself in such a vulnerable position? At this point of the interview, Courtney's answers begin to sound like a collection of pop culture signposts—*Scarface*, blaxploitation, street dancing. "You can't be out there and not have the money to buy the things you like," he says. "Maybe I want to go to the movies, buy a pizza or new sneakers. That's when the b-boy stuff started to happen. To hang out with the b-boys and the breakdancing and all that, you actually had to be fly. You had to *stay* fly."

For most of the 1980s, Courtney was in and out of state prisons, including Riker's Island, and in and out of dealing weed, cocaine and crack. He and one of his sisters (she died of cancer in 1988) ran a crack operation out of her apartment in the Bronx. After Riker's, Courtney went solo and chose a different part of the city to deal from. With an army (his word) of six men—three pushing and three on the lookout—and a work schedule that ran from six in the evening to six in the morning, Courtney had complete control of his new domain. He got married in 1991, and the couple welcomed their only child a year later.

His success irked rival gangs, however, and they started to divert customers away from him. A turf war erupted. Courtney had already learned all about guns in prison, and during a chance encounter, he used his to shoot one of his rivals. The bullet lodged in the man's head, causing cerebral damage that left him disabled. Courtney was charged with but not convicted of attempted murder, possession of more than half a kilo of cocaine and possession of weapons. In what he believes to be a police setup, he was convicted in 1993 of a C felony (possession of marijuana). Because he had a previous felony, he faced the possibility of twelve years in prison. He ultimately spent six years in Riker's Island and an upstate New York jail, followed by two more at an Immigration and Naturalization Service (INS) detention centre as he unsuccessfully fought a deportation case he would likely have won just a few years earlier.

In 1996, two of Bill Clinton's toughest pieces of legislation came into effect. The first, the Illegal Immigration Reform and Immigrant Responsibility Act, closed loopholes and allowed for the deportation of undocumented immigrants who had committed misdemeanours or felonies. The second, the Antiterrorism and Effective Death Penalty Act of 1996, narrowed the scope of habeas corpus as a means to challenge criminal convictions. (Habeas corpus petitions were frequently used by prisoners to contest the constitutionality of their convictions in federal courts.) Both acts meant that someone like Courtney, without extensive legal resources, could no longer fight deportation.

In 2001, Courtney, then thirty-six, was sent back to the country he had left at age nine. Although he had obtained a US green card in the 1980s, he'd never applied for citizenship. One of his sisters had returned voluntarily many years earlier, and she eased his way back into the homeland. "I didn't know what to expect when I came home," he tells me. "You read in the newspaper and you hear from my sister that Jamaica has changed, that there's no work, that there's violence."

While in prison in New York, Courtney had learned about HIV and AIDS prevention, and once back in Jamaica, he used that knowledge to land some work in counselling and sexual-health education through an international program run out of the USAID offices in Kingston. He and I meet on a Saturday afternoon because that evening, he plans to visit the parts of town where men who have sex with men hang out. Courtney will reach out to them with tips on safe sex and harm reduction. The funding for such programs can be erratic, and Courtney tells me he supplements his income with conflict-resolution work, which pays him a monthly stipend of $10,000 Jamaican (less than $100 Canadian).

A shortage of money concerns him more at this stage of life because he's the doting father of a four-year-old girl, Kourtney-Ann, from a new relationship. "All she talks about is her daddy," he says as he shows me her pictures and explains that she lives with her mother in Spanish Town. (He's separated but not divorced from his New York–based wife and estranged from their son.) For now, Jamaica is home, but he'd like it not to be.

"I feel that there's more to offer than this in Jamaica where life is concerned—opportunities for my daughter and for myself as I reach a certain age. I can't work forever, and I like to have something. I can't penny-pinch forever."

With help from the Family Unification and Resettlement Initiative, a local organization that helps deportees "adjust positively" to their new lives, Courtney plans to get back to the US under a rehabilitation program. Deportees who have worked, paid their taxes and contributed to their home societies have an opportunity to reverse course and return to America, especially if sponsored and supported by US-based family members. "What I have to offer can be a contribution to the United States of America," Courtney says confidently.

But it's hard to see how the US can open its doors again to Courtney after four years of Trumpism. Perhaps the Biden administration will take a different approach. I can't help thinking that he had his chance—and his green card—and blew it. But I also can't imagine what it's like to live on so little after getting used to a more financially rewarding life in North America—even if he got his share of the American dream through illicit means. The stories of people like Courtney and the others I met at the Peace Management Initiative reveal the harsh reality of going home as a deportee. These men have returned to a homeland fraught with economic and social problems. But the America they were deported from is undergoing racial and cultural convulsions of its own, and that makes a return to it dangerous and unpredictable.

***

Yvonne Grant knows first-hand what coming home voluntarily feels like: in 1997, she returned to Jamaica after twenty-five years in England. Her work as the director of Open Arms, a rehabilitation centre for Kingston's homeless, also gives her insight into involuntary returns. Since many deportees have no family members to stay with when they arrive, they are counted among the homeless. About half the beds in the all-male Open Arms compound—which sleeps up to ninety people—are occupied by deportees. To return to your homeland only to find yourself without a home increases the depression and anxiety among deportees, says the former mental-health nurse and educator.

When we met in 2018, she was just six weeks short of her seventy-fifth birthday and scoffed at the idea of retirement. "I tried it before and it didn't work out. I'd just rust up," she tells me. She refrains from calling herself a workaholic, but her work ethic and determination helped her survive a move from Kingston in 1962, at the age of eighteen, to London, where her father had lived for a few years after the Second World War as part of the Windrush generation. (He eventually decamped for the United States because it was closer to his beloved Jamaica.) Yvonne's Kingston boyfriend, also eighteen, soon followed her to London, and the two were married within a year. To survive, she worked as a milliner in an immigrant-friendly East London hat shop and began to adjust to the cold and bleak climate. "I never saw daylight," she says as she describes—fondly, I must say—her long shifts. "They wanted us there. They needed people to work."

Nursing offered many Jamaican immigrants, and women in particular, a chance to move into a professional career. For Yvonne, it was a lifelong dream. She started nursing school after giving birth to the first of her three boys and had completed her training by the time the second was delivered. She recalls "difficulties" on the job, not because of outwardly racist doctors or patients—although she recounts a story about a patient who wouldn't take his medication from her "Black hands"—but because she had to prove herself over and over to be treated as equal. "You have to shine. You have to work twice, sometimes three times, as hard."

By and large, she lived uneventful family and professional lives. She and her husband, a woodworker, moved around different neighbourhoods in south and northwest London, raised three "alright" boys and dealt with her homesickness by taking regular trips back to Jamaica. She introduced her sons to the food, the culture, the sights from a young age. For the children, Jamaica became a second home; for Yvonne, it remained first. Looking back at her twenty-five years in England, she describes it as home only "partially" or "most of the time." Coming back to Jamaica, however, was a "dream." Many of the early waves of Jamaican immigrants, she says, worked in England just to save enough money to come home. "I think it's in your blood," she says. "Maybe it's the way of life. You feel freer. Something in your spirit, in your mind. Yes, there's poverty, all sorts of things. At the same time, there's a sense of freedom."

Her dream came true in 1997, when one of her brothers, who was living in Canada at the time, suggested she meet with the nursing school faculty at the University of the West Indies in

Kingston. As it happened, the school's expert on mental-health nursing was leaving. By the time Yvonne made it back to London, she had received an offer to teach full time. She prayed on it, but the final push came from the children. "They wanted somewhere to stay," she says with a knowing smile, when they go on vacation. Although she had travelled back to the island many times, she still underestimated the difference between visiting and living there. Red tape, disorganization and a slower pace of life irritated her. If she missed England at all, it was because of its "discipline" and the grandchildren.

Yvonne worked full time until 2001 and then part time until 2005, when she had her unsuccessful first stab at retirement. By 2006, the homeless situation in Kingston had reached a crisis point. As part of a five-year strategic plan spearheaded by the government and the private sector, Open Arms began operating as a drop-in centre to feed, clean and counsel the homeless and the destitute. The demand quickly exceeded supply. Yvonne volunteered to run Open Arms with an eye on expanding its services. Over the years, it became less of a drop-in centre and more of a homeless shelter. The *Coming Home to Jamaica* booklet lists it in the emergency accommodation section.

Yvonne's job takes her to the island's different airports and processing centres to greet deportees and guide them through customs and passport retrieval. "I make them feel welcome," she says, but that takes a long time and draws on all her training in mental health. "They're angry, resentful, sad. Some of them are very frightened. Some of them are happy to come home because they have been in prison for a long time. Each person is different, but there's a lot of anger. They're angry with Jamaica for taking them . . . The anger is always projected [outwards], not towards themselves."

Despite that anger, Yvonne says that very rarely do any of the deportees revert to a life of crime or join gangs. Her experience on the ground echoes the results of independent studies, which contradict the government's position on this issue. Some may reoffend, but most deportees are as vulnerable to Jamaica's violence as the people who have never left. What's worse, some Jamaicans target deportees because they're seen as possibly richer than the average citizen—having come from foreign and all that.

The shelter runs on a strict daily schedule. The dorms close between 8:00 a.m. and 4:00 p.m., but residents may stay on the premises, provided they don't congregate in the kitchen or the entrance. Breakfast is served between 7:30 and 8:30, lunch between 12:30 and 1:30, and dinner between 6:00 and 6:45. Gates close and lights go out at 10:00 p.m., except on Fridays and Saturdays, when the participants (the preferred term for residents) may stay up an extra hour. The shelter emphasizes social enterprise, with some participants tending to the fruit and vegetable (okra, pumpkin) garden, while others take on beekeeping or staff an affiliated thrift store. As Yvonne guides me through the premises, she points out the kitchen, where one participant is preparing a lunch of mackerel, vegetables and rice.

Since some women drop in during the day for training, the shelter offers a beauty salon, in addition to the barbershop for the men. A classroom that seats sixty doubles as a lecture hall some evenings. British deportees are assigned to a section called

Maureen's Place, which was inaugurated in 2011 as a joint effort between Jamaica's Ministry of National Security and the British High Commission. Each of the thirty residents there has a room of his own—a higher level of accommodation than other men enjoy—although the proximity of the units makes them look more like locker rooms than bedrooms. In his book *Deporting Black Britons*, Luke de Noronha suggests that the shelter helps the Jamaican government deal with the influx of deportees but also facilitates the UK government's deportation efforts because the Home Office uses it to demonstrate that the people it sends home will survive the initial shock of their return journey.

"Sometimes you do feel sorry for them because they would have left young children and families behind," Yvonne says. "Some of them are bewildered, lost souls. They don't know what's happening to them." Open Arms provides a place to sleep and a transition back into life in the homeland. But many believe that they have been deported unfairly and will one day return to England, Canada or the United States. One of the men I spoke to lived illegally in England for twenty-five years until he was deported in early 2018, just as he turned sixty-seven. "England was my home," he tells me. "I don't feel adjusted here." Maybe things will change when he starts making money, he tells me, but nine months into his return, he hasn't received his Jamaican ID or a passport. He still hopes to be reunited with the girlfriend he left behind in Brixton.

An optimistic outlook gives deportees the means to survive their new reality. Their move may have happened against their wishes, but they have to make peace with the fact that this is their homeland—the same one that draws wealthy retirees and their life savings. In the novel *A Brief History of Seven Killings*, one of Marlon James's narrators writes that in Kingston's violent ghettos, "Reason is for rich people. We have madness." I suspect the same applies to the division between deportees and retirees. I'm just not sure I can tell who is following reason and who has gone mad with their homeland returns.

PART II

Chapter 4

THERE'S NO BUSINESS LIKE RETURN BUSINESS

As the United States, Britain and, to a lesser extent, Canada fumbled their responses to the COVID-19 pandemic in the first few months of 2020, a handful of countries in East Asia and the Pacific reacted with what one public health expert in Britain described as a winning combination of alarm and thorough preparedness. Taiwan, South Korea, Singapore, Hong Kong and Vietnam have confronted epidemics in the past, including MERS and SARS, and drew on lessons learned from previous encounters to contain the virus. Vietnam, with a population of nearly ninety-seven million, lasted until July 31 before it reported its first death. As impressive as that sounds, it pales in comparison with the achievement of New Zealand, a country that has not just flattened the curve but crushed it.

Under the firm, science-backed leadership of Prime Minister Jacinda Ardern, the country of almost five million people barred entry to travellers from China, mobilized a sophisticated test-and-trace operation, and went into lockdown early and enforced it rigorously. Just three days after the WHO declared the outbreak a "public health emergency of international concern," on January 30, the country introduced containment measures and promised to strengthen them as needed. By the end of 2020, the death toll from the pandemic stood at a relatively negligible 25, with total cases at 2,144.

Global responses to this stellar performance overshadowed another good-news story out of the country: there's been an influx of highly qualified citizens who have chosen to return after living abroad for years and even decades. Many have come back to wait out the pandemic and seek shelter from a world riddled with "destabilizing populism and nationalism which, like the virus itself, seems mercifully absent from these shores," reported the *New Zealand Herald*, calling this influx a "once-in-a-lifetime talent shock."

An estimated 33,000 New Zealanders made their way home between the first and third quarters of 2020. In the year to June 2020, the country reported 79,400 in net migration (measured as the difference between those arriving for good and those leaving for good), a figure not seen since the early 1990s. The final numbers will likely trend up as temporary returnees decide to make their move permanent. One of the returning New Zealanders, Peter Gordon, a world-class chef who lived in London for thirty-one years, started a business with his partner to sell the country's produce globally. They named it Homeland.

New Zealand has built a reputation as a host country that draws highly skilled immigrants from around the world. That achievement lives alongside another, less dominant narrative of the country, however, as a place that routinely loses its talent to cosmopolitan centres, particularly London and New York. Travelling and working abroad has become a rite of passage for educated New Zealanders as they compensate for growing up in a place so physically remote from international hubs. The country has one of the largest offshore communities per capita among member states of the Organisation for Economic Co-operation and Development (OECD), according to Kea New Zealand, an organization founded in 2001 to "connect and engage" the diaspora to benefit the homeland.

As journalist Duncan Greive wrote in a story about the returnees in the *Herald*, the departure of the country's best and brightest has always been discussed among decision makers with a "wounded pride." After all, few places can rival New Zealand's spectacular scenery, mild temperatures, tolerant social attitudes and universal healthcare coverage. Yes, New Zealand sits on an arc of seismic faults in the Pacific known as the Ring of Fire, making it prone to earthquakes. But so does California, home of Silicon Valley, which is built atop the San Andreas and other faults.

As the pandemic ushers in a temporary reversal in population trends—more New Zealanders going home, fewer new immigrants coming in due to restricted border controls—the country faces the challenge of matching job opportunities to the skill sets of its returnees. The agriculture sector, for example, is unlikely to benefit from this particular talent surge, given how many repatriated New Zealanders have been working in the technology and service industries.

Taiwan, which has recorded just ten deaths and fewer than one thousand cases of COVID-19, has pitched itself to overseas citizens and dual nationals as an escape from the pandemic. In 2020, about 270,000 more people came to the island than left it, and the phrase "Covid migrants" is making its way through the local culture. "The influx of people," the *New York Times* reports, "helped make Taiwan one of [2020's] fastest-growing economies—indeed, one of the few to expand at all." The tech sector has benefited the most from this particular return story.

What New Zealand and Taiwan have gained as an unintended consequence of the pandemic, many other countries around the world have been actively pursuing for decades. Return is a big business.

Whether through nationally mandated campaigns or public–private partnerships, the return of diasporic communities fuses politics and economics, business needs and personal longing, individual and mass movements. While the outward migration of people with skills to sell can be determined by, among other measures, financial need, individual returns are governed by such hard-to-quantify factors as the desire to reunite with family and a need to reconnect with the homeland.

Measuring the economic impact of return migration on host and home country can be tricky, however. Host countries in particular don't keep records of what researchers refer to as the "outflow" of residents—even though, on average, two out of five migrants will leave the host country within five years of arrival. As Jackline Wahba, an economics professor at the University of Southampton, points out in various publications, including the

International Handbook on Migration and Economic Development, this makes the data on returns "sparse and inconsistent," and therefore difficult to analyze.

The multiple routes that return takes further complicate the process of quantifying its economic effect. While returns from the Global North to the Global South tend to receive the lion's share of critical and media analyses (and this book is no exception), the flow of capital is generally not as one-directional. In her research into the return of Senegal's diaspora, ethnographer Giulia Sinatti demonstrates that many migrants "sustain transnational ties with the former country of immigration" after homecoming. Some returns are not final—many migrants choose to divide their time and resources between two homelands, natal and adopted. Returns also take place among countries of similar or relatively small economic differences, as the mobility of migrant workers within South and East Asia suggests.

Despite the above challenges, there are a number of economic benefits for people who decide to go back to where they came from, as Wahba and other return scholars have shown. And governments of both developed and developing countries are paying attention to what's being said and liking what they hear.

Return migrants by and large invest their savings in local businesses, creating jobs and opportunities for compatriots who never left. Studies indicate that return migrants also transfer skills acquired in the host country to their homeland. The same applies to new ideas, management styles and norms they've picked up abroad. While some locals will inevitably resist these changes—and red tape, corruption and bureaucracy present their own problems—researchers note a healthy exchange between returnees and non-migrant communities that benefits the home country as a whole.

None of this negates the narrative of "failed" immigrants returning to their homeland without savings or job prospects. The "successful" ones, studies show, are just as likely to return to their home country after reaching their target savings, a sum they believe will go a long way back home, as either the basis for retirement or capital for a new business.

The biggest and most noticeable economic benefit of return migration is that it happens, for the most part, from developed and wealthy countries to less developed and poorer ones. Return therefore should be considered one of the most direct and impartial transfers of wealth—or at the very least a redistribution of it—on a global scale. Even though it frequently takes place when migrants reach the end of their careers, return as a process often covers different generations, as it impacts children or younger family members. In this sense, return pays long-term dividends.

I've been thinking about my own return mostly in emotional and selfish terms. What do I get in return, as it were? But as I was researching the business side of this issue, I began to see going back to Yemen as something less self-involved and more as a way to pay back my land of origin—a personalized program of reparation and repair. I have no experience with and no interest in running a business, but perhaps I can support the next generation of journalists, playwrights, filmmakers, fiction and non-fiction writers as they try to reach an audience outside Yemen. My niece Yousra, a talented documentary director, is part of a generation of gifted artists whose work—always polit-ical, invariably passionate—deserves a bigger platform.

I dream of restoring my Arabic to a level where I gain back my own voice in that language, but I also imagine shining the spotlight on young creatives in Yemen by translating their work into English. That would be my way of transferring skills I gained abroad to my homeland. And if there's a small business opening in doing that, so be it. I may lose my shirt, but whatever I stand to gain will be divided more equally and equitably, or so I like to think.

* * *

Engaging the diaspora in conversations about the development and economic growth of the homeland has emerged as one of the defining aspects of managing migration globally. At least half of United Nations member states have established public authorities to connect with the diaspora, according to Oleg Chirita, head of global initiatives at the International Centre for Migration Policy Development (ICMPD). The African Union even defines the word "diaspora" as "people of African origin living outside the continent . . . who are willing to contribute to the development of the continent and the building of the Afri-can Union." Various studies estimate the number of Canadian expats to be somewhere between 2.8 million and 3.5 million. In his book *Planet Canada*, journalist John Stackhouse calls them an "undeclared eleventh province" that's "quietly shaping" Canada's global identity.

When migrants become involved in development and economic

projects, it creates a link with the homeland in which their money and expertise travel home before they do—*if* they do, of course. This explains why several countries have changed the wording in official documents to recast the diaspora as either a "region" or a "national asset." Chirita has described oft-cited narratives of the diaspora as "key actors for maximizing the positive impact of migration for development." This recasting erodes the distinction between home and host country. More Lebanese, for example, live outside their homeland than within its borders.

The more blatant monetary aspects of the homeland's call on the diaspora are usually tempered with a few civil and political privileges, such as voting rights and dual citizenships, and even some cultural rights (guided trips home, language retention classes). We'll see a striking example of this from Taiwan later in the book.

Seeing return through an economic lens raises two major concerns. First, it reduces varied and complex human experiences and mobilities to a formula. Second, it inadvertently elevates the contributions of men over those of women, since the former dominate in-demand sectors such as industry, technology, biomedicine and finance. Measuring return and diasporic worth by business practices and their effect on GDP is an exclusionary act.

Other models do a better job of balancing the needs of the homeland with the skill set of the returnees. In 2001, for example, the International Organization for Migration (IOM) started a Migration for Development in Africa program that has facilitated the return of 150 doctors and nurses to various African nations. According to IOM's senior specialist on migration and human development, Tauhid Pasha, the returnees have helped train more than fifteen thousand local health workers. IOM has also helped nearly two thousand skilled migrants from various African countries return to their homelands through its Return and Reintegration of Qualified African Nationals program.

Homecoming Revolution, an executive search firm based in South Africa, bills itself as a "brain gain" company. It searches for talented African workers around the globe to "bring them home to their respective home countries in sub-Saharan Africa." Its focus is on anglophone countries such as Kenya, Tanzania, Ghana, Nigeria and South Africa, which tend to have higher living standards and relatively fewer conflicts.

Homecoming Revolution has also played a role in the return of white South Africans who left their homeland in the post-apartheid era. It's estimated that as of 2016, eight hundred thousand white South Africans had departed for New Zealand, Australia, the United States, Canada, the United Kingdom and other parts of Europe, as well as the Gulf economies, to escape rising crime and what they perceive as the reverse discrimination of Black-empowerment policies. Angel Jones, CEO of the firm, believes that nearly half have since returned to South Africa. The country also welcomed back a significant number of its Black citizens who had left to escape violence and to seek a better life.

At the European Union, the management of return has become part of a security-driven campaign to protect member countries from waves of migration over the past decade. As Anna Triandafyllidou and Alexandra Ricard-Guay wrote in the *Journal of Immigrant & Refugee Studies*, in a review of recent essay collections on irregular and return migration, the categorization of return into forced or voluntary shows how politicized and misleading the discourse has become within the EU. The voluntariness in the EU's Assisted Voluntary Repatriation Program, they wrote, comes only after the migrant "has been apprehended and faced with the tough dilemma of absconding or departing 'voluntarily.'" The EU's aggressive investment in returns is underscored by the fact that by 2018, almost 22.3 million people with citizenship in a non-EU member state and 38.2 million born outside the EU resided within it.

Many countries encourage returns to stay competitive in economies that have rapidly shifted from the industrial or agricultural to the knowledge-based, particularly in digital industries. In contemporary China, this pattern has acquired a geopolitical twist.

* * *

When it comes to encouraging and attracting (or coercing) return migration, no country comes close to China's record over the past four decades.

For the Chinese Communist Party of the People's Republic of China, inducing students and professionals born or educated overseas to return to the mainland forms part of an official policy to address gaps in innovation, technology and management. In its early stages, the Cultural Revolution of Mao Zedong (1966–76) targeted students, intellectuals and anyone else the party classified as an elite in favour of an ideologically pure proletariat.

Mao's attempt to control his party and reinvigorate the Communist revolution plunged the country into a decade of violence, starvation and economic mayhem. A generation of scientists, thinkers and innovators was almost wiped out. Although the Chinese economy and its industrial and technology sectors have made great strides in the past forty years—vaulting the country into the world's fastest-growing and second-largest economy, after the US—the perception of an innovation gap between China and Western democracies persists.

Early returnees played a role in China's modern transformation, and the economic opportunities that came with that transformation continue to draw new returnees at a high rate. In 2009, just 42 percent of Chinese students studying abroad returned after graduation. Since 2014, the rate of return has averaged 78 percent. This increase reflects the larger number of Chinese students pursuing degrees outside the mainland—662,100 in 2018, up 8.83 percent from the previous year, according to figures from the education ministry—but it's also proof of how resilient China's economy was to the financial credit crunch of 2008–09. Of the nearly 6 million Chinese who studied abroad between 1978 and 2018, 3.65 million returned to the homeland.

Facts and propaganda mingle in some high-profile return stories. In 2017, the Chinese Academy of Sciences (CAS) announced that Yang Chen Ning, a 1957 winner of Nobel Prize for Physics, and Andrew Yao, the 2000 winner of the A.M. Turing Award in computing, had renounced their American citizenship. Both had returned to China as Americans but were inducted into the CAS as domestic citizens. The news of their renunciation was announced two years after both had given up their American passports, but the academy didn't provide an explanation for the delay. As an article in *Science* magazine explains, China has often complained that its people are awarded recognition only when they hold foreign passports. At the very least, repatriating internationally recognized scientists increases China's Nobel Prize tally. In their introduction to *New Thinking about the Taiwan Issue*, political scientists Jean-Marc Blanchard and Dennis V. Hickey argue that should China secure Taiwan, it will inherit its "advanced technology, an educated workforce, and its managerial and productive expertise"—applying a business lens to a geopolitical conflict that often gets lost in discussions of China's territorial overreach.

China's survival as the world's second-largest market and as a global and regional superpower depends on how it maintains international returns. But internal returns may play as important a role in the future.

For years now, one of the big stories coming out of China has been the development of megacities, including Beijing and Shanghai, the two reigning champions. When the coronavirus was first reported in Wuhan, the capital city of Hubei province, many people (me included) were surprised to learn that this relatively unknown (in the West) Chinese city had a population of nearly nine million. The building frenzy that changed China's landscape over the past two decades was largely the work of internal migrants who, like their Indian counterparts, left their villages in pursuit of better-paid opportunities in urban areas. In 2016, an estimated 286 million Chinese workers moved to cities.

Every Lunar New Year—until the coronavirus struck and the Chinese Communist Party issued one of the most severe lockdown orders in the world—a remarkable mass migration took place as migrant workers returned to their villages and rural communities for an extended holiday. A report from 2018 puts the number of new year passenger journeys (mostly by train and bus) at three billion. In 2019, I was transfixed by TV footage of these journeys during a two-month visit to Hong Kong that coincided with the Lunar Year festivities. News anchors and experts explained the meticulous planning it takes to orchestrate the safe return journeys of millions of workers every year.

This logistical feat underlined some unsettling facts about life in modern China. Its overcrowded and increasingly unaffordable cities make little to no room for the people who build them. Migration to cities has had an adverse effect on rural communities and their centuries-old way of life. To mitigate the situation, China has encouraged the entrepreneurial work of return migrants in their home villages. According to the ministry of agriculture, five million returning entrepreneurs account for two-thirds of all new businesses in rural China. Between 2015 and 2017, an average of 391 businesses were registered each day.

As a report in the *South China Morning Post* in 2018 suggests, Beijing's investment in new motorways and in expanding internet access to rural areas has radically altered life in Chinese villages. They are now "more connected than ever, making it easier for residents to start businesses and reach customers far away." These return migrants close the wage gap between cities and villages, and bring with them skills they learned while living away from home. As international demand for goods and services slows due to the pandemic, Chinese economists have been seeking growth opportunities and a bigger consumer share at home. This domestic version of return migration is now one of the country's multiple economic engines.

The timing couldn't have worked out better, as a ten-year international talent-recruitment initiative known as the Thousand Talents Program. It was part of an extensive effort by Beijing to lure diasporic citizens back to the mainland and invite recognized experts to "maintain the Chinese growth locomotive," writes Wang Huiyao, a researcher and past vice president of China Overseas Returned Scholars Association. He suggests that these talent-recruitment plans brought more than twenty thousand high-level experts to China. The one from 2008 alone attracted more than three thousand high-quality professionals of Chinese origins.

While high tech, business and science draw the largest number of ethnic Chinese returnees, almost all sectors of the economy and public life have been changed by their homecoming. Education, health, culture and government have felt the impact. Aggregate figures from the past decade suggest that 78 percent of all university presidents and 72 percent of directors of key laboratories identified as returnees. Many have become the chief architects of Beijing's Belt and Road Initiative, an enormous infrastructure project designed to spread its global influence. China has been on a shopping and building spree, buying ports in Israel and the Horn of Africa while setting up railways in Saudi Arabia and investing in Iraq and Iran. It's difficult to understand modern China, and leader Xi Jinping, without absorbing the full impact of its return policies.

China's only legitimate Asian rival for regional and global supremacy is India, which has also seen the return of business leaders and entrepreneurs as its strong economy—at least by pre-pandemic measures—has lifted millions out of poverty and reversed the country's brain drain. While exact numbers on returning Indians (sometimes referred to as non-resident Indians, or NRIs) can be hard to find, a study from Duke University, Berkeley and the Kauffman Foundation for Entrepreneurship suggests that as many as 60 percent have returned to India to start new businesses. By 2015, half of all NRIs were involved in their own ventures, and according to *Franchise India*, nearly 80 percent cited demand for their skills as a reason for their return. Like Silicon Valley, India has embraced start-ups and business ecosystems with a religious zeal. Read any articles about or studies of returning venture capitalists and you'll note the proliferation of such titles as "accelerator evangelist," "angel investor" and "tech guru."

NRIs from the United States, Britain, Canada and Australia represent the largest group of returnees, but others have come back from Japan, Hong Kong, the Gulf States and Germany to be part of what they invariably describe as a duty to the home country as it tries to recast itself as a superpower under (or despite) the nationalist imprint of Prime Minister Narendra Modi.

After years in Silicon Valley, including stints at enterprise software companies such as Oracle and his own software venture, Deepak Gagneja returned to India in 2013 to launch a healthcare technology business. "After spending a decade in Silicon Valley, it became clear to me that technology has the potential to impact every industry and every person on the planet," he told *Franchise India* in 2015. "And for me, there was no place better than my home country to witness this change."

Ultimately, that's what it comes down to: pride in the home-land and a desire to see it do better. Politicians will tout new policies at press conferences, public–private partnerships will be set up and, when travel resumes, conferences on attracting the diaspora will fill banquet halls. But it's all transactional and on some level theoretical until everyone on the migration and return policy watch understands the complex appeal of a homeland.

Chapter 5

NORTHERN IRELAND

Call My Brother Back

The courteous immigration officer at Dublin International Airport asks me if I plan to spend "any time" in the Republic of Ireland. Fatigued from my overnight flight, I mumble a series of clumsy responses: "I'm afraid not. I was hoping to. Maybe next visit." I'm certain he doesn't care how or where I spend my time, but I feel sheepish all the same. I'm using Dublin as an entry point to Belfast, which has no direct flights from and to Toronto. I'll take advantage of the frequent bus service from its airport to Northern Ireland's largest city and pass through the open (at least for now) border between the Republic of Ireland and Northern Ireland, which remains part of the United Kingdom. As I wait in line to board, an elderly fellow passenger tells me to prepare for the noise, as the bus originates in the city centre and will be full of young people going home to Belfast for the weekend. The majority are studying in Dublin's post-secondary institutions.

The free flow of people and goods across that border was in limbo when I visited Belfast in late November 2018, almost two and a half years after the UK voted to leave the European Union. The historic but unexpected win for the Leave side meant Britain would withdraw from the single market and customs union of the EU, which would necessitate the return of a hard border and customs checks between Northern Ireland and the republic for the first time since the two governments began to phase them out in the 1990s. Brexit, the outcome of distinctly English hubris, false narratives and miscalculation, was set to leave a damaging legacy on Northern Ireland, a region that voted Remain with a comfortable majority (55.8 percent).

For many Northern Irish, the idea of a return to army posts along the border with the republic stirs up memories of decades of explosions, gunfire and political assassinations that saw an estimated 3,739 people die in what came to be known as the Troubles—a thirty-year period bookended by a civil rights march in Londonderry (Derry) in 1968 and the signing of the Good Friday Agreement in Belfast in 1998.

Although bombings and deadly confrontations continued past 1998, Northern Ireland had been enjoying a relatively peaceful and prosperous twenty years. Conflicts between the Unionists, who are loyal to the United Kingdom and largely Protestant, and the Republicans, who believe in a unified Ireland and are largely Catholic, became more about ballots than bullets. (In counting and accounting for the dead, the Republican side, through the various factions of the Irish Republican Army, either claimed or were accused of 2,167 deaths; the Unionists' share came to

1,115; security forces logged 362; and the remaining 95 were attributed to various other groups.)

For the business, technology, tourism and venture-capital industries in Northern Ireland, the possibility of a hard border throws into question the economic future of a region in the midst of reinventing itself as a digital hub and a hot destination for foreign direct investments. Northern Ireland has also been enjoying a tourism boom that includes fine dining, a *Titanic*-themed museum and tours of the twenty-five locations where all eight seasons of *Game of Thrones* were shot. The region—and Belfast in particular—wasn't spared the economic downturn of 2008–09, but it weathered it better than most economists could have predicted, thanks in part to what came to be known as the peace dividend—major investments by the European Union and other parties to revive Northern Ireland after its three-decade encounter with terrorism and sectarian violence. The economy of the republic, on the other hand, collapsed after nearly two decades of a supposed economic miracle that saw it emerge as a "Celtic Tiger." Once the property bubble burst, its GDP dropped to "one of the worst ever recorded in peacetime in the developed world," writes journalist Fintan O'Toole in *Ship of Fools*. Of twenty-seven European cities, Dublin had the worst investment and development potential. For a change, Belfast looked like the smarter investment opportunity on the island.

The UK and the EU would eventually reach a deal that kept the border between Northern Ireland and the Republic of Ireland open. But a new regulatory border between Great Britain (England, Scotland and Wales) and Northern Ireland was set to come into effect in 2021. According to the terms of what's come to be known as the Northern Ireland Protocol, the region will continue to be part of the United Kingdom politically but will follow most of the EU's strict rules, especially on food items such as eggs, meat and fish.

Belfast's success hinges on another kind of flow across its borders: leveraging the power of the Irish diaspora, funnelling their investments back to the homeland *and* tempting a select few of them to return for good. According to the United States Census Bureau, an estimated 32.7 million Americans (10.2 percent of the population) claimed Irish ancestry in 2015. That figure is seven times larger than the 4.7 million who live in the Republic of Ireland. (Northern Ireland's population in 2019 was 1.9 million.)

Call My Brother Back, by Belfast novelist Michael McLaverty, captured another period of troubles: the early 1920s, which witnessed the creation of Northern Ireland on one side and the Irish Free State on the other. The plea of the title has been heeded by the Belfast International Homecoming Conference, and Connla McCann, its director, believes it to be part of Northern Ireland's new story. "[S]ummoning home the brothers—and of course, the sisters—of the Belfast diaspora," she writes in the conference's program, "was among the first actions taken to underpin the nascent peace process."

Now in its seventh year, the business and investment conference serves as one of the lead initiatives to connect members of the "global Irish family"—code for well-heeled Irish Americans—with the local one "to boost the peace through economic development." Politician, author, newspaper publisher, businessman and former mayor Máirtín Ó Muilleoir created the conference to help

Belfast transition from a city "mired in the past" to one "brimming with hope for the future."

Although his Twitter handle is @newbelfast, I can't tell if the sixty-year-old Ó Muilleoir is ushering in the future or clinging to the past. He's more energetic than many people half his age and his faith in Belfast's prospects feels messianic, but as a Catholic and Republican, he bears the scars of decades of Irish nationalism. When I mention the documentary *66 Days*, by Irish director Brendan J. Byrne, about the 1981 hunger strike of the IRA's Bobby Sands, he admits that he just can't watch it. It'd be too painful, he says.

Almost everyone I spoke to at the homecoming conference remarked on Ó Muilleoir's energy and appetite for extreme networking. "I get tired watching him," says John Donovan, a lawyer and chair of the Boston/Belfast Sister City Initiative. "I tell him, 'My exercise is following you.'" I spent some time with Ó Muilleoir before the start of the conference and have to agree. I followed him around a charity bazaar on a Sunday and joined him for a weekday stroll through his riding and an interview with a local channel on the Brexit negotiations a few days later, all in the hope of a sit-down interview (which he promised but never seemed to find the time for). Ó Muilleoir is the South Belfast representative in the Northern Ireland Assembly (often called Stormont) for Sinn Féin, once the political front of the IRA and now the leading nationalist party. When I visited, the assembly had been suspended for nearly two years because talks between Sinn Féin and the Democratic Unionist Party (DUP) had collapsed over the latter's mishandling of a green energy plan. Other contentious issues included same-sex marriage, which is not legally recognized in Northern Ireland, and DUP's refusal to grant official status for the Irish language. (The assembly resumed session in early 2020, after the DUP and Sinn Féin reached a deal.)

Despite border worries and periodic government shutdowns—this was the fifth suspension in the past twenty years—investors, entrepreneurs, legal scholars and security experts from the Irish diaspora share a positive view of Belfast's future. Before Brexit, they may even have been bullish. Although conference delegates are a mix of fourth- or fifth-generation Irish and some who have "reconnected" with Northern Ireland in the last two or three years, they're all motivated by a desire to help the homeland recover from its troubled past—to literally and figuratively pay back. (Belfast's coat of arms features the motto *Pro tanto quid retribuamus*: For all we have received, what shall we give back in return?)

While it focuses on the future, the conference makes no attempt to gloss over the past. The itinerary includes guided bus tours to the two areas most affected during the Troubles: Shankill Road, the Protestant enclave, and Falls Road, its Catholic counterpart in West Belfast. These tours come complete with visits to the "peacewalls" that once segregated each community but have since become a tourist attraction, thanks to a constantly changing array of murals. (I found the murals on Falls Road so compelling that I returned to them on two separate occasions. Their salutes to liberationist movements, including the Palestinian and Basque people, brought together three of this book's homeland quests in one spot.) Conference delegates stay at the Europa, once famous for being the continent's "most bombed" hotel but one of many properties of the local Hastings chain. Another Hastings hotel is the new Grand Central, a sleek glass tower that, with an Asian dragon as its icon, wouldn't look out of place in Hong Kong or Singapore. The company's CEO, Howard Hastings, declined my request for an interview because he thought my focus on return was "too sentimental," but he told me on the last night of the conference that it was simply in his blood to invest in Belfast, no matter what the future holds for the city. "What else is there to say?"

"We're very unique," says Jayne Brady, an electronic engineer and Belfast native who worked in Canada, China, Japan and Germany before returning to her hometown in 1997. "We have lived through an extraordinary and horrific history." To her, the beauty of Northern Ireland is that everyone from the community is trying to make peace last. "Northern Ireland has progressed despite the lack of progress in the assembly."

It all sounds very convincing, and I'm inspired by the resilience of the people and their desire to move on from their past. Maybe the same will happen in Yemen one day. But the conference proceedings sparked more questions than answers. Does the homeland return of the Northern Irish diaspora depend on how well the economy does? What happens if the good times end—or worse, the bad old days of political clashes restart?

John O'Doherty, an activist and director of the Rainbow Project, an LGBTQ group, believes that much of this new-found financial confidence in Belfast masks a more unsettling reality. "No amount of external investment or people returning home or new people coming here is going to change the fact that we have a troubled history that needs to be addressed," he tells me when we meet in his office before the start of the conference. "There are people in Northern Ireland today who are unsure if the state had a hand in the murder of their family members. They deserve an answer to that."

How do you return to a homeland that's still struggling to understand its past? Where sectarianism, although somewhat better managed, is never out of the picture? The extremes of wealth and destitution, hope and despair, war and peace in this return story left me exhausted by the time I was back on the bus to Dublin Airport to catch my flight to Toronto. Although I've seen tangible evidence of the much-touted Irish spirit, I still don't know how the people of Belfast manage such uncertainties and grievances, which seem rooted in one geographical fact: proximity to England, the country that has controlled their political fate for centuries and continues to do so today. It was difficult to separate the return stories I heard from the contested nature of Northern Ireland and the loyalties of its people to both Britain and Ireland, their twin motherlands.

* * *

If you're looking for a recipe for a hearty Irish stew, you will not find it on the website of Northern Irish Connections, the body that oversees the return of the diaspora, or at least the repatriation of their investment dollars. For Anne Beggs, the head of operations, the story of contemporary Northern Ireland that she and her colleagues prefer to tell is of a "very modern, very progressive" society.

We're sitting in a small breakout room in the relatively new glass-and-steel headquarters of Invest Northern Ireland, the main economic development agency for the region, so at least the message and the messenger are consistent. Instead of recipes, the site features news of Northern Ireland's being named best food destination at a world-travel market event; in place of sepia-toned images of downtrodden ancestors leaving the harbour for the New World, the homepage is filled with the smiling faces of men and women who have returned to Northern Ireland to take on top corporate positions or start their own businesses. The goal is to remind the Irish diaspora of their home connection "without, I suppose, being too twee about it," says Beggs, a twenty-year veteran of Invest Northern Ireland, but a new recruit to its relaunched Connections division. Northern Irish Connections has twenty-three offices around the world, some of which are housed within the business or foreign-trade missions of the Republic of Ireland. Many in the diaspora claim ancestry from both parts of Ireland. "We're not necessarily looking to export the border or be identity-focused," Beggs says.

Unlike the Basque cultural centres, which tend to emphasize an emotional and visceral connection to the region through language and landscape, the Northern Irish agency prefers to focus on economic prosperity. I recall hearing comments in Bilbao about how diasporic Basques are not as rich, as well connected or as numerous as their Irish counterparts. In Massachusetts, almost 22 percent claim Irish heritage. There's an art and a science—and a limit—to calling such an overwhelming number of brothers and sisters back home, and Beggs knows where to find the sweet spot. "Look, we're not trying to get everybody back," she tells me. "Because then we wouldn't have a diaspora."

So which returnees are more favoured? The answer may seem broad at first, but it narrows down to those who are well connected in sectors and regions that Irish companies wish to break into. On the list are those who can bring direct foreign investment, enhance business tourism (including conferences like the Belfast International Homecoming) or establish ties in the educational and research sectors (with international students filling up boarding schools or research-intensive PhD programs). When I mention how much overlap I've noticed between Ryerson University in Toronto and Ulster University in the creative and digital industries, Beggs cites that as an example of a connection worth pursuing. Within a week, I'd received an email introducing me to her colleague in the Toronto office so we could start a conversation about possible collaboration between the two institutions.

Digital and social media platforms play their parts in drawing in the global Irish family, but this remains a business of personal and one-on-one interactions. To that end, the organization throws events that appeal to a subset of people in key locations—"You can't invite ten million people to an event," Beggs says—and from that select guest list, a process of analysis by sector and opportunity follows. Think matchmaking for the business elite. Among the most sought after are Irish executives and entrepreneurs who have reached a stage where they want more work–life balance or a place to raise their children.

It's a testament to how much things have changed in Northern Ireland in the past twenty years that what was once the setting of Western Europe's longest and bloodiest conflict has transformed into a homeland of tranquility and stability. Good public education and lower housing prices—compared to, say, London—sometimes make this return feel less about a deep-seated desire to go home and more about an affordability index. "A number of them will absorb a salary decrease because all of these other factors compensate for a salary differential between London and here," says Beggs. The homeland factor remains the strongest draw, however.

Philip McAleese, the co-founder and CEO of the cycling-technology company See.Sense, is among the executives who decided to return to Northern Ireland for the reasons Beggs just cited: family ties, quality of life, affordable housing. An awareness of his Irishness helped, but as he tells me, ties to a homeland are subject to other conditions, including political stability and good government. Both were in a state of flux when we sat down for an afternoon tea in Belfast.

McAleese lives in and works near Newtownards in County Down, a few miles east of Belfast. He grew up there in the 1970s, after his Protestant parents moved to escape the worst of the Troubles and to give him and his sister as normal an upbringing as was possible at the time. "It was a fine childhood," he recalls. After almost sixteen years as an expatriate in England and Singapore, he resettled in the same relatively quiet town. Philip was the adventurous world traveller, while his sister has never left Newtownards. She has worked for the same employer for decades and lives close to their parents. But now that this jet-setting brother is back, the original family is reunited—not just in the homeland but within walking distance of one another.

"I've always prided myself on being North Irish," Philip says. "It's a nationality I really like. I like the identity. No matter where you go in the world, people generally have a good perception of it." He discovered that positive association when he left the country in 1996, having graduated from Queen's University Belfast with a degree in electronics and software engineering. By his own admission, he wasn't a star student and had no idea what a university education entailed—"I thought it was research. I didn't realize it would be three more years of school"—but he stumbled upon a major that was in high demand as the internet and computer programming changed business practices in the late 1990s.

His first job—integrating radar systems and flight simulators for the National Air Traffic Services in Bournemouth, England—took him all over Europe. He recalls sitting in the third pilot seat on many a British Airways flight to Rome, only to turn around and go immediately back to London (give or take a few duty-free purchases).

Then came more than a decade in London as a software engineer in the financial sector. He moved jobs regularly, starting with a contract at a third-party company that created trading software. Eventually, he was hired to do the same for banks and investment firms directly. In 2005, Philip met Irene, his now wife and the co-founder of See.Sense, while he was working for a Dutch investment bank. An Australian whose grandparents on one side were among the original Ten Pound Poms—British citizens who accepted ten pounds sterling and free passage to Australia after the Second World War—Irene was exploring life in London as a professional in human relations and organizational change. The two "instantly liked each other" and got married in 2008, with the financial crisis as the backdrop to all their plans.

As Philip recalls, the two were married for only a few days when his employer, Lehman Brothers, went under. As competitors bought divisions of the multi-tentacled global company, Philip remained employed. After a short stint at Barclays in London, he accepted an offer to work for its Singapore office in 2010. Their first daughter had been born the year before, and the couple knew that they couldn't afford to buy a larger apartment in London. So instead of moving farther out of the city and commuting, they decided to start over thousands of miles away. He still felt Irish and she Australian, so there was little to keep them in London.

Singapore offered a halfway point between Northern Ireland and Australia, making it a neutral place for two sets of grandparents to visit. In reality, none of them could cope with the long flights or Singapore's humidity. Not even the birth of a second granddaughter in 2011 could sway them to visit more. Philip and Irene knew that it was time to return to his or her homeland and give the children a permanent base. "Irene and I were very close to our grandparents, and we wanted our children to have that," he explains. "Lots of people in Singapore loved them, but not unconditionally the way grandparents do."

Because Irene's extended family lived all over Australia, and they knew they were likely to find work in the more expensive cities of Melbourne or Sydney, a move there made little sense. Northern Ireland emerged as the clear choice. "We can afford to come here [and] buy a house outright, which reduced our costs greatly. It has a good education system. A relatively good healthcare system. It's generally perceived to be a good place to raise children. The weather is not great [and] it doesn't have the beaches, but on the whole, it represents a good balance." Philip says that his decision had more to do with practicalities than sentimental attachment; as the founders of a global tech company, it makes no difference where they're based.

I note that he resettled in the same small town he grew up in. To me, it felt like not just a homeland return but a re-creation. "Again, just practicalities," Philip insists. "We're a mile and a half from where my parents live; we're a mile and half from where our business centre is, a mile and half from the school where my children go. We're never more than a ten- to fifteen-minute drive from where we need to go." As an added bonus, his two daughters picked up the Irish accent, which gives their father a "sense of pride."

Now if only Philip can be as proud of his elected officials. It didn't take long for him to realize that some of the underlying issues that turned Northern Ireland into a war zone during his youth have resurfaced as a power grab. While the day-to-day operations of See.Sense may not be immediately affected by the shutdown of Stormont, the uncertainty it creates and the shadow of no-deal Brexit (still a possibility when we talked in late 2018) are starting to affect long-term plans. He doesn't rule out a move to Dublin. "If things deteriorated in Northern Ireland, we wouldn't stay." Philip and Irene keep their three passports—British, Irish, Australian—up to date and have given their children the gift of their triple nationalities. He prefers that politicians "set aside their differences," but he's resigned to the political interruptions for the time being.

Beggs knows how frustrated returnees like Philip feel. When I ask her about the prospects of no-deal Brexit, she acknowledges that the business community is talking about it, but adds that she's in no position to comment on it. This region is no stranger to political crises, she says. "The other part of our psyche which stands us in good stead is that we have a real strong ethic of getting on with things," she tells me. "Making the best of a situation and carrying on regardless . . . Business is continuing here. We are not pressing pause in any of our efforts to attract foreign direct investment."

The Northern Irish will keep coming home and will continue to send money. Whether that's the resilience Beggs and others have talked to me about or an irrational emotional attachment to the homeland is up for debate. It may be a combination of both. Homeland returns straddle money and idealism, hopes and fears. In this case, they also involve a certain level of denial. For those who never left, Northern Ireland's economic renaissance seems partly based on a confidence trick.

"Many people say we're a post-conflict society. I'm not convinced," John O'Doherty from the Rainbow Project tells me. "I think we're still in conflict. We're a *post-violence* society." To this day, he explains, the vast majority of children in Northern Ireland go to single-identity schools, perpetuating the very cycle that the peace process tried to address. (According to 2018 figures, 93 percent of children attend schools that identify as either Protestant or Catholic.) "Some people have opportunities—going to university and in terms of their career paths—that take them to the wider world and allow some of these misconceptions to disappear. But for many of us, that's not our lived experience."

O'Doherty doesn't understand how politicians and those in

the business community can talk about a "shared vision" for a new and forward-looking homeland without first agreeing on this vision. And if that shared vision continues to be elusive, how can it be achieved in the first place? His words sound like more than a series of conundrums and reflect the contradictions of politics as usual in Belfast. Asking assembly members who represent two opposing views to work together, he notes, is akin to handing over the American Congress to the Tea Party and the Green Party and leaving them to duke it out.

And yet, O'Doherty has never been tempted to leave Northern Ireland. The closest he came was considering a move to Dublin. "I love this part of the world. The reason I stay here and try to make it better is because I want it to be the best that it can be," the self-described "Irishman through and through" tells me. His tone of voice changes once he starts talking about what he loves about his homeland. Earlier in our conversation, I felt his frustration—partly directed at me for asking questions about Belfast politics that he has fielded many times before—but now I can hear the pride. Northern Ireland people are "wonderful, great, friendly people." He says there's a lived experience to being Irish, whether in the homeland or in the diaspora, that's not shared by any other nation. "For this little piece of land to have such a great influence—find me another country of our size and our population that does as well as Ireland. Vatican City is the nearest."

His dream homeland return story is to resettle in his birthplace of Maghera, County Derry, where his family lives. He and his husband talk about moving somewhere they can have as many animals as possible—more than the three dogs they share in Belfast, at any rate. O'Doherty is part of a small but expanding number of LGBTQ people who consider returning to the communities they ran away from after coming out. "Leaving home is part of our story, a chapter we tell a lot," writes Colin Crummy in the *Guardian*. For most of the gay liberation movement, the city was where people found a home. But as Crummy notes—and as I began to realize as I got older—"the global city is proving less of a safe haven." As the number of gay spaces shrink and gentrification erases our neighbourhoods, many members of the LGBTQ community are rethinking their relationship with their cities. The thirty-something me viewed Toronto's gay village as the prize for winning my sexual liberation, but now I avoid the neighbourhood. As its bars and restaurants hollow out, the village feels less safe, more like a microcosm of urban decay than a place to call home.

"Sometimes when you find what you're looking for, it gives you the opportunity to realize how much you have and how much you had to give up," O'Doherty says. He misses his family, his siblings (who still live in or around Maghera) and his nine nephews and nieces. "There are multiple aspects to my identity, and being LGBT is a big one of them. But I also come from a very working-class background and a community which is still a working-class community."

Replace Maghera with Sana'a or Aden and O'Doherty might as well be reading my mind. Of course, his Irish family and community may be more accepting of this gay son's return than mine would be, but the sentiment is identical, and it warms my heart to realize that I'm not alone in hoping to reconcile my sexuality with my desire for a homeland return. My journey will be longer, farther and more dangerous. More than thirty years ago, I let my sexuality alter the course of my life completely by moving to the West. I will never regret that decision, but I wonder if it needs to be an irrevocable one. O'Doherty—in Belfast, of all places—has opened my eyes to a scenario I never thought would apply to me.

* * *

Steve Orr doesn't think of himself as a particularly religious person, but his return to Belfast after eighteen years away feels like the "the reason I was put on this planet," he tells me. We're chatting in a conference room at the premises of the tech incubator Catalyst Inc., of which he's the CEO. It's late Friday afternoon, and the building—a massive two-storey warehouse-like space decorated in that quirky-but-designer aesthetic, with vintage aeroplane models and old-timey collectibles—looks more deserted than its location on the edge of Belfast's Titanic Quarter normally suggests. During the week, at least two hundred independent and non-profit organizations and up to three thousand workers share offices and facilities to capitalize on Northern Ireland's strength in engineering and technology. Life needs a purpose, the "most blessed man in the world" says, and this innovation centre has become his.

I've worked long enough in both journalism and academia to earn my stripes as a tech-disruption heretic. What sets Steve's digital gospel aside from that of many of his counterparts is the way it all relates to his homeland—the time he spent in it, away from it and back to it. And how much has changed and remained the same.

Like many Northern Irish of his generation—he's forty-seven—Steve grew up with the Troubles not far from his doorstep. Although he was born in a suburb outside Belfast, he went to school in the city centre. His parents, like Philip McAleese's, moved out of their Shankill Road home to provide him and his brother with a safer environment. Steve, however, rarely paid any attention to his surroundings. "I loved growing up here," he says. "My friends and the cracks and the fun. All the bad stuff was going around, but we didn't know any different. It was hard for my parents to be raising a kid who didn't care."

When I ask if going to university in northeast England, as he did to study business and information technology (and French), was his way of avoiding the Belfast reality as he grew older, he instantly shoots down that theory. "Like any kid at that age, you want to get away from your parents. You want to party, explore and have an adventure." It all sounds like a very improbable origin story for a tech prophet, but being at the right place at the right time in the late 1990s sped up his character conversion. Steve found his niche as Europe and North America competed in building mobile networks to allow data to travel wirelessly. He worked in Buckinghamshire, England, for four years and then in California for nine.

After spending some time in San Francisco with an English company, he moved to San Diego to start Kineticom, a talent firm for the tech industry. It became one of the fastest-growing start-ups in southern California and made it to number thirty-three on the Inc. 500, a ranking of privately held small companies in the US. His key to success? His Northern Irish upbringing. Growing up close to a core group of friends made them all competitive by nature. "Not just that," he continues, "but also the values, the honesty, the integrity. We want to inject a huge amount of fun whenever we are dealing with people."

In England, the Protestant-raised Steve identified as British. In the United States, he was Irish. So Irish, in fact, that his misgivings about California life kept growing alongside his company. He knew that if it reached a certain size, he'd have to step away from it and set up a non-profit of some kind. By his seventh year in San Diego, despite its "amazing" lifestyle of sunshine and year-round surfing, he and his now-wife (from Donegal, Ireland) knew that the next logical move was home.

"We had a conversation about what we want to do with our lives. She said she wanted to go home," Steve recalls. "That was a big realization for me, as I thought we'd be there a bit longer. Then I actually realized that what I wanted was to get married. I didn't want to raise kids in Southern California." He explains that the body-conscious culture and the ready availability of drugs made the two of them rethink plans of starting a family in that setting and book their one-way tickets to Ireland. They flew back in 2007. He's now the father of three, a seven-year-old and five-year-old twins. "I just love the depth, the warmth of the people here. The resonance. I probably could have been a better global citizen elsewhere. But I love the effortlessness of being home, of raising kids here. For everything that was wrong here growing up, there's so much more about it that's right."

San Diego's transformation from a government town in the 1980s to a technology hub by the 2000s inspired Steve to transplant that model to his hometown of Belfast. The city had just begun to recover from its violent past, and calls for the Irish

diaspora to come home and rebuild grew louder and more frequent as peace took hold. "My values have changed over the
years. It was more about making money when I was younger.
Now I just want to make an impact for my community."

I tell Steve that he's like the poster child for the Northern Irish
Connections campaign to draw back the diaspora with an aggres-
sively modern image of Belfast. What could be more twenty-
first century than the tech hub he leads? Its goal is to incubate
two industry clusters that Northern Ireland will lead the world
in over the coming few years. He nods in agreement, but he
also tells me to be aware of the government hype. Northern Ireland remains divided along the same old sectarian lines, but in
less confrontational and violent ways. The economic-prosperity
agenda continues, but so does the "carve up" culture, which
insists that any amount of money coming in must be distrib-
uted equally. Each side keeps an eye on not just what it gets but
also what the other one does. "I think the difficulty here is that
the past keeps competing with the future for attention, and the
past keeps winning." In his day-to-day work at Catalyst, Steve
says, the subject of the sectarian divide has never come up. What
matters is not where workers went to school or what neighbourhood they grew up in, but what ideas they bring and how they
plan to make them happen.

"My starting position is that the people of Northern Ireland
are as good as, if not better than, the people from anywhere else
in the world," he says, regaining the upbeat tone of the earlier
part of our conversation. "If we can provide an environment
which is as good as, if not better than, elsewhere in the world,
then the rest of the world is in trouble. Because we're coming,

baby." ("Watch out, the Irish are coming," I tease. "The *North-ern* Irish," he responds.)

Part of the shift from a business-driven to a purpose-driven life is ensuring that his children enjoy and pass on the Northern Irishness he loves. "I love for them to maintain a strong connection to home. I'd love if they lived and raised their families here, but I also would understand if they felt the need to go and explore." He may regret the American passports he secured for them, but what matters is that their lives, like his, have a purpose.

* * *

Much of Steve's work at Catalyst falls under the "giving back" agenda of the Belfast Homecoming Conference. Jayne Brady, the electronic engineer, tells me that contributing to her community takes up much of her spare time. As the daughter of working-class parents and the first to go to university, she makes a point of going back to her old school on Falls Road once a week to tutor some of the students in maths and science. When she was their age, she says, she didn't know what an engineer looked like.

In a morning conference session, titled "Philanthropic Pioneers: It's About What You Give, Not What You Get," at the Belfast Harbour Commissioners building, several Irish and Irish American executives seem to suggest that it's not hard to find those who want to give back to the homeland—but managing the wealth and expectations that come with them can be a challenge. Belfast needs to liaise better with those who "give back relentlessly," one panellist insists. Mary Sugrue, a CEO at a Boston-based organization called the Irish American Partnership, says it all comes from the heart, in some kind of primal urge that diasporic Irish people can't control when they think about the homeland. "They feel strongly connected and want to give back," she says. They try to find "tangible ways of giving back. They are motivated because this is where their heart is." (Research suggests that Northern Irish people lead the rest of the UK in charitable giving. A 2017 study ranked Northern Ireland sixth in a prosperity index but first in charitable donations.)

Perhaps what I found most revealing about the philanthropy aspect of this diaspora story is the way its members sustain a link with the homeland, even if they can't relocate to it for good. As Beggs said, there would be no diaspora if everyone returned. Several generations of Irish migrants left with very little to their names; their descendants seem to respond by creating, as the panel description put it, "life-transforming opportunities" for those who stayed behind. Part of me sees this as an attempt to rewrite history, another as paying back dues. I like to think I'll do the same (and whatever is within my means) when Yemen calls on its diaspora to uplift the country from six years (and counting) of war. Those years have cost more lives and created more devastation than anything Northern Ireland experienced in six decades. Even if the Yemeni diaspora comes nowhere close to the Irish one in numbers or in wealth, the thought of using homeland return to rebuild and give back makes me feel that there may be a larger meaning to what I've been dreaming of. Of course, it might just be the guilt I'm feeling about the privileges I have in Canada—privileges denied to my family and millions of others in Yemen. And maybe I do want to feel good about myself after all: a brown saviour for a troubled part of the brown world.

Returns rely on multiple and at times contradictory messages, my time in Belfast confirmed. The highlight of the homecoming conference's closing gala came not in the form of a dazzling business announcement or a preview of a disruptive new technology developed by one of the returnees. For twenty minutes, four young locals and an older narrator presented a set of traditional Irish songs, dances and stories about ships, fishing, fog and journeys. A banquet room packed with stuffy businesspeople danced and clapped along to this most stereotypical, definitely twee, but ultimately joyous representation of the Irish homeland. There was something very visceral about the performance. I lost count of how many men and women in tuxedoes and evening gowns were wiping away tears by the end of it. I'd be lying if I said I wasn't among them, even if the show got me emotional about another homeland thousands of miles away.

Chapter 6

TAIWAN

The ABCs of Return

The population of Laomei Village, a coastal community at the northern tip of Taiwan, has thinned out over the years. Once a popular choice to house Taiwan's naval officers and personnel, and then a retirement quarters for them, the village is now mostly deserted as aging residents move to live closer to their children or to access better elderly care.

The government of Taiwan has embarked on a large revitalization project of former military communities around the country. One has been transformed into a cultural park and another into an art colony. Laomei's turn will come, but for now, its glut of available houses makes it a cheap place to rent and use as a base, of the non-military kind, for Hsiao-Wei Yang. The fifty-year-old Taiwanese teacher and educator (and daughter of an army veteran) turned a two-storey house in a laneway that branches off the main road into a not-for-profit school. Children in the economically depressed surrounding area receive private tutoring, hot meals and emotional support. After nearly thirty years in England and the United States as a student and teacher, Hsiao-Wei returned to Taiwan in 2016 and set up iPower Alliance, an NGO of which iSchool—"to sound like 'ice cool,'" she points out—is the flagship and only branch (for the time being).

The parquet floor gives away the house's vintage, but everything else showcases Hsiao-Wei's forward-thinking approach to education. You won't find a blackboard or dog-eared textbooks here. Instead, students get creative and problem-solve with the props, toys and tools (from buckets to yarns to masks) that line one wall. On the other, Hsiao-Wei has arranged two white tables and several metal benches in a half circle to facilitate conversation and collaboration. In Taiwan—home to a public educational system that drums dates and facts into students' brains—this freewheeling method remains a novelty. Some parents have been converted to Hsiao-Wei's style, but appreciation from "people in power" remains elusive.

I travelled to Laomei Village to spend time with Jay Chen, a Toronto-born and -raised thirty-five-year-old teacher of mixed Taiwanese and Chinese heritage who moved to Taipei in 2010. On this windy and damp Monday in December, Jay plans to guide three at-risk youth at the local elementary school with some extracurricular activities: a little lesson in structuring a simple rap-style rhyming couplet in Chinese. In exchange, and in line with Hsiao-Wei's preference for bartering instead of paying, the young men will teach Jay a dance routine and some basic drum patterns they've picked up from one of iSchool's assistants. Jay and Hsiao-Wei first met through a network of English-language teachers in

Taipei. I include the two as returnees here, even though their stories, and the monikers given to them, differ.

Jay represents the second or third generation of what some East Asians call CBCs (Canadian-born Chinese) and ABCs (American- or Australian-born Chinese). These terms encompass anyone born in the West to parents from mainland China, Taiwan, Hong Kong or Singapore. The abbreviations are staples of Chinese culture in the West, but they gained pop-culture traction with the 2018 film adaptation of Kevin Kwan's novel *Crazy Rich Asians*. They extend to include those who left their home countries at a very young age and grew up in the West.

Chinese culture has a different slang for people like Hsiao-Wei, who were born locally but received their post-secondary education and started their careers abroad before returning to the homeland. They are called *hai gui*, or sea turtles, a reference to the air-breathing reptiles' extensive migration routes. Despite travelling long distances, female turtles invariably return to nest on the beaches where they were born. The term *hai gui*, however, refers to any returning student or professional, and mostly captures the experiences of men working in science and technology, upper management and finance.

Such is the ubiquity of homeland returns in China that more specialized terms have been coined to capture the variations within. *Hui jale*, which translates to "returning home," describes any ethnic Chinese who live in or visit China after spending time abroad. As highly paid jobs among sea turtles became more competitive and less common, a new term entered the vocabulary: *hai dai*, or seaweed. It refers to unemployed returnees. Seaweeds deplete resources and contribute little of significance, the thinking goes. And recent research suggests the emergence of another category—overseas returnees, or sea turtles who came back to China, made some money from the economic boom (or found adjustment to the homeland difficult) and left again.

In Taiwan, the repatriation of sea turtles, as well as ABCs and CBCs, unfolds against a more pressing homeland-return geopolitical crisis. As far as China is concerned, Taiwan (formally known as the Republic of China) is not a sovereign state but a breakaway province that will eventually be returned to the motherland, by peaceful or military means. As political scientist Lowell Dittmer suggests in *Taiwan and China: Fitful Embrace*, Taiwanese intellectuals see their national identity as constructed and evolving, but President Xi Jinping takes a more primordial approach. "No force can pull us apart," he insisted, addressing a summit in Singapore in 2015, "because we are brothers who are still connected by our flesh even if our bones are broken. We are a family in which blood is thicker than water."

The cross-strait tensions between China and Taiwan are the result of seven decades of military hostilities, diplomatic pressures, friendly overtures and, above all, startling ambiguities. This "nexus of interrelated puzzles," as Dittmer called it, has the potential to rewrite power dynamics in the Pacific in the twenty-first century. And return lies at the heart of it all.

* * *

Despite having many characteristics of an independent, democratic nation, Taiwan is almost a rogue state in terms of its legal status and presence on the world stage. As of late 2020, only fourteen countries in the world—mostly in the Caribbean, South Pacific and Central America—recognize Taiwan as a sovereign state. (In 2019, Kiribati and the Solomon Islands, both in the Pacific, switched sides to Beijing.) The Vatican is the only state in Europe to recognize it. In Africa, it's Eswatini (the former Swaziland). This figure is likely to go down as China continues its campaign to pressure countries to break ties with Taiwan. The United States supports Taiwan's right for self-defence but opposes its independence. The policy has come to be known as "strategic ambiguity": acknowledging China's status as a regional power on the one hand and supporting Taiwan's transition to a democratic and free society on the other. Between 1979 and 2017, the US also supplied Taiwan with nearly 75 percent of its imported weapons.

I visited Taipei in December 2018, at the end of one testy year between the two nations and on the eve of a number of significant anniversaries that raised the level of both China's aggression and Taiwan's defiance.

In 2018, China stepped up international pressure by insisting that trading partners and corporations with deep ties to its economy list Taiwan on their websites and in their business plans as part of the People's Republic of China. Beijing also reduced the number of Chinese tourists allowed to visit Taiwan and suspended existing mechanisms for communications, official and unofficial, between the two. In Taiwan, the pro-independence Democratic Progressive Party (DPP), which swept back to power in 2016 after eight years in opposition, suffered a setback in regional elections in 2018 but triumphed again in 2020.

The 2018 loss reflected a poor performance on domestic

issues, but China viewed the news as a fitting punishment for the DPP's anti-unification sentiments. President Tsai Ing-wen—the first woman to lead Taiwan—has refused to embrace the 1992 Consensus, which her pro-unification predecessors relied on to establish a warmer relationship with China, according to a report by the Council on Foreign Relations. The Consensus holds that there's "one China," which Beijing understands literally and Taipei has interpreted differently.

On January 2, 2019, Xi Jinping marked the fortieth anniversary of China's "Message to Compatriots in Taiwan," which accompanied its suspension of a bombing campaign against Taiwan-controlled islands. The 1979 speech was delivered in the name of the standing committee of the National People's Congress and marked the start of the reform era in modern China. In his own stern missive, Xi warned that Taiwan "must and will be returned" to China by any means necessary. The "great rejuvenation of the Chinese people," he said, requires as much. Former Chinese leader Deng Xiaoping once said that a Chinese government that greenlit Taiwan's independence would be the first to lose power. Most experts agree that independence for Taiwan could intensify calls for more autonomy in areas that China controls, including Hong Kong, Macau and Tibet.

As the thirtieth anniversary of Tiananmen Square approached in the spring of 2019, China's crackdown on domestic freedoms increased to include shutting down lifestyle bloggers and social media stars who normally talked about food or fashion but were viewed as distracting or stealing audiences from the government's official communication channels. Although Xi had described the Taiwan situation as part of a domestic agenda, some experts saw his hardened foreign-policy stance in 2019 as a way to shift attention from the country's slowing GDP and as a warning shot to the US, which in 2018 passed the Taiwan Travel Act to encourage visits to the island by high-level Washington officials.

Another fortieth anniversary in cross-strait relations came and went in 2019. In a 1979 communiqué, the Jimmy Carter White House moved to recognize the People's Republic of China and derecognize the Republic of China (Taiwan). Diplomatic relations between the two nations followed. At the same time, the US continued to "acknowledge" the Chinese position that Taiwan is part of China. The legal difference between recognizing and acknowledging allows the US wiggle room to maintain its official relations with China and its unofficial ties with Taiwan. As diplomat Richard Haass writes in a report for the Council on Foreign Relations, "Such ambiguity was meant to dissuade either side from unilateral acts that could trigger a crisis." If China were to launch a war on Taiwan, it would do irreparable damage to the very people and land it has been trying to bring into the fold. In 1979, the US Congress also passed the Taiwan Relations Act to safeguard American military and commercial interests on the island. The act includes assurances that any effort to determine the future of Taiwan through tactics ranging from boycotts to military intervention will be of "grave concern" to the United States.

As these ambiguities, contradictions and diplomatic games mount, some facts remain uncontested. Most Taiwanese descend from Hoklo Chinese (Fujian) or Hakka Chinese (Guandong). (The indigenous population is estimated to be just 2 percent.)

Historians on all sides agree that the Chinese Qing dynasty ruled over the island of Taiwan from 1683 to 1895, when it ceded it to Japan in the Sino-Japanese War. After Japan's surrender at the end of the Second World War, Taiwan was placed under China (then known as the Republic of China and ruled by the Kuomintang, or KMT). In 1949, the KMT lost the Chinese Civil War to the Communist Party.

Chiang Kai-shek, the KMT leader, retreated to Taiwan and established Taipei as the capital of a government in exile. His ultimate goal was to recover the mainland and unify China under his leadership. For the following two decades, Taipei and not Beijing was broadly recognized as the official base of the Chinese government. In 1971, Beijing took over China's seat at the United Nations. The next year, Richard Nixon's historic visit to China ended the country's diplomatic isolation on the world stage and formalized the so-called One China policy, which Canada also recognizes. ("Canada does not recognize Taiwan as a sovereign state and does not maintain official, government-to-government relations with Taipei," according to a factsheet on the government's website.)

Despite the KMT's stranglehold on Taiwanese politics since the end of the Chinese Civil War—martial law was finally lifted in 1987—the island's experiments with parliamentary democracy came to fruition in 1996 with its first free and open presidential election. In 2000, the KMT lost power for the first time since 1949 with the election of the DPP's Chen Shui-bian as president. The KMT returned to power in 2008, when Ma Ying-jeou campaigned on a more China-friendly platform. Ma did more than any of his predecessors to establish political and economic relationships with China and dial down talk of independence. His eight-year tenure as president overlapped with the first four of Xi Jinping's rise as general secretary of the Communist Party and president of China. Xi embraced a more nationalist stance toward Hong Kong's and Taiwan's aspirations for independence, which in 2014 erupted in student-led protests—the Umbrella and Sunflower movements, respectively. During Ma's time as president, China became Taiwan's largest trading partner. By 2017, bilateral trade was estimated at US$181.76 billion.

As governments changed, most people on the island—55.8 percent, according to a 2017 survey—were emboldened to think of themselves as exclusively Taiwanese. About 37 percent in the same survey saw themselves as both Chinese and Taiwanese, while the only-Chinese camp had shrunk to 4 percent from double digits two decades earlier.

The chaos-prone White House of former president Donald Trump further complicated the relationship between China and Taiwan. As president-elect, Trump broke with tradition by calling President Tsai, the first direct contact from an American leader in decades. He backed this gesture of support with a host of policies that included imposing tariffs on products from China and sanctions on a number of companies. It's hard for security experts to predict what, if any, action the United States would take to defend Taiwan from military, economic or digital aggressions from China. All three countries (and the rest of the world) would probably prefer to maintain the status quo of designed ambiguities than engage in a confrontation along the Taiwan Strait. Early signs from the Joe Biden administration suggest a rebranding of Trump's policies but not a complete departure from an economic confrontation with China.

These many contradictions resurfaced in my conversations with returnees in Taipei. And yet everyone I spoke to either ignored or underplayed the threat that China's aggressive regional policies pose to their careers. The recession of 2008–09 emerged as the significant global event in their return decisions. A generation of new graduates or early-career professionals in Canada and the United States saw their future employment plans upended by the twin poles of a bear market and austerity measures. Some enrolled in graduate studies to wait it out; others advanced (retreated?) to homelands they knew only as children, as visitors or, as in Jay Chen's case, from family lore.

* * *

Rats the size of cats.

Whenever Jay's father reminisced about his childhood in Taiwan of the 1950s, which wasn't too often, he'd mention the well-fed beasts that traumatized him. Growing up in the 1980s in Scarborough, on the east end of Toronto, Jay didn't know what to make of his father's musophobia—or his entire Taiwanese heritage. The signals he received were faint and mixed. His mother's relatives, who came from mainland China, had lived in Canada for three generations and were assimilated to the point where she and her brothers (Jay's uncles) spoke hardly any Mandarin. The father, who studied in California and then immigrated to Canada with his parents and siblings in the early

1970s, "carried the culture," the introspective and soft-spoken Jay told me.

We had just returned from Laomei Village and settled down for late-afternoon tea in Taipei. For privacy reasons, I couldn't observe his teaching, but I caught a short performance in which he and the students swayed to a Drake song and used drumsticks, wood boxes and rubber balls to make percussive sounds. The scene could have played out in Scarborough as easily as it had in Laomei, with the possible exception that the teenagers described as "at risk" in this instance merely spent too much time playing video games. (Hsiao-Wei rewarded their performance with a few minutes of computer time at the end of the workshop.)

At their age, Jay and his younger brother Adam—who, for the record, is a former graduate student of mine—lived in an exceedingly multicultural Scarborough, where hip-hop and urban music were the lingua franca. The Chinese community in the Greater Toronto Area in the late 1990s and early 2000s consisted of mainland families with different immigration histories, a smattering of Taiwanese and a steady stream of new arrivals from Hong Kong. Fleeing the handover of their island to the Chinese in 1997 and seeking a new home in Toronto, Hong Kongers became an easy target for teasing as FOBs, for "fresh off the boat." To stand out and ingratiate himself with the more established Chinese and street youth, Jay began to identify as Taiwanese for the first time in his life. "You look for something that makes you different when you're a teenager," he tells me. "I feel bad because I joined in on the teasing of the FOBs. I was such an ass."

If you add pretending to be sick to avoid the weekend Mandarin classes his father enrolled him in when he was around seven, his embarrassment at bringing aromatic Chinese food to school in his early teens and a brief and uneventful dalliance with Asian gangs in his late teens, you have all the tropes of a classically non-white upbringing in suburban Toronto. After he graduated with a degree in kinesiology from the University of Waterloo in 2008, Jay planned to return to the city and share a downtown apartment with his then-girlfriend. The idea of going to his father's birthplace, even for a short visit, never crossed his mind. And yet, when I met him in Taipei in December 2018, he was closing in on the nine-year anniversary of his homeland return. What happened between 2008 and 2010 to make him take this journey—his first trip to Asia—and stay so long?

Like many Canadians who graduated from university just as the global recession decimated their employment prospects, Jay found himself taking short-term contracts and dead-end jobs. When he landed a full-time position at an orthodontics company, it meant doing the "same thing every day." On the personal side, his long-term relationship sputtered and his confidence hit bottom. "I was in a shell, not meeting people and forgetting about myself." When his brother, Adam, "an instigator," convinced him that the two should relocate to Taiwan, Jay saw it as a way out of the doldrums. "My goal was to learn Chinese," he recalls. "What can I do to further myself? I'll go to Taiwan, learn Chinese for a year, come back and it'll increase my job chances, open up the job market for me."

There was little sentiment and all practicality in that decision. No homeland attachment caught from his father, no desire to "reconnect" with his cultural roots or retrace the steps of his Taiwanese ancestors. None of the intensity that author Jessica J. Lee brings to her own return journey to Taiwan in *Two Trees Make a Forest*, where she describes finding "constancy and comfort" in walking the hills of her homeland. I had detected the transactional nature of this kind of return in other ABCs and CBCs throughout my stay in Taiwan. Missing was the folkloric appeal of the land and the protective attitude toward the language that Basque returnees often displayed. Or that indefinable Irish quality of life, sometimes referred to as a value system, that draws top executives back to the homeland. Or the yearning for a home in the yard, as Jamaicans explained to me. Instead, most returnees in Taipei talked of an unfamiliar land that took some time to get used to and occasionally required an official intervention. To ease his slide into Taiwan, Jay secured a ticket on the "love boat."

The Taiwanese government formally calls it the Study Tour Program for Overseas Youth. Applicants between fifteen and twenty-five who live abroad and are of Taiwanese or Chinese descent are eligible as long as they meet academic and health requirements and can adapt to a group setting. Each tour lasts three weeks and includes meals, board and activities such as language training, museum visits and martial-arts classes. The website of the Overseas Community Affairs Council of the Republic of China lists the program's goals in unapologetically evangelical terms: "To enhance the knowledge and understanding of Taiwan's multicultural character as well as the current situation in the Republic of China (Taiwan) of overseas youth; to foster social interaction between young people in Taiwan and participants from overseas so that the latter can become a new force in their overseas community; and to promote relations between overseas youths' home countries and the Republic of China (Taiwan)." Think the Taiwanese equivalent of the Birthright Israel heritage trips.

The love boat moniker comes from the program's reputation as a dating pool for horny ABCs and CBCs. Jay's memory of the program as a place for frat boys and sorority girls confirms that. "Everybody was going crazy, hooking up." Because he and his Toronto girlfriend had reconciled just before he left for Taiwan, Jay wasn't looking for love. At twenty-five, he was the second-oldest person in the program and did his own thing. The trip failed as the cultural indoctrination the government intended it to be, but it provided the soft landing that Jay needed until his brother joined him a few months later. "As much as the love boat tries to expose you to Taiwan and Taiwanese culture, when I look back, I don't remember anything that we did . . . When people ask me, 'Have you been to this place?' I don't remember. I don't know where I was. I didn't learn anything." Homeland connections happen organically or not at all.

The love boat did introduce him to the possibility of teaching English as a way to earn a living—a job he took on reluctantly, "until the next thing happen[ed]." It happened in the shape of a juice bar franchise that Jay, his brother and three other friends co-owned for a few years. WooGo, Adam told *Asian Entrepreneur* in 2013, offered "a genuine American juice bar experience." Its main product line, a California-style smoothie, blended Taiwanese fruits with sorbet and yogurt.

The business took off, especially among Taipei's health-conscious youth. For Jay, it freed him from the stigma of being just another CBC teaching English to adults or in so-called cram schools (*buxiban*), which offer tutoring in the afternoons and on Saturdays to groups of students. After two reasonably successful years of blending and slurping, differences among the partners and their collective lack of business know-how forced them to sell the juice franchise at a loss and go their separate ways. That meant a return to teaching for Jay, a setback. Except that by then, Taiwan had become more than just a place to find himself; it had become home.

"I want to say I made myself again here," he says. "When I was in Canada, I was very lost. I'm not saying I'm not lost now. I was way out of sorts, in a weird place in Canada. When I got here, it forced me to meet people. You've got to survive, do this or that . . . I built an identity here, and I associate that with Taiwan." His brother, Adam, he says, found the country's conservatism a poor match for his "very expressive" personality and returned to Canada.

Earlier in our conversation, Jay described himself as 100 percent Canadian and said he occasionally wears his Blue Jays hat as a sign of hometown pride. Now that his inner life is at peace—and his professional one is on the rise since he joined a venture capital firm as the Taiwanese representative—I ask if a reverse return to Canada is imminent. This homeland has served its purpose in healing a wounded Canadian millennial, no? "If you dropped me off in Canada, I wouldn't know what to do," Jay responds. "I haven't been working in a company developing my skills, working my way up. What would I do? I've saved some money, but not enough to live in downtown Toronto. I like living here. I feel that there are opportunities for me."

Like its mainland rival, Taiwan is placing more emphasis on the tech sector and developing new business ventures now that manufacturing jobs have moved to cheaper locations in Vietnam and Bangladesh. The days of "Made in Taiwan" are numbered, and that's probably a good thing. Despite the threat of a confrontation with China, there's a sense of promise here, of new directions, of things turning around. The economic situation in Canada and the United States doesn't always seem to offer that to millennials. While Taipei is one of the least affordable places in Asia to buy a condo, rent remains reasonable. As Jay says, he can live very comfortably in the heart of a big metropolitan city on what he earns from the venture capital work (which is not much at the moment) and his part-time teaching job. The low cost of living makes up for the lower income. Compared to his peers in Toronto (where the average one-bedroom rent in 2019 was $2,260), Jay comes out ahead in savings and quality of life.

Returning to Taiwan began as a career move, but as Jay talks about his future, I can detect patriotic notes in his decision to stay. "Something that I always have the urge to do: How can I make Taiwan a better place? It has given me so much over the years. I feel like I've taken a lot, so I want to give back." I'm taken aback when I hear him say this. So much that for some reason, I feel like sticking up for Canada. Do you ever think how you can make Canada a better place? I ask. "I feel that Canada is such a massive place, whereas . . . it's easier to help Taiwan." I press on, suggesting that he left Canada, where he was born and raised, during a recession to go to a place he hadn't visited before but where the job market, at least in teaching, remained strong. The opportunism rankles. "Not really fair to say you're here for the good times, gone for the bad times," he responds, pointing out the proliferation of Western expats and ABCs/CBCs in the country. This is true. I've noticed the increasing presence of the first group since my first visit to Taipei in 2005, when they stood out. In 2018, they seem to be everywhere. "Everybody is gone for the bad times," Jay says. "Not like I chose to be born in Canada." But he notes that as his parents get older (his father is sixty-five, his mother sixty—both relatively young in boomer terms), he can see himself opting to live closer to them.

For now, Jay's bigger culture clash lies in negotiating his new relationship with a Taiwanese woman. Her English is not strong, and despite almost a decade living in Taipei, he says his Chinese is at the level of a six-year-old. He can read most menus and direct taxi drivers to where he needs to go, as he did when we took a taxi from a subway stop at the end of one line to Laomei Village. He can express how he feels about her in ten different ways in English but only knows one way in Chinese. "I don't get to know her in Chinese and she doesn't get to know me in English."

Can you still call a country your homeland if you don't speak like the locals? Many returnees seem to manage and feel integrated with only rudimentary language skills. But does it mean they're home in an emotional or psychic sense?

Perhaps ambiguity and complexity seem intrinsic to Taiwan. More likely, many of us who think about or make the homeland journey view it as a way to piece together fragmented lives, dual languages, the here and there of our existence. We seem to think of the connection between our bodies and the places we came from as innate because we share blood or a common language.

While my Arabic is at a much higher level than Jay's Chinese, I know I'm a long way from regaining enough of it to navigate conversations around love, sex, emotions or belonging. I can watch Arabic dramas if they're in the Egyptian dialect, and with struggle, I can read the newspaper. But I use English for my inner and professional lives. Being forced to use it in other, more personal contexts will not make me more at home and may in fact draw attention to my outsider status.

Many studies of sea turtles and ABCs refer to a syndrome called the fake foreigner, someone who's Chinese but speaks English as his or her first language. I've come to call myself something similar—the ethnic fraud—whenever I'm asked to comment on Arabic language and culture as if my relationship to them is immutable. It may seem perverse, but I found some comfort in Jay's linguistic challenges with his partner. As I heard his story, I felt more prepared psychologically for my own return and my inevitable failure to communicate.

* * *

Like Jay, English and yoga teacher Jen Chen attended school with students of different ethnicities and immigration histories. Her close friends in a district of Virginia Beach, Virginia, were Black, white and brown. Unlike Jay, Jen wouldn't be caught on the love boat if her (romantic) life depended on it. The Taiwan-born American never had much luck befriending other Asians. "To be on a boat with all ABCs is horrific to me," Jen, now thirty-eight, tells me with as straight a face as she can muster. We are sitting in the living room of the Taipei apartment she shares with a Taiwanese woman, someone she quickly describes as a roommate and not a friend. "I always date Americans," she clarifies. In the years since her return to Taiwan in 2008, only one local person has flirted with her.

Identity, belonging, citizenship and homeland are all complex and fraught concepts. For Jen, this complexity is filtered through a gendered lens. The "very feisty, very American" teacher sports a trendy bob, wears leggings and neutral-coloured sweaters and doesn't fit the image of the delicate, passive Taiwanese woman that, she says, men on the island idolize. Her Western and mixed-race friends eschew frilly dresses, pricey makeup and accessories. "If you look at us under a Taiwanese microscope, we're a bit rougher around the edges. We have opinions." Jen also has a history of family estrangements, separations and tragedies that have shaped her character and her journey home.

She was five years old when her parents left Taipei to start a new life in Houston, Texas, in part to salvage a bad marriage. When she turned eight, her father moved her and her younger brother to Virginia Beach without telling their mother. Shortly after, the mother took her own life. "My dad moved us while she was sleeping," Jen recalls, preferring not to go into too many details about this loss.

She studied creative advertising and graphic design at college, then followed that career path in Richmond, Virginia, and San Francisco, where she art-directed print ads for an alternative weekly and the *Wall Street Journal*. When one of her colleagues was diagnosed with a brain tumour and another quit, Jen's workload doubled while her salary stayed the same. In addition to taking on bartending and catering gigs to boost her income, she signed up for yoga classes and completed a training course in teaching ESL. In 2008, she quit her various jobs and travelled to India for a year of yoga. "When you're in your twenties, you jump without a parachute," she says.

The global recession hit while she was in India, so Jen decided not to go back to pricey San Francisco. "I've been unemployed twice. I'm so capable of getting a job, but I knew it would be harder." Her father had already returned to Taipei, remarried and started a new family. Jen, then twenty-eight, saw her proximity to him in Asia as a sign to mend their relationship and an opportunity to reconnect with the city of her birth, which she hadn't visited for about seven years at that point. The ESL teaching certificate made her recession-proof. "I'm in an industry where there's always work. Someone is always looking for a teacher." (Long-term expats recall a time before the recession, when school representatives stood outside bus stations to try to convince Western tourists to consider a career in teaching.)

The yoga and teaching panned out; her relationship with her father didn't. Not only did their personalities clash, but his conviction on perjury charges (or money laundering—she's not sure which) not long after her return derailed any fantasy of a father–daughter reunion. She carried on with her life without him, thanks in part to a new relationship with a man she describes as a "white American from Indiana." They met in 2012 and lived together for a year and a half before he was diagnosed with lymphoma. Anticipating the costs of medical bills in the States, the couple decided to stay in Taipei and rely on local healthcare. Jen's "angel" of a boyfriend died a few months later.

Paradoxically, this new tragedy and her unsalvageable relationship with her father strengthened her resolve to stay in Taiwan. Her long-term commitment to a Buddhist meditation group had its ups and downs, but it has taught her about impermanence, an idea she has incorporated into her yoga classes and her life.

I want to know if she conceives of Taipei as a home and Taiwan as a homeland, with all the certainty and permanence that these words imply. The long pause that follows suggests not that she has to think hard about my question but that she has turned it over in her head many times before. For most ABCs and CBCs, these questions tend to encompass more than just a philosophical, internal debate.

"I don't have much of an identity as far as place," she says. "I associate with Taiwan as my birthplace. I feel a connection to it. I feel like I've come back to my roots, as an Asian, as a Taiwanese. In America, you're speaking English and eating American food. Here, I'm with the people I look like and speaking the same language." Pressed to come up with an answer to my "Where do you want to be buried?" test question, Jen says she would like to be interned in Taiwan because that's where she has found friends and a new boyfriend—a man of European heritage, naturally. But her homeland attachment more accurately reflects how disconnected she feels from American race politics in general and the Trump administration's anti-immigration policies in particular. She experienced some racism as one of the few Asian kids in her Virginia school, but the racial battle lines of contemporary America go beyond anything she remembers from her teen years.

As an ethnically Chinese English teacher in Taipei, Jen knows all about a different kind of race-based discrimination. Language schools in Taiwan (and elsewhere in Asia, but it's acute on the island) have an open preference for teachers who are white native speakers. ABCs and CBCs for whom English is the first language are often denied employment, and those who do get jobs can expect lower pay than their white counterparts. Most managers of these schools justify their hiring practices by insisting that they're acting on parents' wishes. Some parents believe that Asian teachers speak accented English that's been contaminated with exposure to Chinese at home. Black and brown native speakers of English have it much worse. A Black Canadian friend who taught in Taipei in the early 2000s told me that parents withdrew their children from his class when they met him in person. It took several classes and a lot of hard work on his part (and his employer's) to convince parents that he's a good teacher because he *is* a native speaker.

The memories of bad interviews where she was dismissed out of hand or told that the job had been filled still sting. Whenever Jen spoke with her perfect American accent to a school manager on the phone, she got one kind of response. When she showed up at interviews, she got another. She learned to declare her ethnicity during phone inquiries to save herself the trouble. "'Look,' I would say, 'I'm actually Taiwanese. I'm ABC. Is that okay?'"

Two days after our first conversation, I spend an afternoon with Jen as she teaches a class of seven kids. To give their children an academic leg up, parents in Taipei enroll them in private language training in one of the city's hundreds of cram schools. They believe their children need to speak English to be successful, Jen tells me. They also fear that China could seize Taiwan and they would have to leave, so improving their children's English serves as an insurance policy against that possibility. I was curious to see what these schools look like, since almost everyone I spoke to during my trip seemed to work in one, either full time or as a side hustle. Jen tells me the Giving Tree Academy, where she works, is a progressive school that hires both white and Chinese teachers. It operates out of what looks like a large two-bedroom apartment on the fourth floor of a nondescript office building in the Da'an area of Taipei.

Jen's smaller classroom is separated from the larger one by a glass partition. A white teacher who looks like what happens to surfer dudes when they hit middle age has the school's unofficial motto scribbled on the whiteboard: Always Speak English, or ASE. In her own class, Jen incorporates this idea as best she can. She rarely uses the Chinese equivalent to explain a new word to the class—sometimes because, despite her much-improved Mandarin, she can't think of it. Her command of the room is impressive when you take into consideration the disruptive behaviour of the only boy in class. With his Justice League T-shirt, he's acting more like a super-brat than a superhero, but Jen is firm with him when she needs to be and encouraging when he completes one of his tasks. The obedient but curious and, without a doubt, smarter girls seem unfazed by his antics. My presence in the back of the room is their only distraction this afternoon. While I'm sure there are numerous exceptions in Taiwanese society, Jen's views on relationships between genders are beginning to take shape for me.

When she teaches yoga to adults, Jen has more freedom to switch between English and Chinese. The former stays in the background until she gets tired and her facility with the latter wobbles. The more she flips between East and West—the language of her birth and the one she picked up in childhood—the more her in-between status is made real to her.

"I think there are a few kinds of people who come here," she says. "The ones who live here very long and never learn the language. And [then] there're the ones who fully immerse themselves in the culture. I would say I'm somewhere in the middle . . . I've accepted the fact that I get [both] 'Why is your English so good?' and 'We don't hire Chinese people.'"

* * *

Eric Ma refused to accept the fate of other American-educated Chinese in Taiwan and decided to change things from within the teaching profession.

When he was twenty, Eric went on a trip to Taiwan. It was his first visit since 1985, when, as a seven-year-old, he, his younger sister and his mother entered the United States on a tourist visa and overstayed. He'd gone thirteen years without seeing his estranged father and the landmarks of his early childhood. The scene was set for an emotional reunion, a return to the homeland where, as a child in an air force family, Eric lived a happy and secure life running up and down alleyways and taking part in lantern festivals in a government-provided housing community, much like the one in Laomei.

"It was a foreign country," Eric, now forty, tells me when we chat in Taipei. Being close to his father did little to make him feel at home. "It smelled different. Things were designed in a crazy way. Sidewalks would end. Traffic was crazy." He could never understand why shop owners screamed into megaphones to attract passersby. And the summer heat and humidity came as a shock to his system. "I knew I couldn't wait to go back to my home in the US. It was almost immediate."

That was in 1998. Eric would return a few more times before he moved to Taipei for good with his wife, Stacey, and their daughter, Emily, in 2009. The move came with a career change from landscape architect to English teacher and later human resources manager of a language school—and a pay cut of about 75 percent. He's never been happier, he assures me, and has no immediate plans to go back to the States. "The more I grew up, the more I realized that even though I'm an American citizen and I speak native English and my [cultural] background is American, I never truly felt like America was my home." His feelings about the US stem from personal, family and health struggles.

Eric's mother had worked as a nurse in Hsinchu in northern Taipei, but she had to put aside her career when she joined her sister in the family's Chinese restaurant in the Hamptons, on the eastern end of Long Island. Eric and his sister grew up in a house in the East Hamptons—the part where locals live and serve the wealthy who summer there. Some of the restaurant's workers and their families would stay with them until they could afford their own apartments. He attributes his retention of Chinese to the fact that most of his housemates spoke barely any English.

Like many working-class immigrants, Eric's mother eked out a living, working long hours and having very little to spare. "She didn't make time for a lot of things parents do," says Eric, who describes his mother as a tough woman. "She was about making money. She was a single parent. Our only source of income was from her . . . It was not an easy life. She didn't take time to [ask] about how we felt. But she made sure we had money to buy what we wanted: bags, clothes for school. And obviously food and a roof over our head." When Eric was diagnosed with lymphoma at age twenty-four, his mother sold her share of the business, retired and focused on her son's recovery.

I interviewed Eric at a time when his mother was visiting Taipei for the funeral of her brother, so I got to meet her when he invited me to his home. That toughness and an unmistakable imperiousness have survived, but they're now coupled with an adoration for her granddaughter, Emily, who was born in the States, and her grandson, Emerson, born in Taipei. She encouraged Eric not to waste his money on rent and instead buy the small two-bedroom apartment he shares with his wife, two kids, his wife's grandmother, Benji the dog, an Indonesian maid and, for a few months now, his mother. It gets intense there, but Eric avoids confrontations like the ones he says marked his relationship with his mother and sister for many years.

One of his major fights with his mother came when he switched majors from pre-med to landscape design, a profession she didn't think was worth the many sacrifices she had made for her children. She may have had a point. While Eric's career took him from one highly paid job in Irvine, California, to another outside New York City, landscape design and architecture were among the first budget items cut by local governments during the financial crisis. He lost his New York job and found another that didn't work out. For the first time since he arrived in America, he began to talk seriously about going back to Taiwan.

By then, Eric had already married Stacey, a Taiwanese woman who worked in the hospitality industry. It started as a long-distance, online relationship, but the two got married at Taipei city hall eleven days after meeting in person. Eric then flew back to California and returned a few months later for a proper wedding ceremony. Within a year, he had to deal with another major health scare when he learned he had an autoimmune disease that he put down to stress, family fights with his mother and sister, and possibly a tick bite from working outdoors. He had his spleen removed, and after he recovered from the surgery, he, Stacey and Emily embarked on a reverse journey from the one his mother had taken in 1985.

"Because of the [economic] instability and the lack of family support, we decided we'd move back to Taiwan," Eric says before he corrects himself. "Back for Stacey. Not for me." Although he had visited Taiwan a few times since the trip he'd found so bewildering at twenty, he felt conflicted about the move. There was a finality to it that he wasn't prepared for. Stacey resumed work in the hotel industry, but Eric "felt like a bum."

It's difficult to imagine Eric unemployed. He had energy to spare after our long day together, during which he also helped me find a place to get a haircut and arranged for me to meet a friend of his, who was contemplating a move to Toronto, later in the evening. He's the kind of big personality who loves to sing along, loudly, to Elton John and Billy Joel songs in the car, as I discovered when he drove me to the nearest metro station from his suburban apartment.

After exploring job opportunities in landscape architecture, Eric realized that it was no longer a viable career because his Chinese was too limited to allow him to read manuals or communicate clearly in a sector where the government is the biggest employer. Had he worked for an international corporation, he would have survived and perhaps even thrived on his perfect English and functional Chinese. "That's when I decided to teach English."

By his own admission, he should be the last person to take on teaching—and especially teaching English. He hated it as a subject in school and never considered himself much of a book reader. If you want to punish him, ask him to write an essay. But he wanted to contribute to his household expenses, so he started to substitute teach at cram schools, mostly for children in the twelve-to-thirteen age range. His experience as an ABC was mostly positive—just a few weird looks when he showed up at a school after a phone interview and some "I didn't know you were Chinese" comments. After class, students would occasionally say, "You speak very good English for someone from Taiwan." He recalls being paid less than what white teachers normally get for the same work: Asians can expect to receive NT$525 (about C$23) an hour, compared to the NT$600 (just under C$28) a native white speaker pockets.

In short order, Eric became the go-to sub for Jump Start, one of the larger recruiters of teachers in the industry, and started a website (now defunct) to connect employers and other substitute teachers. After six months, he received a call from Jump Start's human resources department to see if he'd be interested in a managerial position where he'd spend more time in the office and away from the classroom. His main task would be to hire and retain teachers to feed the fast-growing cram schools on the island.

He took the job and soon discovered that many schools actually like ABCs because they understand local culture, even if they were born and raised outside it. It's the parents who insist on white teachers—known as NETs, for "native English teachers." In 2012, Eric became involved with a local group of ABCs and CBCs who had come together to change attitudes around teaching and race. This grassroots organization, Teachers Against Discrimination in Taiwan (TADIT), was "created for the purpose of promoting equality in the hiring practices of English teachers in Taiwan." According to its Facebook page—a closed group that Eric helped me access—discrimination happens on a "daily basis."

The page offers links to newspaper articles and YouTube videos about language acquisition, definitions of terms such as "native speakers" and accent discrimination. Mostly, however, it's a platform for those with ABC or CBC backgrounds to share horror stories about being qualified teachers and yet getting turned down for work. In one post, a BBC (British-born Chinese) writes that his interviewer offered him a job—but only until she could find a native speaker to replace him. A white teacher urges the group to press employers on their definition of "native speaker" and their "unofficial racist policies," and to name and shame the bad ones on the forum. Eric posted a link to a story from *Taiwan News* in which a kindergarten teacher tried to help a friend by posting a job on another forum. She, however, apologetically added a side note that the school had informed her they wouldn't hire "black or dark-skinned" teachers.

A few years ago, members of the group conducted a little informal experiment. They showed parents a poster featuring four pictures of teachers posing with local students. Each teacher represented a different ethnicity: European, African American, Chinese and South Asian. When asked which one would make the best teacher for their children, the parents overwhelmingly chose the white European.

Eric's employers understood the problem, but they shrugged it off as a local custom. "I would still invite ABCs, African Americans, Indo-Canadians to the interviews just to rub it in their face," he recalls. "I was the manager. If I thought they were okay, I'd send them to schools. The ultimate decision is made by the school manager." Schools rarely hired African American applicants, he says, but ABCs and CBCs fared better. As more middle-class families ramped up their investments in their children's education, luring white teachers became a competitive sport. Taiwan offers a lower salary package than mainland China or Singapore, but that hasn't stopped many returnees from taking a chance on a career in teaching. Eric believes many of them have completed "generic majors" in university (humanities, arts) and struggle to find jobs in North America. It can be worth it for them to return to Taiwan. For those in a more advanced stage in their careers, a homeland return solves the problem of the so-called Bamboo ceiling, the Asian equivalent of the glass ceiling. It's another immigrant experience in the West that Eric doesn't have to deal with anymore.

"I now really feel at home. I look like the rest of the society here," he says when we resume our conversation in his apartment. "Nobody looks at me funny. If they do, it's because they think, 'This guy speaks English. This guy is an ABC.' . . . I don't have to stand out if I don't say anything. I stand out with my career, language ability. I actually feel more at home now more than I ever did in the US."

While his parents' generation thought the best thing they could offer their children was the privilege of Western education, Eric believes that staying together as a family is a better long-term investment for him and for his homeland. He wants to help Taiwan gain some economic resilience. To that end, he quit teaching to spread the gospel of bitcoin and blockchain, which he believes to be his biggest career opportunity to date. "It would be dumb for me to pass this up. After ten years in the old economy, it was a simple decision." His homeland return story rejects the wisdoms of the past and the belief that leaving for the West makes you happier or better prepared for the world. "Yeah, my children are not getting the American education. But to me, having got that, it's not a big deal."

All the same, he'll keep Emily's American citizenship and will work to get Emerson his (that may take a while because he was born in Taipei). "It's an extra option for them to have in the future." No ABC in Taiwan can afford to sever all ties to the West while China keeps a watch on the island.

* * *

Buy Bob Cheng a few drinks in Taipei and listen as his southern American drawl creeps up on him. Because we're sitting in a coffee shop on a late afternoon, after work and before his dinner commitment, I didn't get to test the true southernness of this Taipei-born businessman who lived in Athens, Georgia, for twenty-five years. I can verify his all-American boy status, however, just from glancing at his stocky figure and the muscle mass he built up after years of playing football in high school and college.

Bob's parents moved to Athens in 1985, when they heard about an opportunity to buy and run a Chinese restaurant. Although neither had any experience in the restaurant business, they saw the move as an investment in the future for Bob and his younger sister. "They felt that Taiwan was to a certain extent restricting in terms of education and opportunity," Bob, now thirty-seven, says, pointing out that his parents were already in their late thirties by then. "Not sure they moved to create opportunities for themselves."

In moving to America, his mother and father, both born in Taiwan, had also left behind a long family history of supporting China–Taiwan reunification. The family moved to Taiwan after the 1949 defeat of the Kuomintang Party. Bob's paternal grandfather had served as a lieutenant general in the army, and Bob's father was assigned to be a bodyguard to Chiang Kai-shek's son as part of his mandatory military service. "They were nostalgic—my father, particularly—about [their] days in the army," Bob tells me. "He was more the outdoorsy type. He used to tell those stories when I was watching too much TV."

In Athens, his parents spent their days and nights serving mid-priced Americanized Chinese food for nearly two decades to put Bob through an undergraduate degree in international affairs at Georgia Tech and send his sister to an out-of-state university. Bob, who went on to earn an MBA, didn't know how they would react when he told them about his plans to go back to Taiwan in 2009 to avoid the "economic tsunami" of the recession. But the parents were completely understanding. "They accomplished what they wanted," he says, in giving their children an American education.

It helped that Bob had paid back his debt to his parents in 2005, when he took over the family business after completing his undergraduate degree. "My parents were getting older, and the restaurant was stagnating. So I went in to try to revamp it, bring in a younger college crowd." He added alcohol, which attracted the tailgating crowd before and after football games. The centrally located business thrived, and his parents sold it two years later to a franchise. That had been their retirement plan all along.

Although Bob had visited Shanghai and other parts of mainland China, where before the recession the GDP was growing at double-digit rates (in 2007, it was an unimaginable 13.7 percent), he chose to return to the place where he was born. Having relatives close by helped, and so did a firm job offer in Hsinchu, where he worked for two years in the processing and distribution arm of a major manufacturer of semiconductors, one of Taiwan's leading industries. Looking back at those two years, Bob says that he gained no real advantage from being American by upbringing or Taiwanese by birth. "Being more local, people wanted to talk to you. Seen as a foreigner, your vocabulary faux pas were forgiven." While he wanted to practise his Chinese, his colleagues saw in him a chance to improve their English.

He found the one-way exchanges mildly irritating, but what he couldn't tolerate was the cautious corporate culture.

When his two-year contract came up for renewal in 2011, Bob took a pass. By then, he felt comfortable enough in Taiwan to pursue a riskier career in venture capital. Shanghai, Singapore and Silicon Valley were hopping, but Bob saw Taiwan's slower pace of tech adoption as an opening. Less competition meant more opportunities. When we met, he was raising money for two funds that invest in companies producing hardware and software to allow objects to communicate and share data with a range of devices—the Internet of Things.

"Our investments are in essence to grow Taiwan," Bob says. His words remind me of Jay's talk of helping Taiwan and Eric's of making it a stronger place economically. You can hear the notes of protectionism and homeland pride in Bob's career ambitions. Maybe it's genuine and maybe it's just an excuse to avoid the more competitive work environment in Canada or the US. I couldn't really tell, and perhaps I'm trying to read too much into their experiences in the hopes that they'll provide some guidance about my own. All three men have been back in Taiwan for almost a decade now. They talk about the place in words that suggest how much they love it, but also how often it feels like an experiment, a work in progress. I ask Bob for words to describe his nine years in Taipei. "Ever-changing," he offers. "Dynamic. Always learning. New experiences. Transition." And when I ask him about unification versus independence and China's policies, he confesses that he doesn't follow local politics too closely. "I'm still in a wait-and-see mode."

Bob's plans for the next ten years include meeting a woman

who shares his values and starting a family. His parents keep expanding the criteria for the first half of the plan—at first they wanted him to marry an Asian woman, but they're more flexible now. They've already picked out the best school district in Athens, Georgia, for his children, though. They believe he should come home. To America. When they gave him their blessing to move to Taipei, they didn't expect his "adventure" to last this long. Bob hasn't ruled out his parents' dream scenario, but he's open to others as well. "To me, what's the best for my family?" he says, clarifying that he includes his parents in his definition of family. "What's the best option where they would have an easier time for all of us to be together, and eventually in terms of education for my kids?" He stops and then pre-empts what I was just about to say: "I've already given up on not sounding like my dad."

It may read like I was trying to trip Bob up, to undermine his homeland return narrative and reveal him as another American kid who's living in an Asian bubble, but that wasn't my intention. If anything, my conversation with him confirmed the strength it takes to live with transition, to flip-flop, to reconcile ambiguity, the unknown and possibly the unknowable with my desire to see grand narratives in return stories. Ambiguities define Taiwan's story as a nation-state, after all. For some, drifting can be as good a plan as a purpose-filled life.

Hsiao-Wei, the teacher from Laomei, had already planted that seed when she and I talked about her own return and possible departure. She has saved enough to pay the rent for iSchool for the next ten years, as long as she doesn't expand and focuses on helping one or two students at a time. Her next goal is to build a library to give children books to read. One of her former students in New York told her that Taiwan needs her. "There's so much to be done here," she says. Her itchy feet and plans to start a PhD and write a book about curriculum design clash with the idea of settling back and helping the homeland, no matter how noble and altruistic that sounds. She loves to picture herself living on a cargo ship, just floating and working on her books and doctoral thesis. "Perhaps that's my next journey," she says.

I don't know if I'll ever feel comfortable with this combination of detachment and unpredictability, but it's something to remember should my own homeland return materialize. What could be more unpredictable—and literally more explosive—than going back to a place that has been mired in a war for six years now? The contexts are different, but if ABCs and sea turtles can manage Taiwan's political instability and accept the risk of a military intervention from China, maybe I can survive the crisis in Yemen.

PART III

PART VII

Chapter 7

ANCESTRAL HOMELANDS

In July 2016, Larry Mitchell started a GoFundMe petition with one request: "Send me back to Africa." The Indiana-based Black man added the hashtag #putyourmoneywhereyourhateis and set his goal at $100,000. The request went viral. As Mitchell told reporters at the time, the idea of the fundraising campaign came to him as America faced another summer of police brutality that had taken the lives of more Black people. He wanted to subvert the "Go back to Africa" calls that white supremacist groups spread on social media at times of heightened racial tension.

The campaign's irony went over the heads of some Americans, who took Mitchell's plea at face value and donated small amounts, before tossing in a racial slur or two. Someone called "Fedup white guy" spared five dollars and sealed it with a personal message: "You better not come back." Most contributors were in on the joke, however, and helped Mitchell raise $2,152 before the campaign stopped accepting donations.

I was in the early stages of thinking about a book about returns when I first came across Mitchell's campaign. I had read reports of Black Americans visiting Africa to trace their roots or pay tribute to the spirit of their ancestors, but I didn't know enough about the long history of such journeys. Or whether these trips had increased in volume and urgency during the Trump presidency. Three years after Mitchell's campaign ended, I found myself in Ghana, meeting Black Americans and Canadians who'd returned to Africa to escape racism, to reconnect with their heritage or just to see what would happen. These returns built on more than two centuries of Back to Africa movements that had straddled Black empowerment and disenfranchisement in North America.

The journey to Africa is one of the more startling examples of ancestral returns, which fall under the wider category of ethnic return migration. The mass migration of millions of Jews to Israel after the Second World War is another. The next two chapters investigate what these return movements have meant for Blacks from North America, Jews from around the world, Palestinians in the West Bank and Africans on the continent. Their stories illuminate historical moments that have been centuries in the making, but they also underscore present encounters with race and migration. But before we get to the present, though, we must look at the context of these returns and examine briefly why the "ancestral" part makes them contentious.

* * *

The Back to Africa movement began more than two centuries ago. Paul Cuffe (also spelled Cuffee in some sources), a Black businessman and descendant of a freed slave, made his fortune in maritime trading and used his influence to advocate for a "prosperous colony in Africa" for freeborn African Americans and freed slaves. In 1811, he founded the Friendly Society of Sierra Leone to capitalize on the establishment of the first African colony made up of returning British and American freed slaves. The first group of African Americans who returned to Africa through the efforts of other members of the Black community arrived in Sierra Leone in 1816.

The Friendly Society distinguished its efforts from concurrent resettlement plans motivated not by altruism but by fears of how this new freedom could threaten slavery as an institution. The white-dominated and -led American Colonization Society, for example, helped thousands of freeborn Blacks and freed slaves resettle in what's now Liberia as part of a controversial repatriation program. Between 1822, when the society began operations, and the start of the American Civil War in 1861, it arranged return passage to Africa for an estimated fifteen thousand Black men and women. Historians and activists continue to parse the intentions of the society, with some suggesting that the mostly Quaker members acted out of a strong belief in equality, a desire to abolish slavery and an impulse to spread the civilizing message of Christianity. Others believe the society was a convenient outlet for slave owners to mitigate the risks freed Blacks posed to their businesses and their sense of security.

There's more consensus around the society's operations in

Africa in the first few decades of its existence. It's known that its representatives used heavy-handed techniques to buy lands and offered inadequate compensation. Once the first settlement was established, at Saint Paul River, its population of eighty-eight freed Americans came into conflict with native Africans. A two-tier system of Blackness ensued. The returning Americans asserted their superiority based on a structure that privileged their Christian faith, their lighter complexion and their language. They viewed local beliefs and languages as "primitive" and "barbaric."

As new waves of returning Blacks joined the expanding settlement that would eventually become the Republic of Liberia, Americo-Liberians recreated the land they'd left behind in the one they returned to, building Methodist churches and acting like the slave masters they'd escaped. The oversized influence of Americo-Liberians continued for a century and a half, only ending in 1980 with a violent coup led by Samuel Doe, a native solider.

Other Back to Africa movements originated in the twentieth century, including one championed by Marcus Garvey, the Jamaican-born, Harlem-based founder of the Universal Negro Improvement Association (UNIA). Garvey believed that self-emancipation for Blacks can happen *only* when they return to Africa. All other quests for equality, he insisted, were delusional. UNIA sold shares in the Black Star Line and bought three steamships Garvey hoped would carry African Americans to their new homeland in Liberia. In 1922, however, charges of financial irregularities and mail fraud led to a five-year prison term for Garvey. He was deported to Jamaica in 1927. But the Back to Africa dream continued after his death in 1940 and resurfaced in the 1960s, almost as a parallel strand of the civil rights movement.

The success of Alex Haley's book *Roots: The Saga of an American Family* in 1976 and the TV adaptation the following year transformed the "going back to where we come from" narrative from a personal quest into a national, if not global, pastime. I recall watching the show as a teenager in Cairo in the late 1970s. My siblings and I were transfixed by the journey of Kunta Kinte, the young man sold into slavery and shipped to America. Haley, explain Marianne Hirsch and Nancy K. Miller in *Rites of Return*, "set the stage for the performance of roots seeking and the climactic moments of recovery that have become common features of American collective self-fashioning."

Although there's reasonable doubt about what counts as fact and what has been fictionalized in *Roots* (its publisher first touted it as fiction, but many booksellers placed it on the non-fiction shelves), its legacy lives on through companies that can follow your DNA to a specific region within any continent and in TV shows that track the ethnic roots of public figures. The PBS series *African American Lives*, hosted by Henry Louis Gates Jr., and its spinoffs "attest both to the seduction of the quest for a direct link to deep roots and family bloodlines, and to what appears to be a widespread longing that crosses the boundaries of ethnicity, gender, and social class," Hirsch and Miller write. "The very definition of diaspora depends on attachments to a former home and, typically, on a fantasy of return." The word "homegoing" as a synonym for a funeral in Black American culture draws on an old saying that conflates the afterlife with a journey or a crossing back to Africa.

Stories of a return to Africa continue to inform more recent creative works, in which Black Americans project more than origin fantasies on the ancestral land. They resurface in the superhero narrative of Marvel's *Black Panther*, for example, with Wakanda standing in for what many Black Americans view as a lost past that needs to be reclaimed. And in her 2020 visual album *Black Is King*, Beyoncé explores "severed ties and return to the ancestral"; its themes of royalty recast Africa as a place that can be "returned to, a place untethered to the world's political economies." In an insightful essay for *Africa Is a Country*, Malawian writer Takondwa Semphere argues that the complicated and entangled histories of Black Americans and Black Africans continue to be "deeply problematic, hewing to old, frustrating tropes." At the heart of all these representations of a regal Africa lies a literal and metaphoric return journey.

A more recent parallel return story for the African American community is unfolding within the country's borders: Blacks from cities in northern and western states are moving back to the South in a great reverse migration. Most are descendants of workers who left for job opportunities in the industrial north between 1916 and 1970. Others are lured by cheaper housing and the slower pace of life. This reverse migration paid political dividends for the Democrats in the 2020 US elections, with Georgia voting blue for the first time since 1992. The Black population of the metro Atlanta area increased by 251,000 between 2010 and 2016. Charles M. Blow, a *New York Times* columnist and author of *The Devil You Know: A Black Power Manifesto*, believes that this reverse migration could create the kind of density that "would translate into statewide political power."

He should know; he moved to Atlanta after twenty-six years in New York City.

* * *

In *Diasporic Homecomings: Ethnic Return Migration in Comparative Perspective*, Takeyuki Tsuda defines this movement as "later-generation and descendants of diasporic peoples who 'return' to the country of ancestral origin after living outside their ethnic homeland for generations."

One of the most dramatic return movements of the twentieth century involved the repatriation to postwar Germany of about twelve million ethnic Germans expelled mostly from Poland, Yugoslavia, Czechoslovakia and Hungary. While many of the expellees could trace their roots in these countries to centuries of German expansion into eastern Europe, others found themselves classified as ethnic minorities once borders were redrawn at the end of the First World War. At the Potsdam Conference in 1945, the United States, Britain and the USSR agreed that this mass return migration should "be effected in an orderly and humane manner." The opposite happened, as Europeans engaged in a violent expulsion campaign that claimed the lives of between half a million and two million ethnic Germans between 1944 and 1950. Their arrival at the motherland hardly ended their troubles, as shortages in housing and resources led to life in government-administered camps or as forced guests in the homes of their fellow Germans. As political scientist Anil Menon writes, the return of this group of ethnic Germans shaped the postwar politics of

West Germany in particular, and their legacy remains "active in German politics to the present day."

Other prominent ancestral homecomings in the twentieth century include the return of 2.8 million ethnic Russians from Eastern Europe, the Caucasus and Central Asia to their homeland between 1990 and 1998, after the collapse of the Soviet Union.

Ethnic affinity with the host country (also known as "co-ethnics") channels the migratory flow to specific countries, but as Tsuda argues, most ethnic return migrations are motivated by economic disparities. He cites, among other examples, the return of ethnic Japanese Brazilians (*nikkeijin*) to Japan in the 1980s, after the downturn in Brazil's economy. An aging population and a booming industrial cycle in Japan, a country that has historically resisted the idea of foreign migrant workers, made the return of this co-ethnic group mutually beneficial.

Closer to home and in a reverse (and minor) example of ethnic migration, the first two decades of this century witnessed a significant increase in the number of French people relocating to Quebec to take advantage of a better economy, cheaper housing and a common language. At least in theory. According to several reports in Canadian, French and American publications between 2007 and 2017—a period during which these immigrant groups more than doubled in numbers—the French find Quebec too North American and Quebecers find them too French. In 2007, the Delegation of Quebec in France estimated that about one in five (18 to 20 percent) returned home within five years. Demographer and University of Montreal professor Marc Termote told the *Wall Street Journal* that in fact one of every two French immigrants to Quebec returns to France within eight years. One Frenchman who was among that early wave recalled in an interview that many French immigrants and students were told to go back to where they came from. Differences between French newcomers and native Quebecers often revolve around the belief that the former have isolated themselves instead of integrating in their new home—an observation that would befuddle anyone with a passing knowledge of the many cultural and legal wars Quebec has started in the name of integrating new immigrants.

During my reporting trips to Israel and Ghana, I didn't always find economy to be the main pull for returns. The desire for a better life may explain the movement of some African, East European and Arab Jews to Israel, but most of the Canadians and Americans who moved there or to Ghana traded higher salaries (and in some cases a better standard of living) for the dream of living in the ancestral homeland. The trade-off serves a more primordial purpose when return becomes a corrective to historical wrongs.

While returns in general offer no guarantees of spiritual or financial fulfilment, the ancestral ones come with a higher probability of culture shock and disappointment. What some writers call the "longing to belong" feels either unrealistic or misplaced. Returnees share an ethnic connection, but they often lack a common experience, language or civic identity with the nation-state in which they seek membership, if not validation. This takes place despite the fact that the return of co-ethnics tends to be tied to "deep-seated and relatively fixed ethnic conce of nationhood," as Christian Joppke and Zeev Rosenhek argue in their comparative study of ethnic immigrations in Israel and Germany after the Second World War. Israel's establishment as a Jewish state and the postcolonial rebirth of Africa as a continent for Africans place those outside these religious, racial and ethnic confines beyond the reach of national projects or unity. Muslims and Christians in Israel, as well as whites or South Asians in, say, Uganda or South Africa—many with deep ties to the same homelands—hint at the troubling nationalist nature of this particular return story.

Since ethnic returns fall under a family of immigration policies that screen newcomers based on predetermined criteria of ethnic, racial, religious or national origin, they tend to be subject to contested identity claims. Africans from Somalia or Ethiopia go to great lengths to prove their Jewish identities to be eligible for a return to Israel. "Creative ethnic reidentification" refers to the different ways some returnees re-engineer their personal histories to fit into the nationalist or ethnic demands of their new (which technically means ancestral) homeland.

Whether it's the Promised Land or Africa, the motherland, something other than economics governs this particular kind of return. How do you call a place your homeland when you've never set foot in it? Or when you know that your ancestors either fled or were forced to leave centuries before? How much of that homeland lingers in the DNA, and how much resides in the narratives that have been kept alive by descendants?

* * *

The Arab-Israeli conflict, as mystifying and violent as it reads to outsiders and is experienced by those in the region, may be better explained as the competing narratives of two returns.

The preservation of Israel as a Jewish state is sustained through its Law of Return. This law gives almost all people of the Jewish faith the right to leave their natal homelands and return to Zion, a land that appeared on world maps as Palestine until 1948. (Some provisions exist to bar people who have serious criminal records or who pose a threat to the state, among other exclusions.) Palestinians' resistance to what they believe is the illegal occupation of their lands and the current displacement of six million people (a number that includes descendants) manifests itself through a doctrine called the right of return—the return of Palestinians to their lands and the restitution of properties to their owners.

As journalist Ian Black notes in his comprehensive book *Enemies and Neighbours*, "Zionists have tended to focus on their *intentions* in immigrating to Palestine; Arabs on the *results*." Within this framework of duelling returns, Palestinians view themselves as the land's "indigenous inhabitants" and as a Muslim majority who co-existed with Christian and Jewish minorities. The establishment of the State of Israel and the wars that followed, they believe, created a refugee population, currently well into the fourth or fifth generation, whose right of return was recognized by the United Nations in 1949 but not by Israel, then or now. Israelis, Black writes, are in turn on a quest for self-determination following centuries of antisemitism through the "'ingathering of the exiles' who 'return' from the Diaspora to Zion to build a sovereign and independent Jewish state in the ancient homeland." (I explore the notion of "making aliyah"—which literally means going up or rising but is understood as a homecoming to Zion—through the return stories of my interviewees in the final chapter.)

The subject of Palestinian return remains misunderstood and has proven to be the biggest obstacle to reaching a peace agreement between the two sides. As political analyst Dahlia Scheindlin writes in a far-reaching 2020 report, "Neither Intractable nor Unique: A Practical Solution for Palestinian Right of Return," it's among the "most emotionally and politically charged issues" of the conflict. Israel insists that Palestinians' right of return to areas under its sovereignty has no basis in reality and denies responsibility for creating the refugee problem. The return of six million Muslims and Christians understandably presents an existential crisis for the Jewish state. Palestinians, on the other hand, view the right of return as a claim based on international law and historic justice.

Scheindlin recommends a "pragmatic balance" between the principle of return and the requirements of its implementation. She argues that other ethnic minority refugees have "successfully sought the right of return," as recognized by international law and conventions. The idea of refugee return, contrary to Israeli views, is not a Palestinian invention, as evidenced by the return of ethnic minorities in Rwanda, Cyprus, Bosnia and Kosovo.

Both sides, Scheindlin suggests, need to re-examine their entrenched views of returns if any peace agreement is to succeed. Israel should change its "fundamentally rejectionist" position, which includes denying Palestinian history and suffering, international law and norms for redress. At the same time, Palestinians must recognize that a "maximalist" expectation of "full implementation of return" for all refugees and their descendants has little precedent.

For other commentators, the Palestinian right of return is a dream that has stood in the way of achieving peace because it represents a historically inaccurate claim. In *The War of Return*, self-described left-leaning journalist Adi Schwartz and politician Einat Wilf argue that the return of Palestinian refugees is *the* issue of this conflict, and yet it remains "relegated to the sidelines." The right of return captures Palestinians' "most profound beliefs about their relationship with the land and their willingness or lack thereof to share any part of it with Jews."

Schwartz and Wilf believe that Western diplomacy and UN structures have indulged this return fantasy and, as a consequence, sustained the refugee problem. The Palestinians have then used that as a bargaining chip to extract other concessions in peace negotiations. Schwartz and Wilf go as far as advocating the dissolution of the United Nations Relief and Works Agency (UNRWA), which they see as a major obstacle to peace as it tends to cave to Palestinian demands and perpetuates a one-sided victim narrative. Their argument may seem extreme to moderates from both sides, but it tracks with the opinion of the majority of Israeli Jews, who no longer believe that Palestinian returns and a one-state solution are viable options. In a 2018 poll, 70 percent of Israelis rejected the very idea of Palestinians returning to form a state of their own. A 2020 poll found that only 12 percent of Israeli Jews supported the idea of one state based on full equality between the two sides.

Reconciling the Jewish and Palestinian narratives of return

may hold the key to peace in the region. As I write this, the two sides seem further apart than at any point in the past two decades. Peace deals between Israel and some Arab countries brokered during the Trump administration's twilight months, mostly to shore up an anti-Iran alliance, have done little to address the Palestinian dreams of return.

* * *

Whether in the context of slavery or the Arab-Israeli conflict, return becomes part of a reparation-seeking mission in the original sense of repairing damage or making amends. These amends are for people captured in their own lands and sold into slavery, and for their descendants on whose shoulders many empires have been built. They cover a religious minority that has confronted prejudice and discrimination so extreme it culminated in the extermination of six million people. And a population that found itself displaced from the only land its people and their kin have known.

Antisemitism, Palestinian erasure and anti-Blackness figure large in the next two return stories I tell. Each person I met carries the burden of history with every act or dream of return. Whether the homelands that receive them offer a sanctuary or merely an escape route remains unclear.

Chapter 8

GHANA

The Year of Return

The Door of No Return holds a special place in the narratives of slaves and the imagination of their descendants in the Americas and beyond. The door marked the final stretch of African land to touch the feet of millions of enslaved men and women before they boarded ships bound for the Caribbean and North and South America. (In reality, there were multiple doors at different castles and dungeons along the west coast of Africa.) For Canadian poet and author Dionne Brand, the door is not a physical place but "a spiritual location" and "perhaps a psychic destination." It's the "creation place" of the Black diaspora, and it marks the end of "traceable beginnings." When visiting Ghana in 2009, US president Barack Obama echoed Brand's words as he described the door as a birthplace of sorts, a "portal through which the diaspora began." The door, he added, is where "the journey of much of the African American experience began."

While an exact number is hard to establish, it's believed that ten to twelve million Africans travelled on these ships between the sixteenth and nineteenth century. In August 1619, one of them arrived in Jamestown, Virginia, becoming the first slave ship to reach what's now the United States of America. Four hundred years later, thousands of African Americans returned to the continent to mark the anniversary and take part in Ghana's Year of Return.

First announced in 2017 by President Nana Akufo-Addo, the Year of Return was a marketing campaign by the Ghanaian government to cast the West African country as a fun destination for holidaymakers, an investment opportunity for businesspeople *and* a spiritual pilgrimage for members of the Black diaspora seeking their roots in Africa. The Year of Return fell in the middle of the United Nations' International Decade for People of African Descent (2015–24) and coincided with the biennial Pan African Historical Theatre Festival in Cape Coast, where Elmina Castle and Cape Coast Castle, both World Heritage Sites, have been transformed from slave dungeons to historical landmarks and tourist attractions.

While most studies estimate that only 10 percent of outbound African slaves departed from ports in what is now Ghana, no other country on the continent has been as successful or as aggressive in rebranding itself as a destination for tracing the origins of transatlantic slavery—or recasting the Door of No Return as a revolving door of entries and exits. In early 2020, Ghana announced a ten-year project to promote tourism and homecomings called Beyond the Return: A Decade of African Renaissance. Much of that plan has been upended by the COVID-19 pandemic, but for now, the 2019 Year of Return campaign seems destined for the (tourism) history books.

Barbara Oteng Gyasi, Ghana's minister of tourism, told the BBC that the Year of Return had injected almost $1.9 billion into the local economy. Idris Elba, Cardi B., Naomi Campbell and other celebrities enlisted to draw attention to the campaign visited Ghana and left a long digital trail on social media. So did a number of Black influencers and YouTube celebrities, whose videos of swanky villas and dance parties feel disturbingly close to a reality show on the E! network. The number of visiting Americans alone increased by 26 percent over the previous year. British tourism went up by 24 percent.

I was one of the estimated eight hundred thousand people to visit Ghana in the first nine months of the Year of Return. I arrived in the capital, Accra, with many questions for the return-ees I'd arranged to meet. What does it mean to return to a place of origin? To the site of an ancestor's (and their own) trauma? The Back to Africa movement is at least two centuries old, so why does the current moment in African and American history seem so ripe for a more meaningful and lasting return?

I visited Ghana one year before the global protests and calls for racial equality that marked the spring and summer of 2020 almost as indelibly as the pandemic. Much of what I heard from the women and men I talked to in Ghana revolved around the origins of this racial reckoning. Many Black Americans and Canadians have taken to the streets to change the narrative on policing, injustice and economic inequalities; others, like the ones you'll meet in this chapter, have turned their backs on North American racial politics and travelled to Africa through the doors of return that Ghana and other countries have thrown open.

* * *

"One of my goals in life is to help Black people, whether they're African American or Caribbean or from the UK, to come to Africa," says Annabelle McKenzie, the project manager of the Year of Return campaign. "Doesn't matter which country. Just for one time in [their] life to step on the motherland." We're sitting in the Accra Tourist Information Centre, in the office that she shares with her assistant, Lucy, who has booked this meeting for me. For Annabelle, this goal is more than shop talk; it's an echo, an affirmation of her own journey to Africa.

Despite a lucrative career that took her from Denver to New York City as a consultant in technology and digital communications, Annabelle says she never felt connected to the United States, the country where she was born and raised. When a previous job for an energy company took her to Africa (Nigeria and Angola) for the first time, she "instantly felt like [she] was home." She followed that visit up with a genome test through African Ancestry, a Washington, DC, genetics company that encourages Black Americans to unlock their family history. The results suggested that her ancestors likely hailed from Ghana and the Ivory Coast. Still, she made no plans to explore West Africa until she met the Ghanaian man who would become her partner in New York City. When she flew to Ghana to meet his family, she knew it would be her new home. "Going to Cape

Coast to see the slave dungeons in Elmina was a very emotional experience," she says. "It's almost like your ancestors are speaking to you through nature . . . Ghana is where I was supposed to be, where I was being led to."

This spiritual realization coincided with a career one: America is a place where, for minorities, the higher they climb in their careers, the more obstacles they're likely to encounter. As Annabelle describes it, there's a racial glass ceiling that many Black Americans know well. Working in technology, she was usually the only Black woman, and often only Black person, in the room.

Dealing with microaggressions and dodging racist assumptions related to her skin or heritage (or hair) drained her. "[This] is the first time in my life where I can work somewhere where everyone looks like me," she says as she points to Lucy and the receptionist in the hallway. "Here, whether you're rich, whether you're poor, whether you're middle class, we all look alike. That's why it feels like home to me. I've never felt like I was sticking out like a sore thumb."

On a personal level, Annabelle prefers to be identified not as a returnee but as a re-patriot—a re-pat. "We're the people who are actually coming back to whatever we consider to be our motherland—to move, to have a life, to invest and to give back." The Year of Return campaign didn't target Black North Americans of explicit Ghanaian heritage. Black people who believed their ancestors came from West Africa and travelled to the Americas through one of the slave ports in the region were invited to this celebration of ancestral returns. But to some participants, there was too much celebration and not enough reflection.

One of the criticisms Black commentators levelled at the Year of Return from the start was the number of high-priced music and wellness festivals, concerts, student summits and exhibitions— few of which local Ghanaians could afford. *National Geographic* and other high-profile publications ran articles about Ghana as the "hottest destination for African-American travelers." The country has always enjoyed a certain reputation as "Africa for beginners" in the travel industry and the voluntary sector, mostly because of its political stability and the fact that English is the official language. But coupling a "hot" travel spot with a history of chattel slavery creates a certain dissonance, at least for an outsider to transatlantic trade like myself. (As a person of Arab origins, I carry the burden of a different chapter in the history of slavery: the enslavement of millions from Africa and elsewhere into former Muslim and Arab empires for twelve or more centuries.)

"The Year of Return is not about anything," Shabazz, co-owner of the Cape Coast resort where I was staying and a returnee (from New York City) himself, tells me when I meet him later in the week. "It's just that somebody heard the grassroots people talking about some pan-African concept, jumped on board with it, invited a whole lot of Hollywood movie stars over here and there ain't no real substance to it. It's just another commercial." He prefers the Joseph Project, a less glamorous faith-based initiative by the Ghanaian government in 2007 to invite Black diaspora to Africa as kin.

Annabelle has heard this criticism before, but she insists that the Year of Return is a broad church that caters to different congregations in a number of ways. "Some people come back because they just want to go on vacation. Other folks are coming because they eventually want to move here and make a life," she explains. No matter the purpose, it doesn't preclude the possibility of a "spiritual experience" or an "emotional journey." The success of the Year of Return, in my opinion, lies in that yoking of business, pleasure and psychological transformation. The nearest model to it is not the Birthright Israel trips but perhaps the hajj to Mecca, one of the tenets of Islam and a boon to the coffers of the Saudi Arabian government and its merchant class.

Return comes with lots of planning and practical steps, Annabelle says, running through a checklist. Whatever their reason for choosing to go to Ghana, visitors had better have some money and have done their research. If they don't plan in advance, they may be left with no option but to go back. Younger returnees and re-pats will want to consider their job prospects and be realistic about salaries in Ghana, which tend to be significantly lower than those in North America or Europe.

Some African American retirees think that their social security payments will be enough, but additional retirement funds will make transition to Ghana smoother. It all depends on what life you want in the new homeland. If you choose a place away from the expensive areas where expats and diplomats are housed— or in other words, live and shop like a local—American dollars stretch further. While all of this may seem worlds removed from tracing origins and unlocking family histories, it's the nitty-gritty of the return process that, Annabelle tells me, many visitors underplay as they plan their journeys to the motherland.

Canadian TV journalist, model and returnee Ivy Prosper has written a book for people considering a move to Ghana, temporarily or permanently, whether they have roots in the West

African country or no connection at all. The second edition of *Your Essential Guide on Moving to Ghana* was published in 2019, to capitalize on the global spotlight on the Year of Return. I arranged to meet Ivy to hear more about her experience and to get the story behind her book.

***

In theory, Ivy is a good pick to write a book on coming to Ghana, but her employment history says otherwise.

She was born in Accra and moved with her mother to Mississauga, west of Toronto, just before her second birthday. They were to reunite with her father, a mechanical engineer who had immigrated to Canada in 1974. Her three siblings were born in Canada, and they all grew up in a household that reminded them of their heritage and served as a drop-in centre for other Ghanaian immigrants. Many even lived with the Prosper family as they found their way in their new country. Ivy was almost thirty-eight when, in 2011, her mother recommended a trip to Ghana after her daughter had experienced a number of career setbacks in Toronto.

When we met in 2019, Ivy had been living in Ghana off and on for almost eight years. (She spent three years in Canada between 2013 and 2016.) In her self-published book, she describes her feelings about returning to Ghana after three years away almost as a case of FOMO (fear of missing out). "I constantly felt the desire to go back to Ghana. Each time I read news about things happening there, I felt something in my spirit that kept tugging at me. I needed to return."

The reality? Until she landed her current position as the social media director of the Year of Return campaign, Ivy had moved from job to job, from one short-term contract to another. She swapped continents but precarity followed. In her first year in Accra, she lucked out with a job as the head of a creative writing centre at a private high school. After some networking, she was offered a job hosting a TV show focusing on maternal health. But "opportunities vanished," she says, after she returned in 2016. One TV station got bought out by another, leaving many of its staff unemployed, and a full-time gig with a production company was terminated when the owners couldn't secure new funding.

"I feel like I want to leave because of all the frustration," she tells me. Much of this frustration has to do with Ghanaian work culture, but some relates more specifically to her awareness of her body as a six-foot-three woman who attracts attention (and unwanted advances) wherever she goes. "I've had people tell me that I'm too aggressive. And also people tell me that I'm intimidating because of my height," she says. When we arranged to meet in the lobby of my hotel, she told me to look for someone "very tall in pink."

Is someone who constantly thinks of leaving the best choice to write a book for people thinking of arriving? I ask when we sit to talk in the hotel's café. Ivy explains that she wrote the book without planning for it. "It got to be repetitive typing the same answer on emails and [direct messaging] on social media." Her sister told her off for "giving away all this free information" and encouraged her to put everything she knew in a book. Ivy would like potential newcomers to learn not just from her experience but from that of the hundreds of returnees and repatriated African Americans who barely stayed a year in Ghana before packing up and leaving for good.

"You have this idealized view of Africa, the motherland," she says, as if addressing one of these people directly or sharing the results of a personality test. "You've always thought, 'I want to go back to my roots,' and then you arrive and you realize, 'These are my roots, but I don't really feel connected because of the experience I've had—my life, my family, my history.'" Thoughts of a *Roots*-like connection quickly crash against the realities of modern-day Africa. Some African Americans, Ivy says, are surprised when local Ghanaians don't embrace them in the way they had dreamed of or read about in other return stories. Some Ghanaians who never left view the returning African Americans as rich and privileged, while others feel resentful of and threatened by what they see as "immigrants coming in and taking their jobs" (and as Western-trained professionals, getting paid substantially more).

While Ivy strongly recommends that diasporic Black communities start their journey to Africa with a visit of a few weeks, she also cautions them not to base their final decision on that one trip. If they do, there're in for a "big surprise" once they make the move. For locals, the novelty of returning African Americans wears off once they transition from visitors to permanent residents. "It's not going to be the same treatment. 'Oh, you live here? Okay, whatever. No red carpet for you anymore,'" says Ivy, this time channelling the local perspective.

Primarily, it's a matter of adjusting to the system. When travellers stay at hotels that have their own generators, they never experience problems with running water or power outages, which remain common even in a country that sells energy to its neighbours. "Learning to exercise patience becomes a big, big thing here," Ivy notes. Patience also applies to such things as recognizing that local traffic sometimes—frequently, actually—means the people you've arranged to meet will arrive later than you expect. On the day of our interview, Ivy sent me two messages to let me know that she was running late—first because the bus she took from Tema, a suburb of Accra, left late, and then because she got stuck in traffic in the city proper.

Running late is part of Ivy's "live like a local" return story. She takes the Ghanaian minibuses known as *tro-tro*. Almost all are privately owned and leave their point of departure when they've reached capacity or near to it. Although she speaks Ga, one of the sixteen official languages of Ghana, Ivy usually keeps quiet on the bus in order to observe and listen to other passengers. Because of her height, most riders assume she's not Ghanaian. Her fashion style, which tends to the flamboyant, marks her out even more. Some passengers wonder why she's riding in the bus when, based on her appearance, she can afford an Uber or a taxi. (Ivy doesn't drive.) "I think if you're always secluded in your Uber or always got your driver from point A to point B, and you never interact with local people, just your returnee friends, then you only have one viewpoint of the country."

This fluency with local culture—her homeland culture—has allowed Ivy to switch between the serious work of hosting the maternal health show and gigs as an emcee for fashion shows or other cultural events. When our conversation returns to her career frustrations, I ask her a direct question: Why are you still here? She may have left Canada after the financial crisis of 2008–09 to avoid the media meltdown that followed, but it's not like she landed on her feet in Ghana.

"Sometimes I ask myself the same question," Ivy says as she collects her thoughts for a longer explanation. "What keeps me going is wanting to change the narrative of Africa, wanting to change that negative view that I was shown growing up in Canada, which was everybody living in trees, everybody's got flies on their face. I want to show that no, not everybody is . . . There is another side that people don't see, and I feel like what fuels me is wanting to show the other side, which I try to do on social media. I've had friends in the States who send me messages and say, 'Oh, some of your pictures look like you're somewhere here. They don't look like you're in Africa.'"

Ivy knows she can have a bigger impact on younger women in Ghana than in Canada. She recalls an event where a Canadian historian who'd discovered some lost documents related to Ghana's roots in the slave trade took questions from the public. One of them came from Ivy, who introduced herself as a journalist. The details of the talk and the nature of the question have faded with time, but Ivy distinctly recalls two Ghanaian girls who came up to her after the talk. One wanted to be a journalist, the other a scientist. They both mustered the courage to ask Ivy about her life and career. She chatted with them for thirty minutes, then gave both her contact information and promised to show the budding journalist the ropes and to connect the future scientist with women in the field.

"Even though there are opportunities here, I find that young people don't have a grasp of 'I should take the initiative if I want A, B, C and D,'" Ivy says. "Because culturally, you are taught to respect your elders and to not challenge authority . . . That means that if you see something that's of interest and you want to ask about it, a lot of times they're afraid to ask adults because they're not supposed to say anything . . . I want to be here to say, 'You can speak. There's a way you can do it without making that authority figure feel like they're being challenged.' Yeah, so that's what keeps me going. I have to think about those moments. Otherwise, I'm back on a plane to Canada."

* * *

In my conversation with Ivy, she mentioned a certain kind of returning American to whom some Ghanaians take exception. Instead of adapting to life in Africa, these new arrivals see their move as an extension of their old life and bring America with them, in an echo of that early group of Americo-Liberians in the nineteenth century. They host events like Black History Month; celebrate Juneteenth, a holiday that marks the end of slavery in the States; and throw Thanksgiving pot luck dinners in November. All three activities rank high on the social calendar of members of the African-American Association of Ghana (AAAG).

When I asked Gail, one of the association's organizers, to choose where we could meet, she recommended the W.E.B. Du Bois Centre in Cantonment, on the way to Accra International Airport. The Triple AG, as the association is commonly called, shares Du Bois's vision of pan-Africanism and facilitates the cultural, social, educational and economic integration of returning African Americans and the Black diaspora at large.

The centre, home to Du Bois's museum and library, includes the association's only physical space—a bungalow with a few stacked chairs, an empty desk and a sofa that looks like it has been handed down one too many times. The Ghanaian government donated the space to the association in the mid-1990s, but it hasn't been used for a long time. These days, the 130 members conduct business through email and WhatsApp group chats. Their numbers may be small, but their association has become the first port of call for returning African Americans. I get the feeling that Gail, her friend Jessica (a long-time member of the association) and I are the first to use the office in months.

Gail and Jessica wouldn't actually call themselves pan-Africanists, even though the two Black women, who are fifty-two and sixty-two, respectively, know the sting of racism in their native America and are married to Ghanaian men who have steered their families toward a return to Africa. They represent a segment of well-to-do Black Americans—Gail is a former lawyer and Jessica a retired computer scientist—who, for economic and generational reasons, have shaped the return narrative to their particular circumstances. Their perceptions of life in Ghana reveal that they've replaced their anxieties about race in the US with new ones about class in Ghana.

Both women know the association has a reputation as a home to mostly older and financially secure returnees, even though they say that they've fielded inquiries from younger people who show interest in work or investment opportunities. Gail explains that the association's activities spring from a desire to let African Americans and other members of the Black diaspora define their own return stories: where and what is their ancestral home, and what to do when they get to it. Irish or Italian Americans can often trace their origins to a specific village or town in their homelands, but that's a luxury denied to their African counterparts, who have to see the whole continent as their home. "I think it's more important to understand the spiritual aspect of coming home," Gail tells me. "It's important to allow African Americans to define for themselves what coming home is." Returns to Ghana don't need to follow a formula or be just about spiritual rebirth.

Jessica's journey to Africa followed a straightforward path. One evening in 1995, her husband, then an executive with Coca-Cola, walked into their home in Houston with news that he was being transferred to South Africa. Apartheid had just ended, and so did the economic sanctions and moral objections that had kept many African Americans from visiting the country. Until then, Jessica had been working on contract as a computer scientist for a range of clients, including NASA. She was also the primary caregiver to their two young girls. The couple had met in 1979, while both were studying at Duke University in North Carolina, Jessica's (and Gail's) home state. She remembered how much fun it was to hang out with her future husband's West African friends. After many years of marriage and raising a family, with "both working, both in the rat race," relocating to South Africa to take up a well-paid job seemed like a safe way to try a new life.

The six years in South Africa had some tensions—particularly around everyday interactions, as some Zulu speakers would refuse to talk to Americans who didn't know their language well enough to carry a conversation—but those paled in comparison to the next corporate posting, in the Ivory Coast. During their two years there, Jessica and her family were evacuated twice because of military and political unrest. The first evacuation took them to Paris for two weeks and the second, in 2003, to Ghana, Jessica's husband's homeland. They've been there ever since, she says, because of support from her in-laws. "Some people have the unfortunate experience that the husband's family doesn't welcome them," says Jessica. "Fortunately, I didn't have that experience. My husband's family is very warm and welcoming to me."

While many other families had been living in Ghana longer, Jessica became a go-to person for newer returnees seeking advice as they navigated life in a new country. I can see why just from the two hours or so we spend together. Of the two women, Jessica comes across as warm and approachable, while Gail seems more hesitant and on her guard with me.

Perhaps I got that impression because Gail, a relative newcomer, having moved to Ghana four years earlier and under more complicated personal and career circumstances, was still discovering her own return story. When her husband, born in the US to Ghanaian parents, was offered a good job in Accra, the couple had to think through their options, especially as parents to two young boys, then fourteen and eleven. There was never a doubt about the boys adapting to a new life in Africa, though. Gail and her husband had taken them on trips to Ghana and fostered a connection to his side of the family. The issue was whether their initial plan—to leave Gail and the kids in Washington, DC, and travel between Africa and North America—made any sense for the family.

"I didn't want to do that because my son is very smart, very perceptive, and [has] absolutely no filter," Gail says, referring to the older of her two boys. "For a Black man, that can be a recipe for disaster." She began to notice that even in their relatively peaceful Washington neighbourhood, her son feared older Black kids. "I'd tell him, 'That's you in a few years. Are you afraid of your future self?'" A few telling encounters with her son's teachers made her realize that as a Black child, he was rarely given the benefit of the doubt and sometimes had to apologize for things he didn't do just to resolve a conflict with other students. Gail had taught her sons never to take responsibility for something they hadn't done. When the teachers challenged her, she said that this method of keeping the peace might work for white children but not for young Black men, who historically face more serious consequences if they admit responsibility. The teachers didn't seem to take her complaint seriously.

The "Oops Binder" was the last straw.

After her son had an argument with another student in the playground, a teacher suggested that he write an apology note and place it in a binder where students' mea culpas are collected. The next morning, Gail stormed into the principal's office. She pointed out what should have been obvious to the teacher: the two children were not in the classroom when they got into it, and they weren't being disruptive to a learning environment. "These things started to happen, and then you read stories about what they do to Black boys in predominantly white institutions, particularly when they're young," Gail says. "These bright kids, they label them. They get pushed to the side." It was then that she decided to give up her career as a lawyer and move her family to Ghana.

"I thought it was a great opportunity for my husband. It was a great opportunity for my children. The jury is still out for me," she says, her voice trailing off. When I say that it seems like quite the sacrifice on her part, she responds at length. "I think mothers in general—some mothers—are used to the idea of sacrifice for their families. And so that's what I look at it as. I look at it as a sacrifice for my children . . . to live in an environment that allows them to be the best that they can be and not have to worry about racism in its purest form. I don't know if I would have made the same decision if I had girls. I don't know. But there is just so much documentation about what they do to Black men in the United States that it felt like a sacrifice that I was willing to take."

Both women moved to Ghana before the election of Donald Trump in 2016, but I ask them if they have noticed a recent uptick in the number of African Americans trying to leave the United States. Yes, Jessica says, there has been more interest, but she notes that ebbs and flows in the number of inquiries are not uncommon. (An older returnee I spoke to recalled a spike after 9/11, for example.) Gail believes Trump's politics reveal the deep racial wound that has existed in America for four centuries. "There's that sense of nationalism, but I don't know whether there are more instances of racism or whether social media allowed for more documentation."

"That's our number-one issue in America—being Black and dealing with racism," Jessica cuts in. "It eats into every facet of our lives there."

Whenever Gail visits her family and friends back in North Carolina or Washington, DC, she shares with them the enormous relief of not having to deal with racism or its psychological effects on a daily basis. There's something to be said about living in a country where everyone—from the president to the children's teachers to the shopkeepers—is Black, Gail tells me. "There's comfort in belonging, in the positive reinforcement of what you could be."

This comfort is also material. Both women live in houses with generators and can afford to buy the diesel that powers them, not to mention several tanks of water when the regular supply is interrupted. The one true challenge, they both say, is the perception that some Ghanaians have of returning African Americans—that they are not just rich but have money to loan, spare for investment schemes or give away. Class issues in the United States are often hidden within more pressing race issues. In Ghana, class is out in the open. I heard a similar conversation in Jamaica, but the Ghanaian version seemed more like low-level grift.

"It makes you harder when you realize you're being taken advantage of," says Jessica. "I think because we are coming from different places, and even though we are used to the environment, there's still that little bit of guilt back there somewhere that makes you feel like, 'Well, you know, they don't have this,' so you can just give a little bit more than you would if you're at home."

Because of the ten-year difference in age between them, and since Jessica has been in Ghana longer than Gail, the women don't agree on whether their return to Africa is a final destination or another stage in life. Jessica's mother was about to turn ninety when we met, and that had started her thinking about her own end-of-life phase. The Ghanaian custom of hiring someone to look after elderly family members is "not really my vision," she says. And if her husband were to die, her roots in Ghana would be cut. "He's my family here." What about being in Africa, in the motherland? I ask. "Land can't take care of you," she notes.

For Gail, it's hard to predict where she'll be in, say, twenty or twenty-five years. But if forced to make a decision on the spot about where to retire or be buried, she says it would probably be back in the United States. "I don't think I've been here long enough to have that sense [of belonging]," she says. If she'd moved to Ghana because of her political beliefs in a stronger and renewed Africa, perhaps she'd stay in the motherland. But, she reminds me, "I moved here because of my kids."

As the kids get older, America's views on race and its attitude to Black men may change for the better, or get worse. Gail doesn't plan to bet her boys' future on either of these scenarios.

* * *

When Foule was thirteen and in a grade 9 geography class in Ottawa, his teacher rolled in the school's bulky TV and video recorder to show a documentary about Africa. Foule can't recall the specific lesson plan for that day, but he thinks it covered either famine or refugees. A few minutes into the documentary, this "really dark guy" began to talk about being persecuted. When the reporter asked him where he came from, the man said Ghana. Everyone in the class turned to Foule, the only Ghanaian in the room, with one question: Is this the country you'll visit during summer break? Foule nodded, but as far as he can recall, he didn't see the inquiry as racist or Eurocentric.

A year later, when his parents decided to relocate him and his two brothers, all born in Ottawa, to Ghana for a few years, he began to harbour doubts about this longer return plan. Why should they leave their prosperous country of birth to return to an ancestral home where electricity and water shortages—a complaint I heard from almost everyone I met—are a fact of life? Foule's older brother had turned into a textbook teenager: skipping school, smoking cigarettes and hanging out with the "wrong crowd." His strict Ghanaian parents figured it would do all three boys some good to go back to their motherland, where "adults are adults and kids are kids," Foule tells me. The wayward older brother was sent to a boarding school, while Foule and his younger sibling attended a private American school in Accra.

I had not planned on interviewing Foule. Instead, he was recommended to me by a Ghanaian contact as someone to call if I need to book a car and driver for trips outside Accra. When I got in touch to make arrangements for a trip to Elmina, I recognized his Canadian accent (confirmed by a reference to the Raptors' winning streak during the 2019 NBA playoffs). A few questions later, he and I arranged to meet that evening in downtown Accra. How could I pass up an opportunity to talk to someone for whom return is a multi-generational, multi-phased event?

Foule's father first returned to Ghana from England in the late 1960s to study medicine. His grandfather was one of the founders of Ghana's first medical school, and he had urged his son to return to fulfil President Kwame Nkrumah's post-independence vision of an educated and involved citizenry. As Foule, thirty-seven, tells me over a drink at his favourite bar, just off Accra's tourist-friendly Oxford Street, his father's return had more to do with family loyalty than national politics. In the late 1970s, he left for Canada to specialize in psychiatry, became a success and never returned, except for short family visits. Foule's mother, equally as ambitious, trained as a nurse in Ghana and worked in Canadian hospitals in Guelph, Ontario, and other places, but she never took to her adopted country. "She felt like she wasn't doing everything that she could."

From the time her kids were young, Foule's mother dabbled in small business deals here and there, not because the family needed the extra income but because she needed to nurture her inner entrepreneur. When the parents made the decision to send their boys to school in Ghana, around 1995, she flew to Accra first to make the necessary arrangements. She never made it back to Canada. She separated from her husband and started a private transportation company offering services ranging from chauffeur-driven limos to the *tro-tros* that roam Accra's streets.

"My mom is really kind of a 'gangster,'" Foule says. "I work for my mom." He recalls conversations with her, even before she returned to Ghana, in which she tried to create a balance between his identity as a Canadian—"You're a Canadian; nobody can tell you that you're not"—and his roots as an African. She played old-school Ghanaian music at home to keep the sound of her homeland alive in her family.

The move back to Ghana lasted two years. It took Foule some time to comprehend his parents' plan for their boys. Looking back, he believes it was their way to prepare them for life in Canada as Black men. His first real glimpse of that reality came in high school. Foule wasn't the most academically gifted student among his circle of friends. He struggled with some of his courses, but he did pass them. His career counsellor didn't think it was worthwhile for him to retake classes to improve his marks. Instead, she recommended a two-year diploma at Sheridan College in Toronto. "I felt very dismissed," Foule recalls. It took him more than two years—he wouldn't say how many more—to complete his marketing diploma. His work prospects were so grim after graduation, he accepted a job as a cleaner in a nursing home. By then, his parents had divorced and his father had remarried another Ghanaian woman. Foule describes his life at the time as aimless and depressing.

His mother invited her sons to Ghana for a two-month visit. It had been a while since all three men took a trip together, and they accepted the invitation. Once there, however, his older brother became "antsy to get back to Canada." The younger one had plans to study at Fanshawe College in London, Ontario. "I felt like I really didn't want to go yet, so they went ahead and I stayed behind." When Foule's application to transfer to university and upgrade his diploma to a bachelor's degree failed, his mother suggested he stay in Ghana for a while longer. "I really liked the idea because I had zero responsibility," he recalls. "So I'll just do that, and I'll try to figure out what I'm going to do next."

He gave himself three months at first. Then he met a lawyer who had returned to Ghana from living abroad and distilled his life experience into one command: "Don't do this back-and-forth thing." He told Foule to "choose something and stick with it." While returns don't always have to be final, research shows that the prospect of coming and going often makes settling in the country of choice much more difficult.

The three-month window became a ten-year plan. Foule decided to give Ghana the best of his twenties. If things didn't work out for him, he would return to Canada. He'd still be in his early thirties and could get a factory or retail job. He admits to having mixed feeling about his decision to stay.

Like the other millennials I'd spoken to in Taiwan, Foule approached his return with a sense of adventure, but he was also leaving behind a terrible employment reality in his adopted homeland and taking advantage of the somewhat better conditions and lower cost of living in Ghana. Unlike most of them, Foule had come to a bitter realization about race. "I came to Ghana because I didn't want to be Black anymore. I was tired of being Black and was ready to be me." In Ghana, he doesn't have to deal with such microaggressions as "You're so articulate," something he's heard over the years in Canada when people meet him for the first time. He doesn't have to wonder if he failed to get a job or a lease on an apartment because he's a single Black man.

With his mother established as a businesswoman, he could also get a leg up on his peers. She had good connections, but what was of more interest to him was that she knew how to do business in Ghana. Foule had to "learn Ghana," which meant picking up the social cues not just of how business is conducted but also of how to build relationships and resolve conflicts. In a typical argument in a bar in Canada, he says, it's likely that the two people involved will escalate matters and get into a physical fight. In Ghana, a third person will step in and try to seek a solution that will allow both parties to save face.

The same rules applied to doing business in Ghana. While he has no point of comparison to how it's done in Canada, despite receiving a diploma in marketing, Foule says that working for his mother's transport company taught him the difference between administering a business and running it. If you're trying to get a contract or a loan, relationship building counts for more than the proposals on the table. If a business decides to go after an existing contract, its owners realize that winning it means taking the "daily bread" of another business and the people running it. He points out the many investment opportunities in Ghana and notes this is one reason he supports the more business aspects of the Year of Return campaign. Corporations and private businesses from China, the Middle East and Russia have had Ghana in their sights for years. It's about time, he says, that well-to-do African Americans, especially those looking to invest their savings, got in on the act. His business experience has solidified his pro-Africa protectionist policies.

From what I can tell, Foule has learned more from his mother than he picked up in a Canadian classroom. He agrees. "It sounds very cocky or arrogant or whatever. But I also feel like I can do a lot more [here]. I'd rather apply that to my people than apply it to Canada." I'm curious about the "my people" reference and ask Foule if he can explain it to me in more detail.

"My people are Ghanaian, African. I'm an African. There's no way around it." He later adds that he thinks of himself as a Ghanaian with a Canadian passport.

When we meet in the late spring of 2019, Foule has been living in Ghana for fourteen years and is married to a Ghanaian woman who used to work for the family company. While they don't have children yet, they're planning on it. Foule doesn't rule out the idea of sending his future children to Canada to get an education. If he has a son, he'll be a young Black man in Canada, so how does that sit with him? "It's important for him to know what's it like to be a Black man in Canada," Foule tells me, suggesting that the experience can be character building in a toughening up sort of way.

Still, he doesn't see any of this as an indictment of Canada. The country did everything it needed to do, he says. It showed him the world through multiculturalism and diversity, something he hopes his children will be exposed to as well. "There's a lot of respect for Canada," he says as he puts his hand on his heart.

But it's not his homeland. Not right now.

* * *

I run into Kwame the day before we're scheduled to sit down for a talk. He assures me he's still up for it, but he insists that we sit at one particular table in the sprawling green grounds of One Africa, the Cape Coast guest house where I'm staying. With its panoramic view of the Atlantic Ocean, there are no blocked or bad spots on the premises. But this particular wooden table, big enough for four people, holds a special place in Kwame's heart and his return story. He visited the resort on his first week in Africa, in 2017.

"I sat here and I had a meal. I was listening to this sound we're hearing right now," he says, referring to the crashing ocean waves on the rocky bottom of One Africa. "There's a powerful energy here, and I think about the spirit of our ancestors." He points at Elmina Castle to his right and the fishing boats in the distance, then stops for a few seconds to take some breaths. "Even now, I'm just full of emotion. Something happens to me here that's really powerful. I think I really connect with the ancestors and with the spirit of Africa. And I feel like I've really, really, really survived. Sixty years in the US and now I'm home."

I've been a journalist for almost twenty-five years and a book author for ten, and I've never had an interview begin on such a spiritually content yet aching note. Or in such a magnificent setting. Kwame tells me that he's very emotional and has no problem with crying. By the time my conversation with him had ended, three or so hours later, I had a better sense of why this returnee calls his story one of survival.

Born in Oakland, California, and raised in adjacent Berkeley, Kwame, now sixty-three, was thrust into the world of racial discrimination when he was just four or five years old. His earliest childhood memory is of a trip to a dime store to buy candy with five cents his mother had given him. As he was mulling his options, a middle-aged white woman looked at him and told him he was ugly. She took a closer look at his nose and described it as flat and ugly. Kwame, alone in the store, felt hurt and intimidated. "I went home and looked at my nose and thought about what she said. I didn't like my nose for a long time."

As he moved into his early teen years in the middle to late 1960s, the liberal politics of Berkeley and the counterculture it birthed "calmed down" the effects of racial violence. As Kwame says, he grew up somewhere "between the race riots and the hippies." The exposure to social justice and the civil rights movement affected him in intellectual and more immediate ways. He recalls the emergence of Black Panthers as a political force but also as a community service. Some Panthers would come into schools in poorer communities and fix breakfast for children. "Those same people that others saw as violent, militant savages were really kind, loving individuals."

Kwame became a hardcore pan-Africanist at fourteen—more in the style of Malcolm X than Martin Luther King, he's eager to point out. At around the same time, he joined the All-African People's Revolutionary Party (AAPRP), which focused on social justice and political education. When the university in Berkeley introduced a course in African Studies, Kwame and his classmates, incoming freshmen at the local high school, protested to get a similar course. They succeeded.

As part of the African Studies program, Kwame took classes with a teacher from Kenya who taught Swahili and a history of the continent that transcended its association with slavery. More powerfully, the teacher gave Kwame the name that he has since legally adopted. Born Gregory Oliver, Kwame longed to be reborn as an African. The new name became part of that rebirth ritual. He has since added the middle name Abdul ("servant of God" in Arabic). Although his teacher chose the name based on the day of the week Kwame was born, as is the custom in some parts of Africa, he also intended it as an homage to Kwame Nkrumah, the father of modern Ghana, whose struggle to liberate the country from British colonialism started in 1955, the year of his student's birth. Although Nkrumah's hold on Ghana came to an abrupt end in 1966, when he was deposed by a military coup after nine autocratic and increasingly repressive years in power, he remained popular among pan-Africanists. Had his new name been a sign to explore Ghana, Kwame couldn't have acted on it back then.

His next move was from California to Nevada, where the very athletic seventeen-year-old was snapped up on a basketball scholarship. (When we met, he was wearing a Golden State Warriors T-shirt under his Ghanaian "up and down," or matching suit. As a Torontonian, I felt I should console him on his team's loss to the Raptors in the NBA Championship earlier in the week.) As he travelled the country for college games, his grades suffered. "Back then, African Americans didn't graduate from college," he says, adding that he missed by a few years the changes that ensured a better balance between academics and athletics. Instead, he joined his mother's real estate business. He acknowledges the long history of housing discrimination against African Americans—a reality he has witnessed over four decades in the business. Although the number of Black realtors in his area was small, he became one of the more successful among them. "I made my money and fed my family from real estate," he says.

The family includes five children—four sons and a daughter—from three relationships and one marriage that didn't last.

Growing up in the "Make love, not war" era, Kwame says, came with an addiction problem that he blames for burning his many relationships. "I started off smoking marijuana and drinking wine in high school. Then I started using cocaine, and briefly, I'd dabble with a little bit of heroin but never got into that, and eventually [I started] smoking crack." He says he cleaned up in time to enjoy raising his children, his "greatest experience in life," and now has seven grandchildren. "I couldn't afford to do things like come to Ghana for a month or two." It took a near-death experience to get him to make a journey he'd been dreaming of since he was fourteen.

Kwame had been suffering from a hernia for most of his adult life. His doctors didn't believe the condition was serious enough to merit surgery. The year he turned sixty, in 2015, he experienced some "emotional stuff" he says he'd rather not get into with me. That either triggered or coincided with an increased irritation from his hernia. A new doctor described the surgery as "real simple—in and out." But when he came to in the recovery room, Kwame learned that he had undergone major surgery. After "sixty years of neglect," the tissues on his abdomen had deteriorated and had to be replaced by a synthetic material that didn't agree with him. The day surgery turned into a two-week stay in hospital and led to other complications.

A few weeks later, while convalescing at home, Kwame suddenly stopped breathing. It may have been for only a few seconds, but it seemed like much longer in his mind. All he remembers now about that evening is that he couldn't take a breath or call on his two younger boys to come down and help him. As he hovered between life and death, his mind wandered into all the things he had planned to do, including take a trip to Africa. "And as I was going through this process, I caught a breath," Kwame says. "Because I didn't think I was going to breathe again, that was an incredible, incredible breath. It was the one I thought I was never going to get. I realized, 'Oh my God, this breath is life.'"

By chance, a friend who had just returned from Ghana visited him a few days later and mentioned that he planned another visit in a few months. Kwame decided to go with him. Six months later, he was on a plane to Accra. "I didn't come initially knowing I was going to stay. I came initially knowing I needed to love myself," Kwame tells me. "I've been taking care of everyone in my life except myself, and I realized it was time for me to love me better." He concedes that the first trip was overwhelming, not because of what he saw on the ground in Ghana but because he had been building it up in his mind. How does any country live up to half a century of longing?

When a friend's son picked him up from the airport and drove him to where he would spend the next five weeks, Kwame struggled to maintain a conversation because he kept looking out his window. "Everybody is African," he remembers thinking, as if that possibility had never occurred to him. Waking up to the sound of roosters and the bleating of goats felt like a spiritual awakening. "And it revealed to me in that time: 'This is where you need to be. You need to be right here.' I made a decision right then—I'm going to move to Ghana." He returned to Oakland to sort out his business affairs, and on July 18, 2018, he re-entered Ghana, not as a tourist but, he hopes, as a permanent resident.

"Nothing is more powerful than a made-up mind," he tells me. He may visit California from time to time to check in on his mother, now in her late eighties, but his message to his children is clear: "You want to see your daddy, you get a passport and come to me." He still worries about the future of his four sons, of course. He's watched many of his Black friends bury their children. He estimates he's been to at least fifty funerals of young men and women in his life. "The trauma associated with that is way too much. We shouldn't have to live like that." In West Africa, he doesn't have to.

As a Black man, Kwame says he's never felt safer or more welcome than he does in Ghana. He realizes that Ghanaians know he's not a local, even though his name and manner of dress are, but they don't treat him as a foreigner. "They see me as I am, a beautiful African man . . . They know I'm real." He loves telling the story of a Ghanaian police officer at the airport who kept looking at him while both were in the area where locals await arriving passengers. The look triggered Kwame's fears of encounters with the police in the US. Mentally he began to prepare for an argument, or at least some questions about his residence permit. Then the officer approached with a folding chair and handed it to an older woman who was standing behind Kwame. He proceeded to ask Kwame if he too would like a chair. The encounter brought tears to Kwame's eyes.

"Something is wrong with me. This is fucked up, man," he recalls thinking. "I brought this shit with me . . . I brought that trauma over here with me. And I know I need to. I need to heal that, I need to get past that."

With each visit to the One Africa resort and each meal at his favourite table, Kwame feels more healed and whole. Like Ivy, he's learning Ga and has mastered the art of the *tro-tro* and other bus routes across the country as he splits his time between Accra and the Cape Coast.

"I'm sixty-three years old. I'm learning how to be an African man."

Kwame is home. I feel his joy. I pray that it's contagious, that all return stories, including mine, will land in that happy place. I know it can't be, but contemplating the possibility of it gives me licence to keep looking and dreaming.

* * *

I saved the trip to Elmina Castle to my last day in Ghana. In the words of Dionne Brand, Elmina and the other castles and dungeons on Africa's west coast have "collected in the imagination as the Door of No Return." I didn't know what to expect from a place she has also called a haunting, a horror and a romance.

On that Saturday afternoon in June, the castle was surprisingly quiet, with just a handful of visitors, all of them of European background (British, Dutch and German), taking the organized tour. My idea of witnessing history didn't include visiting the gateway to slavery with a group of white travellers taking photos on their phones (and in one case, a bulky camera). Still, there's no denying the power that comes from knowing how this space served as the clearing house for hundreds of thousands of Africans before they embarked on the middle passage for the Americas.

The Door of No Return was physically nondescript—just a

rusty, narrow copper door. It was designed so that the slaves passing through it would have to lower their heads and proceed in an orderly manner to the boats that would take them to the ships. As I glanced at it one last time, the thought of their descendants making the return journey to their ancestral homeland felt overdue and necessary.

The Year of Return may have been a big marketing push, but the message it sent to the African diaspora transcended business and borders. It told them that a return passage to the motherland could be one way of rewriting history and restoring the agency that was denied to their ancestors.

As I made my way back to the car, I noticed a plaque in the courtyard of the castle. I make a note of what it said, as it encapsulates the centuries-spanning resonance of this return story:

May those who died rest in peace.
May those who return find their roots.

I wrote these words down in my little notebook, but I also took a photo of the plaque. I needed a visual reminder of this prayer for peace and roots—two things I wish for Yemen and my return to it.

Chapter 9

ISRAEL AND THE PALESTINIAN TERRITORIES

Competing Returns

As the date for my flight to the Middle East drew closer, concerns about my own truncated attempt at returning to my roots turned my already terrible sleeping habits into full-blown insomnia. I don't think I had a single good night's sleep in the six to eight weeks before my flight to Cairo in the spring of 2019.

I had intended to spend two weeks in Egypt and two weeks in Israel and the West Bank. My goal for the first leg of the trip was to meet with one of my sisters and my nephews and nieces, and to see, for the first time in thirteen years, my sister Raga'a, who was flying in from Yemen. I thought of the trip as a small family reunion and a crash course in Arabic. I wondered if it'd serve as a preview of what it would be like to return to the place where I had spent fifteen formative years. I kept alive the possibility of sneaking into Yemen, if and when the opportunity arrived. I thought of the second leg, to Israel and the West Bank, as a regular reporting trip—although regularity and that region struck me as an oxymoron. Each visit to the Middle East, each passport control check-in, always filled me with a sense of dread.

In Egypt, the often-rude officers at passport control take a certain pleasure in asking travellers, in as authoritarian a tone as possible, to declare the purpose of their visit. It feels more like an interrogation, a bad move in a country whose last hope of economic revival is a boost to its tourism sector. The officer who checked my completed arrival card asked me to write my name in Arabic, even though I filled in the form in English, as any Canadian citizen would. When I only wrote my first and last name, he looked at me as if I had given him an alias. "Add your father's, grandfather's, great-grandfather's and great-great-grandfather's names," he commanded. Did I even know what my great-great-grandfather was called?

Eventually, he stamped my passport and handed it back to me without a word.

In Tel Aviv, I wondered if the legendarily harsh Israeli border control would even let me into the country. While I hold a Canadian passport, my ethnicity and religion raise red flags in a country that has been at war with these identities since it was formally established in 1948. Almost every person I know, including some of my white North American and European friends, have shared distressing stories about being pulled aside, interrogated for hours and then admitted or denied entry.

I sailed through immigration at Ben Gurion Airport in three minutes.

I presented letters of introduction from my friend Ayelet Tsabari, the Canadian-Israeli-Yemeni writer, and from one of the women I'd arranged to interview. I omitted mention of any plan to speak with Palestinian activists and citizens. The young man at passport control seemed more bemused by than concerned about my trip. "You want to talk to Israelis about return to Israel? For a book?" He added my name to almost every other question. "Where do you live, Kamal?" "Kamal, where do you work?" "Kamal, how long will you stay and where?" Within an hour of landing at the airport, I crashed onto my hotel room's bed, wondering if this hassle-free entry was a sign of good things to come.

I needed this visit to go well. I had gone through a more challenging time than I expected in Cairo, a city that has become noisy, violent, crowded, angry. My attempts to practise my Arabic and, optimistically, restore what I'd lost of it didn't go well. In all the taxi and Uber rides I shared with my Cairo-based older sister, Farida, and her daughter, Amira, I was instructed to remain silent. If I talked, Farida warned me, the driver might recognize my foreign-sounding Arabic and try to scam us. She gave directions, negotiated fares and handled any small talk, which at times was anything but. No two Egyptians can share a small space without getting into an argument about the wrong turn the country has taken.

While my comprehension has improved, my spoken Arabic remains frozen in time. Colloquial Egyptian has moved on. As I tried to speak it with my sister and her children, they told me I sounded like a matinee idol from the old movies I had watched to restore my Arabic. I relied on phrases and sentence structures that people in Cairo, even ones my age or older, no longer use. Think of someone coming to Toronto and adopting a Cary

Grant cadence. After suffering one too many barbs about my dated Arabic, I decided to talk less and listen more. The practise I desperately wanted came at too high a price. This return story didn't end the way I—like many returnees—had fantasized it would: with a triumphant return and a warm welcome.

There were many highlights to soften the language blow. I loved exploring the city with my sister Raga'a—revisiting the old buildings we'd lived in as a family in the 1970s and 1980s—even though crossing Cairo's streets at times felt like a competitive sport. The fact that my hijab-wearing sister and I looked like everyone around us liberated me from worries about racism or Islamophobia. On one level, I *was* home, among my people. Here, no one can tell us to go back to where we came from, even though neither one of us is Egyptian. Our long family history in this city gives us a pass, a membership card. When I wasn't bombarding my sister with questions about life in Yemen and that mountain house, I simply soaked in the all-Arabic setting—ignoring the English-language billboards and the relentless intrusion of words from French and English into everyday conversation.

In the end, though, I was glad to leave Egypt behind. I knew the trip to Israel and the West Bank would present certain challenges, but I couldn't think of a book about returns without engaging with a conflict that comes down to two competing narratives of return.

For the Israelis, the very existence of their state represents a centuries-long prophecy in which Jewish people return to the Promised Land. To make aliyah is to return as a Jew from the diaspora to Zion on an oleh's visa. Organized aliyahs began in waves in the late nineteenth century, but in 1950, the Israeli Knesset passed the Law of Return, which stipulated that "every Jew has the right to immigrate to this country." The law was amended in 1955 to deny that right to dangerous criminals, and again in 1970 to extend Israeli citizenship to non-Jewish descendants and spouses of Jews.

For the Palestinians, the right of return to land and homes from which they've either escaped or been forcibly removed over the course of several wars and an expanding Israeli state is a defining demand of and a stumbling block to any internationally brokered peace deal. The right of return extends to original inhabitants of the lands and their descendants, anywhere in the world. Marches of return date back to the late 1940s and have been a cornerstone of Palestinian resistance ever since, with the Great March(es) of Return in 2018 and 2019 garnering significant political and media attention.

Nowhere in the world offers such powerful and conflicting testimonies on what return and a homeland mean as the 28,365 square kilometres (10,952 square miles) that make up Israel and the West Bank and Gaza. The people I met and the places I visited bore witness to national and religious aspirations, to everyday joys and to long-held grudges and existential fears. In that part of the world, return means survival or extinction. I left Israel and the West Bank with more questions than I had when I entered—but also with a better understanding of a conflict I've read about in news reports and books since childhood.

An essential disclaimer: My point in writing this chapter is not to summarize the conflict, much less offer solutions to it. I don't have the hubris (or gall) of a Jared Kushner. And although

I think of objectivity as a false idol in reporting, I tried to keep an open mind and heart to both sides—with the full understanding that neither is a monolith. I came to this contested homeland to get a first-hand glimpse into the dream and realities of return.

* * *

Eden was nineteen and studying commerce at McGill University in Montreal when she spotted a poster for a free trip to Israel, generally known among Jewish students and young people as Birthright. Organized by a group called Birthright Israel, it's "a gift of a 10-day educational group trip to Israel for Jewish young adults between the ages of 18 to 32." To date, Birthright (also known as Taglit, the Hebrew word for "discovery") has financed more than 750,000 trips to Israel. At the time, Eden, now a devout Orthodox and thirty-two-year-old mother of two, "wasn't religious" or "a huge Zionist." She grew up in North York, a middle-class neighbourhood in Toronto, feeling proud of Israel as the country of Jewish people and donating to charities that ensured the survival of the state and its people.

"I went on the trip with no expectations, not searching for anything," she tells me as we sit down for a chat in her home in Modi'in, a planned community halfway between Tel Aviv and Jerusalem. The teenage Eden was more attracted to the fun things: the beach, restaurants, nightclubs, making new friends and possibly meeting a future boyfriend. (One of the frequently asked questions on Birthright's website is if an applicant gets a free honeymoon if he or she meets a future spouse on the trip. The answer is "Unfortunately, no.") Eden crossed most of these items from her to-do-in-Israel list, but she also returned to Montreal with a deeper sense of the history of the country and of her religious identity that years of Jewish summer camps and afternoon Hebrew school had failed to instill in her.

"Judaism was taught in a very unmeaningful way," Eden explains, recalling her own experience. "Teaching kids who are so tired at the end of the day and all they want is to watch TV, have supper and play . . . If you're not given a meaningful education, you're not connected [and] you don't feel the obligation to live your life according to your religion. In Judaism, that means the Torah, which is the book that God gave the Jewish people thousands of years ago on Mount Sinai." The same book, Eden explains at a later point in our conversation, tells the Jewish people that Israel is their "homeland," a gift from God. "So if you observe the Torah, my opinion and that of many people is that you have to live here. Because it's a promise made to [Jews], and since we've got a Jewish state since 1948, it's possible to live here."

As I listened to Eden in Modi'in and transcribed our conversation a few weeks later in Toronto, I had to keep reminding myself that I was talking to a Canadian who is the daughter of someone I've known for almost two decades and with whom I've enjoyed many long conversations about theatre and music. Bob, Eden's father, was the owner of one of the last independent record stores in Toronto, Song & Script, which specialized in musical theatre, cabaret, jazz and standards. The store became one of my regular stops on Saturday afternoons. I've also met Eden's brother, Jasen, and chatted with him about postgraduate education and career prospects in academia and journalism.

And although I met Eden's mother, Melanie, only after I made up my mind to visit Israel and asked her and Bob to connect me with their daughter, I always thought of the family as quintessentially Canadian—with a father working downtown, two kids at university, a mostly stay-at-home mother and a house in a safe residential neighbourhood north of the city centre. Eden described her parents to me as "completely assimilated." Even in Modi'in, as I read P.D. Eastman's *Go, Dog. Go!* to Eden's daughter before supper, I could easily imagine this scene playing out in Toronto. Yet here I was, in the spring of 2019, talking to a devout woman who describes Israel as her homeland and Canada as the diaspora.

For Eden, a return to Israel after that first Birthright trip was the fulfilment of God's promise and the perfect marriage between her faith in Judaism and her growing belief in Zionism. "My definition of Zionism is the return of the Jewish people to Zion, which is Jerusalem," she explains. Her Toronto Jewish upbringing felt like going through the motions, a happenstance, she tells me.

Once she returned to Montreal after the Birthright trip, Eden reached out to rabbis on the McGill campus. She lit candles on Friday nights for Shabbat dinners (before, she admits, going out with friends to nightclubs). Gradually, she began to clear a more observant path for herself, taking the bus in the middle of Montreal's notorious winters to buy kosher meat and cheese rather than popping into her local supermarket.

In her third year at McGill, Eden applied for a study-abroad program at Hebrew University's international school. After a summer in a yeshiva (seminary) with a woman teacher, she experienced a "shock to her system" that led her to declare herself an observant Jew. "I was convinced—I was convinced as a Jew—this was right for me, to live a proper Jewish life. I would have felt hypocritical had I not continued to go down this path," she says.

Eden completed her exchange year in Jerusalem and her final one in Montreal determined to return to Israel after graduation. Like many of her peers who finished their degrees on the eve of the financial crisis of 2008, she was motivated by the dire job situation in Canada to pursue a career elsewhere. Her ultimate destination also happened to be a "passion." She approached the Jewish organization Nefesh B'Nefesh (Soul to Soul) to start planning her aliyah. In December 2009, Eden flew from Toronto to New York's JFK airport to connect with a Tel Aviv–bound El Al flight. Everyone on the chartered plane, from babies to the elderly, was making aliyah. The aliyah planes usually land in a different part of Ben Gurion Airport and are occasionally met by high-ranking Israeli politicians, religious leaders or celebrities. On that particular flight, Eden and her fellow passengers were met by Natan Sharansky, author, politician and former head of the Jewish Agency, the world's largest Jewish non-profit.

"It was really emotional," Eden says when I ask her to describe her moment of arrival as a future Israeli. "I was so tired, I don't even know if I cried. It's something that Jews have been dreaming of for two thousand years, and all of a sudden, you can do it. To me, my journey to Judaism and Zionism was only a few years [old]. There were people who lived forty, fifty years of their lives . . . and all they talked about is returning to Israel. For them, it was probably much more meaningful than it was for me. I felt it, but I didn't grow up in a home that ideal-ized making aliyah, a home that talked about the sacrifices [of the Jewish people]." Deep down, Eden says, she knew she could always go back to Toronto if things didn't work out in her new homeland.

Following the compulsory five months in an ulpan (a school to study Hebrew), Eden landed her first job doing marketing and communications for an Israeli high-tech company. Within two years, she'd met her future husband, Daniel, at a group meal hosted by a friend. Daniel became observant at age thirteen and moved from South Africa to Israel in his twenties. As Eden tells me, he left a "very materially comfortable" life in South Africa to be conscripted into the Israeli army, for which he con-tinues to do reserve duty.

For her part, she left Toronto, arguably one of the safest large cities in North America, for a country enmeshed in a protracted conflict. And yet, she says she feels safer in Modi'in than she normally does in most parts of North America. Raising a family without both sets of in-laws can be challenging, but then "you have to remind yourself it's a privilege to live here. I can't reiter-ate that enough . . . Being a Jew and living in Israel is a privilege, to be able to live the life that our ancestors dreamed of, prayed for thousands of years."

Eden and Daniel plan to live in their bright two-storey home in Modi'in until the children leave. Then they may move to a smaller place. Her homeland will always be this country to which she, as a Jewish woman, returned in her twenties. When I ask her if sees returns like hers as contributing to problems in the region, she responds with what felt to me like her last and most passionate appeal to me to understand. "You don't know why Israel is so important to the Jews. Why Jewish people pray to come here. Why there is a deep longing. We didn't grow up with the deep longing because we weren't educated enough to have the deep longing. To know the sacrifices that our ancestors made. Not just from the wars since 1948, but for many generations. Many Jews made lots of sacrifices to be here, to work the land, to protect the land from the enemies."

* * *

The sign on the left-hand side of the Dheisheh refugee camp in Bethlehem, the West Bank, leaves little room for debate. It reads: We Will Return (*San'aoood*). Arabic can be a verbose language, but it allows speakers to join the subject, the verb and its tense to make a single word. I recognize the word on the sign, even if I haven't heard it in this context in decades. As a child growing up in a pro-Palestinian education system, and to the soundtrack of nationalist anthems, I heard many songs about the return of refugees. The repertoire of the Lebanese singer Fairuz includes at least four songs about going back to Palestine (*"Sanarj you'man,"* or "We Will Return One Day," is probably the most popular of them). These songs applied mostly to the Palestinian right of return, but my father would comfort himself and my mother by singing along whenever both felt nostalgic for Aden, the homeland from which we had been exiled.

I manage to take a photo of the sign, but I'm aware of my host's limited time this Friday afternoon. Mohanad, who was born in and lived most of his thirty-one years within the walls of the camp, has a pressing family commitment later this evening. He picked me up from the drop-off point of the "Arab bus" I took from Jerusalem to Bethlehem, travelling through areas controlled by the Palestinian Authority (and therefore needing no permits or border checks). A mutual friend in Toronto recommended I chat with Mohanad if I wanted to understand what the Palestinian right of return really means on the ground. The truth is, I knew very little about Mohanad and showed up for our time together with few questions—some of which he was surprised to hear. The first was to ask him to explain his name, which I had never heard of before.

"Mohanad means the sword you fight with," he tells me when we settle down for a chat over a cup of mint tea in the third floor of his family home in the camp. I'm familiar with Seif, the more common male Arabic name that means the same thing. As he explains to me, Mohanad comes from classical Arabic poetry and ancient tales of chivalry, but he's not entirely sure why his father chose it for him. "I believe we carry some specifics of our names," he says. "I hate violence, but I believe you want to give yourself the character of the name given to you."

Amateur psychology and speculation aside, there's no denying the history of violence and displacement that Mohanad and his family have lived through over the last fifty years or so. His grandfather moved from another camp to Dheisheh in 1970 and served as "principal" of the three nearby Palestinian refugee camps in Bethlehem. As part of his duties, he was given a modest house that Mohanad's father and uncle and their children have been living in ever since, adding a second floor in 1995 and a third more recently. I could tell the third floor, where we were chatting, was new because it felt cold and unlived in. When Mohanad gets married, he's expected to make it his home. Multigenerational homes are not just a cultural norm but a necessity, given the lack of space within the camps and the West Bank.

Mohanad was born in 1988, "one year after the first intifada," he points out. Because the house sits at the main entrance of the camp, other refugees used it for shelter as they threw stones and rocks at Israelis who cut through the main street on their way to Jerusalem. Israeli soldiers eventually used the roof of the family home to protect the street, even if it meant making themselves the target of rocks thrown from within the camp. "Somehow I grew up seeing a fence around the house," Mohanad recalls of a family home that turned into its own mini battleground. "There used to be a lot of soldiers, guns, violence, stone throwing, people getting injured in front of us. We would hide inside."

The "inside" rarely provided a respite from the violence outside. Mohanad's parents and five siblings shared a one-floor house with a grandmother, two uncles and several cousins. At school, up to sixty-five children were crammed into a single classroom. It would get so noisy, it made Mohanad long for his (less noisy) home. "It was rough. Lots of kids in the camp, so there was violence because you're not getting your space in the school, at home or in the camp." He and his friends took turns playing Soldiers and Palestinians, using guns made of wood and whatever sharp objects they could find in the camp. Those playing the Palestinians would throw stones at the boys pretending to be soldiers, who would in turn disarm their "opponents," arrest them and lock them in a room. It was a popular game among children twelve and under. By the time Mohanad had turned thirteen, games gave way to existential questions. "'Why am I in a refugee camp? Why is our house so small? Why is it crowded?' And then my grandparents and my father told me that we used to have a land, used to have a nice village," he recalls. The family hailed from Bayt Jibrin, northwest of Hebron in the West Bank. Today the old houses sit empty, and Mohanad says he's not allowed to go back as the village is now part of Israel. "I'm living in a refugee camp because someone came and took my land. I'm suffering for thirty-one years because I'm Palestinian, and my land is given to somebody else just to enjoy life. From America, Poland or France, they do the aliyah and come here. At the same time, my uncle living in a refugee camp in Jordan is not allowed to come. It's not fair."

Studying psychology at Bethlehem University helped Mohanad understand his own anger and taught him to channel his experiences of violence and displacement into voluntary work with the next generation of refugees. In his early twenties, shortly after graduation, he decided to leave the region altogether and join a branch of his family in New York on a worker's visa. Many highly qualified Palestinians who have given up on a peace agreement and their right of return to their ancestral villages have taken a similar path. As it turns out, it was a terrible mistake—or as he puts it, "[It] wasn't a good choice."

He worked twelve-hour shifts in a grocery store without making any new friends or decent money. Within two years, he'd returned to Bethlehem. "My homeland needs me here more," he says, adding that his social personality fits better with Palestinian society. "A homeland is the place where you were born, where you have the experience, the friends, the heart, the feelings. Even if it's very tough." Since his two-year trip to America, he's visited twenty countries around the world, including Norway, Denmark, Sweden and Holland, for work. For the past six years, Mohanad has been a coordinator for the Olive Tree Campaign. It supports Palestinian farmers by planting their land with olive trees. "Right now, I have opportunities to go [abroad] and do good work. But I still think I'm doing much better in Palestine because there's a lot of work to do here, especially as a young man." Returning to the refugee camp where he was born is an act of resistance, he tells me. So is adding that new third floor. He'll leave the house and camp when he can go to Bayt Jibrin. "Then I'm free to decide whether I want to go to New York or not. I don't want to be pushed away."

Mohanad's responses to my questions explain why the right of return is such a complicated issue. It mixes the legal with the emotional, the personal with the political and the aspirational with the harsh reality. Time hasn't been on the Palestinian side. The more years pass, the more elusive the dream becomes, or so some commentators on the conflict seem to say. I ask him to share with me his own definition of the right of return. He perks up, as if he's been waiting for me to ask him this question all along.

"I see it as very simple. People came to occupy our homes and our lands. And we have the right to take it back. That's it. And it can last another seventy years. That's fine. Everyone should know that. It's our right to return to our homes. We're temporarily living in this camp. Believe me, I'm not delusional about this. I'm pretty sure we will go back."

When I quiz him further on what that return might look like, he hints at a one-state solution. "I also don't have the right to kick out someone who was born here seventy years or sixty-five years ago. We always say that Palestine is a holy land and all people have the right to come live here, peacefully. We never deny the Jewish presence or history in Palestine. But I would stand against anyone who kills someone else in order to take their home because they believe that they are the promised people to come to their land here after three thousand years . . . I don't believe God wants us to kill other people and take their home. That's not how God works. God is better than this."

Mohanad's work for the Olive Tree Campaign preserves the Palestinian ancestral connection to the land. The State of Israel, he explains, asserts that an old Ottoman law gives it the right to claim lands that have not been cultivated for five years. The campaign plants twelve thousand trees every year. People within the West Bank and around the globe sponsor trees, with teams of volunteers planting seeds from December to March and harvesting in October. The trees are invariably uprooted by the Israelis and the volunteers attacked, Mohanad says. "This conflict is about land, so whoever works for the Palestinian lands would come under attack from the Israelis."

This explains why the volunteers come through partnerships with schools and youth groups from Denmark and Norway, among other European countries. It helps to have a bunch of white people on your side, I tell Mohanad. "*Blond* white people," he fires back. "When the Israelis see them working in the field, they don't attack us. They know they're international. We're secured by these people. They would deal with us in a good way."

The theme of the Olive Tree Campaign is "Keep Hope Alive," which, he says, sends a message of support to the farmers "that we will go back to our lands, that we will return." But the biggest challenge to this return dream may come not from Israelis but from a generation of Palestinians born after the Oslo Accords, in the late 1990s. As a child, Mohanad had the return message drummed into his head. But men and women from this new generation, he tells me, are focused on the wider world and not the villages of their ancestors.

"In the camps, we do our best to remind them of our right of return, that we're going to go back one day, that we're temporarily refugees. The identity of a refugee we try to keep alive so that these people believe one day they have a right to go back," Mohanad says. "What brought the Israelis to this country is the dream of the Promised Land. They came back and they are here." That Palestinian refugees can't replicate that return narrative explains the sometimes intractable nature of this conflict.

* * *

The twenty-something Howard wanted nothing more out of life than to recreate the lost vibes of hippie California of the 1960s. It was the early 1980s, Ronald Reagan had just been elected and the "crass capitalism" of the 1970s had left this Berkeley dropout in despair and in doubt over America's future. When I met him in Jerusalem, just shy of his sixtieth birthday, the first thing I noticed was the gun he kept in a style somewhere between secret service and open carry. You can tell it's there and he's ready to use it, but he's not brandishing it.

I don't think I've ever met anyone who owned a gun—at least no one who made a point of admitting to it publicly—and much less carried one about during an interview. Howard lives in Tekoa, a settlement in the West Bank, south of Jerusalem, where attacks on settlers, he says, make him and his neighbours "a target for extremists." Because we'd arranged to meet on the edge of the Arab quarter in Jerusalem, where shop owners had in the past been "not nice" to this visibly Jewish American (his long white beard and yarmulke are giveaways, even before you spot the gun on his right-hand side), he felt he should carry it with him. Later in the day, he told me that he also wasn't entirely sure about my intentions in meeting with him, even though we were introduced by a mutual good friend, Michael from Hong Kong.

In the interest of full disclosure, I'll also admit to being nervous about walking around Jerusalem with him. While I've been mistaken for a Sephardic or Mizrahi Jew (Howard is married to a Yemeni Israeli who could easily pass for any of my sisters), we did look like the oddest of couples, even in a place where different ethnicities and faiths have mingled for millennia. I felt vulnerable and on my guard. Maybe on his behalf. Maybe because I felt overwhelmed by the *idea* of being in Jerusalem, especially coming from Toronto, where a century home is the definition of heritage.

Still, my desire—as a writer and an Arab and someone who's fascinated with stories of return—was to know how a refusenik becomes an observant Jew, a settler and, as I found out in the course of our conversation, a Trump voter (but not a Trump supporter). In some indirect ways, Howard's life journey represents dimensions of ancestral return stories that have sustained the most contested claims to a homeland in history. Over one cup of tea at the Gloria Hotel in Jerusalem and then another at his home in Tekoa, I tried to piece together Howard's life and his many transformations from the late 1970s to the late 2010s.

It took him two years at Berkeley to realize that his hippie-revival scheme wouldn't come true—in part because it "wasn't really me," he says. His parents had moved to California from New York City when he was eight, and in retrospect, his flirtation with counterculture was probably his way of fitting into a place with more overt antisemitism than he'd experienced growing up on the East Coast. By nineteen, he had dropped out of university and hitchhiked across the country. He eventually settled in western Massachusetts, where he earned a degree in agriculture history and economics in 1982. Again, alternative lifestyles held little appeal for him. "There was a lot of mysticism in Amherst and western Massachusetts," he tells me. "Everybody was into shamanism, Sufism. I didn't believe in any of that. I'd always been Jewish and had a pretty strong connection to Judaism: Passover, High Holidays."

He began to read books about the Hasidic ways and became interested in the work of travelling rabbis reviving Judaism with music, folklore and stories. Howard credits the so-called Singing Rabbi, Shlomo Carlebach, with deepening his own engagement with Judaism and convincing Jews around the world to return to Israel. "He was an amazing mind and intellect, but he broke with standard Judaism." His events drew large crowds that weren't separated by a fence between the men and women. Carlebach offered Howard a way out of the same American materialism that had driven him to counterculture in the late 1970s.

The Carlebach way took hold, and Howard set out on a journey through Europe to see the lands that his grandparents had left behind for America a century earlier. The idea was to trace their footsteps through Russia and Eastern Europe. But in the final years of the Cold War, a quest through the Eastern Bloc was both "dangerous and expensive." Instead, he tracked down family members who had settled down in Antwerp, Belgium, and from there continued by train and bus through much of western Europe. The rabbis in Strasbourg, France, suggested a place to learn more about rabbinic laws in Israel. Howard says he wasn't thinking of going to Israel at that point, although he had thought about tracing his family history from America to Europe to the Jewish state. Until that trip, he always saw Israel as "over there." He listened to its music and read books about it but "was never going to it."

He took a ferry from Greece to Israel and made his way to Jerusalem, where he felt an immediate connection with the culture. When I ask him to explain what he means, he notes that his feelings at the time transcended religion. When he was as young as eighteen or nineteen, he wanted to get married and start a family, but women in his immediate circle in California and Massachusetts, he says, prioritized education and career. "Here in Israel—certainly at that time, anyway—there were women who also had the same values that I wanted in my life." Howard also felt that marrying an Israeli woman—as opposed to an American Jewish woman who moved to Israel—would be the closest he'd ever get to a home-field advantage in this new country. "I felt it would be hard enough to make it here. It would be more helpful if one of us had a firm leg in the Middle East."

Enter Noga, an Israeli whose family moved from Yemen to Israel after 1948. Howard met Noga when she guided a group of his Anglo-American friends on a walking tour to historical sites outside Jerusalem. His attraction was immediate but wasn't reciprocated. Noga was the daughter of hard-working academic parents. Howard was still finding his way in the country and at times felt like an "unsuccessful Israeli." He didn't speak Hebrew as fluently (and still doesn't, he later tells me), and he didn't act in a pushy or aggressive way. I tell him that sounds like every stereotype I've ever heard of life in Israel. He dismisses my observation as the product of an overly politically correct culture. There's a context for his comment. "Israelis today are fun-loving, but back then, to smile was a sign that you are novice and naive," he says. "You had to be tough, sly, a survivor, unscrupulous. I was never like that." (At least this side exchange explained an earlier one. On my way to meet Howard, I had received a WhatsApp message from a friend in Tel Aviv who was a bit concerned about my safety. "How has it been? Are people intense and rude?" She was relieved when I noted how helpful everyone had been so far.)

Eventually, Howard won over Noga, and they got married and had their first child, a boy, in Israel. Their four daughters were born in the United States when Howard decided to move back temporarily to pursue a graduate degree in clinical psychology. What began as a two-year trip lasted more than eight. During the tech boom of the 1990s, Howard landed a job at Intel, in Silicon Valley, which paid him a massive salary and came with stock options and other perks. By then, he could cope with the materialism that had driven him out of America a few years earlier because he used this financial windfall to start a big family—a long-held dream of his.

He also says that he wanted to show Noga where he came from so she wouldn't think of him as the unsuccessful Israeli he felt at heart. She, on the other hand, "convinced herself" that she was unhappy in California. She feared that she would end up with "American children"—not Jewish or Israeli. The couple sold their house in Palo Alto and returned to Israel in 1999.

Noga didn't care where they lived as long as they came home to Israel. "I wanted to be able to build a house, a home, not live in an apartment," Howard tells me. This pretty much excluded expensive Tel Aviv from the list and brought Tekoa to the couple's attention.

I hadn't noticed it on our drive to Tekoa, but when we're chatting in his kitchen, Howard tells me that his car windows are made of plastic. Like many settlers' cars, his has been targeted by Palestinian youth (Howard refers to them as "terrorists") who throw rocks to protest settlements. More serious crimes, including stabbing people and cracking skulls with large rocks, sometimes fatally, happen every now and then. The frequency had increased during my trip as a response to Trump's shambolic deal of the century, then dominating the local news. In theory, the deal gives Israel the security it needs and delivers a state to the Palestinians. On closer examination, the deal offers Palestinians "a sort-of state that will be truncated, without proper sovereignty, surrounded by Israel's territory and threaded between Jewish settlements," as BBC reporter Jeremy Bowen described it.

While I had assumed I might visit a settlement and a refugee camp if I wanted to be open to meeting people on different sides of the conflict, seeing both just two days apart brought the extremes of the situation home to me. The Dheisheh camp where I met Mohanad felt underdeveloped and overcrowded. Tekoa struck me as overdeveloped and sparse, more like a gated community in the American Southwest than a settlement in the Middle East. In 1975, it started as an outpost confiscated from the Palestinian village of Tuqu. It was handed over to Jewish residents (French, American and British) two years later for development.

Howard pulled over near a bus stop to offer a ride to a young Frenchwoman who lives in the settlement and explained it as the sort of thing residents in Tekoa do all the time. Adversity has brought the community together. It's also a place where residents periodically get alerts to their phones telling them to stay indoors because of suspicious activities near its fences. While these alerts usually turn out to be a false alarm, Howard always take them seriously. "You have to be careful; you have to be alert." Case in point: while he loves to take his ATV for a drive in the desert, he's excessively cautious about where and when to go. He avoids times of day when there's likely to be increased traffic. If he runs into one or two Bedouins, he'll stop and chat and maybe even sit down for tea with them. But when he sees five or more, he maintains his distance. "Trust, on your guard" has become his motto.

The trust between settlers and their Arab neighbours has built over time and out of a mutually beneficial arrangement. It's cheaper to hire Arab labourers from a village in the West Bank than Arab or Jewish workers from elsewhere in Israel. How cheap? The minimum for a Jewish or Arab-Israeli day labourer is 300 shekels (C$118). A worker from a nearby village would charge 40 to 50 shekels (C$15 to C$20) for the same work. Jewish residents who hire local labour are required by law to carry a gun for protection—although Howard says that attacks on settlers are extremely rare as many Palestinian families rely on the income they collect from working in the settlements.

The home-in-the-homeland dream of so many returnees plays out here against a distinctive story of labour and land. My mind wandered to the Jamaican version that came with a different set of fears around violence.

From the comfort of my quiet home in midtown Toronto, where I'm writing this, it all seems like such a complicated, potentially life-threatening choice that people like Howard (and Eden) make by coming to Israel. On some level, I understand it. I'm the one who wants to return to a country with an ongoing war. But part of me sees the situation in Yemen as fixable. Howard doesn't share my views. I'm thinking practical and immediate, he ancestral and timeless. "I wanted to expand our boundaries and establish a connection to the Judean heartland," he says. "People who live here, my family, are in love with this place and its connection to the ancient Jewish life." He notes that some of the villages have names from biblical times, and that even in some Arab villages, the tradition of lighting a candle on Friday night has survived millennia.

Ethnic and cultural roots are at once fragile and resilient. When I meet Howard's youngest daughter and mention growing up in Cairo, she serenades me with the opening verses of "*Enta Omry*" (You're My Life), a song from the late Egyptian diva Oum Kalthoum that she learned as a child from watching Arabic programming on Israeli TV. I often played the same song on YouTube as I worked on this book. It sounds like home and reminds me of afternoon teas in Cairo. This California-born, Israeli-raised twenty-something chooses to hold on to traces of a heritage from her mother's side. While I can detect some accent, the phrasing and what we in the Arab world call *tarab*—a certain joy and ecstasy in singing—are unmistakable.

Howard says that all his children are grateful to their parents for returning to Israel. He has felt more danger for himself and his family in Palo Alto. "There's physical survival and there's spiritual survival," he explains. "It's important that my children have values that I've transmitted to them, and that my parents transmitted to me. And that they will transmit to their children. Any family, losing their ancestral heritage, that is like death too."

I ask Howard what he feels about the argument that the more Jews return to Israel through aliyah, the more likely additional settlements will have to be built to accommodate them, leading to even more displacement of Palestinians. He responds by saying that new settlements have been prudent by building vertically and organizing in a way that maximizes density, infrastructure and mass transportation. And even though he is a Zionist, he doesn't believe that every Jew should come to Israel, or that those who don't are bad or self-loathing. They should do it if they want it for themselves and not because Israel needs them. He feels confused when he talks to Israelis who believe every Jew must return to the Holy Land. "I have a degree in psychology and I don't know if I should call [that attitude] an inferiority or a superiority complex," he says. "There's so much land, so much space. We [Israelis and Palestinians] can work together in so many ways that are amazing." Howard is talking here on the level of interpersonal relations because he has no faith in the Palestinian Authority as a broker of peace or even a defender of its people. He remains pessimistic about "political elites" who use grievance and anger to "enrage and control" their constituents, including Palestinian leader Mahmoud Abbas. This explains why, in 2016, he voted for Trump—who stopped sending money to the Palestinian Authority as part of his (or more likely, Jared Kushner's) Middle East policy.

"I feel incredibly degraded by voting for him," Howard says as he simultaneously points out how much he hates everything Hillary Clinton stands for, including the liberal world order. "Trump with all his idiocy, all his real despicable behaviour and language, and all his egotism—I don't deny that I voted for a complete idiot. [But he] moved the embassy; he removed the money paid to the terrorists . . . It took an idiot to make the right decision." To be conservative, he tells me, "is to call it the way it is, not the way you want it to be." The old ideas for peace, which compensated Palestinians for their loss of land and sovereignty, are not working, he tells me.

As our time is running out and we both have to head back to Tel Aviv, I decide to end my conversation with Howard with one final question: What does the word "homeland" mean to him? For someone who claims that his Hebrew is not as fluent as his English, he says he prefers the word for it in the former: *mouladak*, the place where one is born. (*Moledet* in Hebrew translates to "homeland" and is the name of a right-wing party that advocates for the "voluntary" removal of Arabs from the West Bank.) Arabic, as it happens, uses a similar word, pronounced differently. A homeland, Howard says, is a "feeling of warmth, a place where other people are building something close to what I want to build. Where we're raising children who can work together and love each other, find spouses and build communities together . . . The core meaning of Zionism is special, something I'm pointed at or pointing at. Something that brings out the best in me and works for me and lets me work with others who are interested in that."

The "others" include Arabs and Palestinians with whom he shares a bond with the land. "I feel more connected to them than I would to a Jew from Tel Aviv," he says, citing a local worker as someone with whom he gets along better than leftists from the city.

"The centre is moving."

* * *

What might the Palestinian right of return look like on the ground? How will it migrate from a demand, a slogan and a folk song into the day-to-day lives of Israelis and Palestinians? Lubnah Shomali, a manager at BADIL Resource Center in Bethlehem, has been thinking about this possibility, living it and preparing others for it for a decade or more. BADIL ("alternative" in Arabic) was created in 1998 at the request of Palestinian refugees and internally displaced persons as an expression of their deep satisfaction with the Oslo Accords. Since Oslo, the Palestinian Authority has been underplaying the concept of return, mostly to keep negotiations with Israel and the West going. The centre was founded to defend the rights of all Palestinian people, but specifically "those who have been or are about to be displaced," Lubnah tells me when I sit down for an interview in her office in Bethlehem.

Return, she explains, "surfaces every day" in BADIL and the community it represents. "We at BADIL believe that without implementation of the right of return or the right to reparation for Palestinian refugees or internationally displaced persons, there can be no peaceful or durable solution. The conflict will continue to be protracted and remain within a circle of violence." Before Oslo and for most of Yasser Arafat's leadership of the Palestinian Liberation Organization and the Palestinian Authority (1969–2004), self-determination was predicated on the right of return of all Palestinian refugees, both inside and outside Israel's territory. Numbers vary, but this is a population estimated to be six million.

BADIL, on the other hand, places return as one element in a "reparation package." The voluntary, physical repatriation (in other words, return) is the immediate and easy part. Other elements include property restitution, compensation and guarantee of non-repetition. "These four elements are indivisible from one another. Say a refugee chooses not to return—that doesn't mean he's eliminated from the other elements."

I had just missed a conference titled "Practicalities of Return" a month earlier, so I wanted to hear more about the conversations that took place and what recommendations, if any, came out of it. BADIL and its staff and volunteers offer a few scenarios, she responds. But first, there are some questions that

explore what return could and should look like when imple-
mented. "Going beyond return as a sacred and inalienable right
to thinking more practically about *how* we will return," says
Lubnah. "What's the state going to look like? What about our
Israeli friends? What about the situation on the ground?"

In the training sessions that led to the conference, Lubnah and
her colleagues would ask Palestinian youth to come up with suggestions for dealing with the Israeli population. The responses
covered a wide range of scenarios, even including sending them
back to their countries of origin or putting them in camps or
ghettos. BADIL staff would have to explain that this is not how
reparations or human rights work. Israelis, Lubnah told them,
have rights. "The goal is to create a situation that's free from
discrimination and apartheid—free from the threat of actual displacement of people. In order to create that, you have to create a
democratic, inclusive, rights-filled society. And so without that,
there can be no chances for return to succeed and for people to
live the kind of lives that they're supposed to live, in dignity."

I had intended to interview Lubnah in her official capacity as
the public face of BADIL, but her American English suggested a
US education or a history of migration, so I switched gears to ask
her a few questions about her life. While not technically a refugee,
she is a returnee to the West Bank. Born in Beit Sahour, a predominantly Christian village east of Bethlehem, Lubnah immigrated
with her family to the States in 1976, when she was three. Her
father made a point of taking his five children back to their home
village for short visits to ensure that they learned Arabic and got
to know their extended family and cultural heritage. Their first
formal return for a longer period took place in 1993 and was

driven mostly by nostalgia and a longing to be in their homeland.

"It was the recognition that we identify as Palestinians, and that Palestine is our home," Lubnah recalls, that made the family return necessary and inevitable. Even though that return didn't last more than a few years, it planted the idea of going home in Lubnah's head. In 2008, by then married and the mother of three young children, she decided to stop waiting "until the situation gets better" and return to Beit Sahour, her ancestral homeland. Her husband agreed. Their oldest child was in grade 6, and the parents felt it would be easier for all three of them to learn Arabic at the same time. Lubnah was already in her second year of university when she'd moved with her family in 1993, and she knew that her children would absorb and retain more Arabic if they learned it at a younger age.

For people like Lubnah—holders of passports from North America or Europe—return can be rough, but it always comes with the option of packing up and going back to the adopted country. She recognizes that this possibility has kept her in the West Bank but insists that her main motive for return is her children. "I didn't want my kids to grow up being ashamed or embarrassed of being Palestinian. I wanted them to know they come from a strong, honourable and just people. I didn't think they could get that from the US." She recalls that whenever she told friends and colleagues in the States that she came from Palestine, she'd get one of two responses. The first was cluelessness—people would confuse Palestine with Pakistan or the Philippines. The other, which came after she explained the Israeli-Palestinian conflict, assumes she was "like a terrorist."

Lubnah's story reminded me of Howard and his family, who

returned to Israel after nearly a decade in California. Lubnah's children, however, were more critical of their parents' decision. Whenever they saw soldiers with uniforms and machine guns, they'd wonder about the wisdom of returning to a conflict zone when they are, by birth and education, American. "I'd say, 'No, you were born there. Your father and mother are Palestinian.'" The years have softened the children's resistance. Nowadays whenever they leave Palestine, they think they're going "abroad," and when they return, they're "coming home."

While Lubnah says she can't compare her first return in 1993 with this one, both are informed by a "longing" for the land, the home. Living in the village where she was born is a scenario millions of Palestinian refugees can only dream of. Her return story meets an essential criterion of the repatriation package she discusses with her community: choice. "The choice to go or to stay, or at the very least not to be forced into going or staying."

In Hebron, the largest Palestinian-run city in the West Bank, and my next stop, the dream of return and the absence of choice resurfaced in the stories of the people I spoke to.

* * *

Every May 15, a date known to Palestinians as the Nakba (meaning "catastrophe") and to Israelis as Independence Day, Youssef makes a point of taking to social media and posting images of land certificates that his grandfather had held on to for over a century. Youssef, now fifty-three, was born to a property-owning family in al-Faluja, a Palestinian village northeast of Gaza. When his grandfather and other relatives were forced to leave the village in 1948, they packed all the land deeds they could lay their hands on and sought refuge in Hebron for what they thought would be a few months at most. Seventy-one years later, the original deeds are hidden, but copies are posted on Facebook to prove that "we're connected to that place to this day, even though we're far from it," Youssef tells me.

We're sitting in the office of a multimedia company that Youssef, a cultural worker with the Palestinian Authority, occasionally uses for online initiatives. His mandate includes collecting and preserving aspects of oral Palestinian culture that can be described as "intangible": folk tales and wedding songs and other artistic expressions that document ancient Palestinian heritage and can be connected to specific villages and territories. He's part of a large contingent of refugees from al-Faluja and nearby Iraq al-Manshiyya who have settled in Hebron in the Palestinian-controlled West Bank. Still, the people I meet from that community identify as refugees. They view going back to the village of their grandparents as their inalienable right of return.

"You have to maintain emotional connection because material connection has been severed," says Youssef, adding that he hasn't been able to return to his ancestral homeland for decades. Instead, he and many other Palestinians have documented the size of the original villages and towns and kept records of the landowners and what each one did for a living. They've also charted relationships to neighbouring villages and built an archive of social life and personal stories. This is culture as a form of resistance, of unearthing and preserving suppressed or endangered stories. The idea is to maintain a connection to the land—and when the time comes, to ease the return to it. Youssef believes that Israel has engaged in acts of cultural erasure of Palestinian identity in the hopes that as one generation dies, the next one forgets. "Anything that foils that Israeli plan is part of the resistance," he says. "Resistance is not just about a weapon. It's culture, it's perseverance, it's thought."

Twenty-three-year-old Raghad, a graduate student at Bethlehem University and a fiction writer, is proof that for now at least, some members of the next generation of Palestinians understand the full meaning of the right of return. I met her (and her father) the evening before I talked to Youssef, and the first thing she pointed out to me was her necklace. It's a key, the symbol of the Palestinian people's right of return. Like Youssef's, Raghad's family moved from al-Faluja to Hebron. Over the years, members of her family have married into and gone into business with people from the local Hebron community. Still, home is elsewhere. "Even though I wasn't born in al-Faluja or Iraq al-Manshiyya, I feel that I always relate to this village. It's my homeland, my original village. I hope one day to return."

I continue to marvel at this concept of returning to a land that you've never set foot in. But if Jews born in New York City or Toronto can call Israel home, why can't a Palestinian young woman whose parents have shown her the land deeds and maps long for the same? Riad, her father, corrects me: "It's not a longing; it's a right." To keep talking about right of return as an emotional or psychological phenomenon undercuts the reality of people who lost their land and became refugees within and outside Israeli borders. Return, Riad tells me, is a "holy right" to him and other Palestinians. "My father died, but he handed me the key—the key of return. It's an actual key. And the paper-work, official ownership papers."

Both father and daughter view the right of return in more categorical ways than those explored by Lubnah and her BADIL coworkers. Riad believes that every Palestinian outside the Green Line has a right to return. (The line marked Israeli borders after the 1948 war and until 1967, when it became the line that sep-arated Israel from territories it had captured, including the West Bank and East Jerusalem from Jordan, the Golan Heights from Syria and the Gaza Strip from Egypt.) Riad suspects that lead-ers within the Palestinian Authority or the Arab world lack the political will or interest to make return happen.

For Raghad, Palestinian return can happen only if all the Israeli settlements are destroyed—not just the ones built after 1967, but everything from 1948 onward. "We are calling for the liberation of the whole of Palestine. We're not calling for splats of our land. We need all the land. This is actually my view. And this is a criti-cal point with the Palestinian leadership. They are asking for the liberation of the borders of 1967. I'm against that."

Raghad's views feed off seven decades of Palestinians talking return—and arguing and fighting about the possible forms it can take. What struck me most about my conversations in Bethle-hem and Hebron was the widening gap between what Palestin-ians in the West Bank said and what their leaders did on their behalf. When I asked Youssef about the Palestinian Authority's dereliction of the right of return, his first response was to deny it. His second? "It's not their right to give away. We have to be consulted . . . Return means going back to the place you came from." In other words, he says, if you take Palestinians originally from one village and resettle them in another, it'll be like going from one form of refugee to another. It's not a solution but a numbing of the wound.

I ask Youssef for a timeline for resolving the return issue, but he doesn't even want to guess. "It can't stay the way it is," he responds. "Rights don't vanish because they're old. They transfer to the next generation. The land of my grandfather may have been passed to my father and then to me, but when I die, it'll go to my sons."

* * *

Whenever the subject of aliyah came up among Palestinians, they would cite instances of Jews from Russia and the former Soviet Union (FSU) moving to Israel and making it home as the ultimate example of how the Law of Return stands in opposition to their right of return, perpetuating their dispossession from their lands. Youssef's question—"You live in Russia. Why come and take my land?"—prompted me to seek an answer from a typical family from the FSU. I wanted to hear their story and know what Israel as a homeland means to them. While this particular wave of return continues, the majority of Russians came to Israel in the early 1990s—more than 330,000 in 1990 and 1991, and 770,000 by the end of the decade—and they're now in a position to look back at their journeys more critically.

Daniela offered to introduce me to her parents, Igor and Lily, both of whom come from Tbilisi, Georgia, one of the republics of the former Soviet Union. Daniela said she could translate for me, as she felt that her parents' English might not be strong enough for a long conversation. Language is always in a state of flux at their household. Daniela and her sister, Nicole, who were both born in Israel, speak Hebrew to each other. The parents still speak Russian. They talk to their daughters in a combination of Russian and Hebrew. The daughters answer in Hebrew. All speak Russian when visiting extended family. To this mix, Daniela and I added English when I visited their apartment in a high-rise in Holon, south of Tel Aviv, two days before Passover.

Igor arrived in Israel as a twenty-two-year-old in 1991, when Georgia's borders opened and the new independent republic allowed its citizens to leave. His father made the decision and surprised his wife, son and daughter with it. "In his mind, it was only a trip abroad," Igor tells me. The open gates and the bad economy in Georgia pushed them toward a new life in Israel. As far as Igor remembers, being a Jew "was never a problem." In the Tbilisi of his formative years, Muslims, Christians and Jews got along. "They even liked Jews in Georgia."

Tolerance? A robust rejection of antisemitism? Neither. Igor's experience of Judaism is marked by its erasure from his family's history. His grandparents on his mother's side died in the Second World War. His grandfather on his father's side served in the Russian military and was a member of the Communist Party. When he died, "all the Judaism, the language and the culture" died with him. Igor recalls his grandparents speaking Yiddish to each other and bringing unleavened bread to his parents on Passover. They weren't afraid to be Jewish, he says.

When Igor was about twenty, his father started taking him to the synagogue in the hopes that he'd meet a nice Jewish woman to marry. Lily, Igor's wife, still gets a kick out of this anecdote because she frequented the same synagogue for a similar purpose. But because she's four years younger, her path and Igor's never crossed.

Lily, an only child, came to Israel in 1994 with her parents. She too recalls a childhood free from religious discrimination. Her family observed a few more Jewish traditions than Igor's, but religion didn't define who they were. "Nobody looked at me and said, 'You're a Jew.'" Lily's family got caught in the civil wars that raged in different parts of the newly independent Republic of Georgia, and in a violent military coup between 1991 and 1993 that ousted the country's first democratically elected president. The civil unrest and imploding economy that followed convinced Lily's father to take his family elsewhere. Because he was working at the Israeli embassy at the time, it took him just one month to secure all the paperwork to perform aliyah with his family. Daniela explains that while her parents weren't religious, "in their mind, they were Jewish."

Both parents say that their families didn't even think of the possibility of going to a country other than Israel. For Igor, it was a case of "We're Jewish people, so we go to Israel." For Lily, the urgency of the situation left them no time to think of other opportunities. Georgians with good professions (engineering, medicine or technology) immigrated to Canada and the United States. For the rest of the country's Jewish population, the choice came down to Israel or a civil war.

The irony of fleeing a civil war to move to a conflict zone didn't escape Lily, who had never left Tbilisi until she flew to Tel Aviv. She had received all her information about Israel from Soviet state television and had heard that "Israel is a bad country because of all the wars and because it tries to occupy lands." Word of mouth from other Georgians who made aliyah before her family, however, was positive. The Israeli economy was strong, and people didn't have to get up at the crack of dawn to line up for milk.

Although they arrived separately and in different years, Igor and Lily followed a similar pattern: studying Hebrew for five months in an ulpan before finding work—he as a paramedic, a new career, and she as a nurse, for which she had been training in Tbilisi. The increased presence of other Jews from the FSU didn't make them feel at home. "We felt like outsiders and didn't know how to communicate," Igor recalls. "Even small things like going to a grocery store [were difficult]. You don't know how to speak to them." Lily's adjustment issues were more dramatic. Her grandmother became critically ill, and her parents had to leave the ulpan to look after her. Lily combined her language training with a part-time job as a sales assistant in a clothing store. She knew she couldn't go back to Georgia, even if she wanted to, so she adjusted to her new life in Israel.

Lily and Igor's first trip back to their ancestral home as a couple came in 2014, long after they'd married and started their family. (Igor returned briefly for a family situation in 1995.) That trip confirmed what they knew on an instinctive level: Israel was now their homeland, and Georgia existed only as nostalgia. "When you move to another country, the only thing that stays in your memory is your house, the tree next to your house and the bench," Igor tells me, as a mortified Daniela sighs. She had warned me that her father liked to speak in metaphors. "He has a metaphor for every situation in life," she says as he smiles and ignores her. On that trip in 1995, he found out that the house was gone, the tree cut down and the bench burnt. "The only thing in your memory and now it's nothing. Even after only four years, I realized that this [Israel] is my home."

Their feelings track with what some scholars of diaspora and return immigration say about the relegation of the country of origin into the realm of nostalgia and memory after just a few years in the new homeland. Both Igor and Lily say that they feel "reborn" in Israel, not just as Jews but as citizens, as people. Admittedly, some members of their extended family moved to Tel Aviv and then immigrated to North America, but to everyone in this household, Israel is "the final destination." Lily says that even during the worst of the Gaza war in 2008 and 2009, she would simply run to a shelter and hide. "It happens a lot. We feel the pressure. But other than that, life is totally normal. You learn to carry on with daily life—yom yom."

I ask Igor and Lily if they ever think about the displacement of Palestinians by people making aliyah, and if so, how that fits into their concept of Israel as their homeland. After an uncomfortably long pause, Igor responds: "There's no need for war. We don't want a war here. So probably everyone needs to have their own country. The Jewish people need to have their own country. The Palestinians need to have their own country. When you think about it, there's now two states."

"It was strange to see all the hate between Palestinians and Israelis," Lily chimes in, recalling her first years of living through the conflict. "I felt that from a very young age, the Arabs are being raised to believe the Jewish people are their enemy. And because of all the alarms and rockets, we also think the people shooting rockets at us are our enemy."

The couple have learned to live with the conflict, to the point where other issues preoccupy them now. One of them is the status of Russian Jews within Israeli society. Early waves of returning Jews from Russia and other parts of the Soviet Union were seen as outsiders. Israelis felt that they started to "take over," Igor explains. Daniela says that Russian Jews of her parents' generation may have benefited from their light skin. She compares her parents' experience with that of more recent waves of Ethiopian Jews. While newer immigrants from Russia continue to take on more labour-intensive or low-paid work (cleaning, driving taxis, stocking supermarket shelves), much of that work is now being taken up by African immigrants. But when there's a war, Lily says, you don't see the difference between races and histories of immigration. "We're all together against the other side."

"We became more Israeli than Russian" with time, says Lily. "In Georgia, we were Jewish. In Israel, we're Russian." Both say that when the time comes, they'd like to be buried in Israel. "We have no choice," says Lily. All their family members who have passed away since coming over are buried in Israel, Igor tells me. No one is buried in Georgia because there's hardly any family left there.

Talk of death and burial is a conversation killer, which is why I keep it until the end of my interviews. I also sensed that everyone was keen to get the apartment ready for Seder Pesach, the Passover dinner, which the family was hosting this year. For

Igor, at least, it's very important to keep Jewish traditions along-side the Russian language. In Israel, he tells me, he doesn't have to choose one or the other.

* * *

It was a familiar smell, the smell of home. That was my first impression of Warda's place in the Ushiot neighbourhood of Rehovot, in central Israel. And why wouldn't it smell like home? Warda is a Yemeni Jew who left her hometown north of Sana'a in 1990. Wafts of burning incense clashed with the aromas of a tangy bread called *lahoh* and a strong, bitter coffee known as *kahwa Sana'ani*. Every other home I knew in Yemen, including my family's, smelled of a similar combination. Yemenis burn incense instead of using air freshener, even when the latter has become readily available, as it does a better job of absorbing food odours.

When I sit down to talk to Warda face to face on the veranda of her home, I notice that not only does she look like my mother but she also acts like her. She insists that I have something to drink. Then something to eat. My "I'm fine" goes unheeded. Just as it did for decades with my mother. And when I don't have enough of the *lahoh* and *laban* (a savoury milky dip), she tells me, in Arabic, that she made them herself, and that I shouldn't be shy and should eat, eat. Like my mother, Warda was married off at a very young age, probably closer to fifteen, and she had twelve children by her early forties. (Mine was married at four-teen and had eleven children the year she turned thirty-three.)

Warda's youngest child was born in Israel, around the same time her eldest two daughters were having theirs.

My friend Ayelet introduced me to Warda because I wanted to meet Yemeni Jews with a more recent history of immigration. Although Yemeni Jews began leaving for Jerusalem as early as the 1880s, the vast majority immigrated shortly after Israel was established in 1948. Their history of migration and transition into the country is well documented. What's less known is the exodus of families like Warda's from Yemen against the background of a stronger Arab nationalism and Islamic fundamentalism from the 1960s onward.

I asked Warda if she had left Yemen because of persecution, which I assumed to be the case, but she played that down. "Nothing was wrong over there, but we were hungry, thirsty. We were thirsty for Israel. In the soul." She recalls owning a big four-storey traditional house with its own synagogue and *mikvah*, where Jews bathe for ritual cleansing and before performing certain religious duties. "We were *mabsoteen*," she tells me, using the very Yemeni word for happy. I was reminded of Igor and Lily, who also talked about a past life free of antisemitism and discrimination. Many experts on Jewish life consider Georgia one of the more tolerant places for Jews in Eastern Europe, so I didn't really question the veracity of their story. Warda's memory of Yemen as a safe, comfortable place seemed more like a reinvention of the past. The modern history of Jews in Yemen tells a story of restrictions on where to live or work and exclusion from public life. (As of 2021, there were about ten Jews still living in Yemen, down from an estimated fifty thousand before the establishment of the state of Israel in 1948.)

Warda's husband, who was at least twenty years her senior and had been married twice before, worked as a silversmith and travelled the country freely to sell his art. I noticed that although I was introduced to him when I came in, he wasn't invited to join us. He greeted me in the traditional way of shaking my hand, then kissing his own before placing it on his heart. I could tell that he was intrigued when I told him about my Yemeni roots between Aden and Sana'a. I thought he might be nervous about speaking Arabic and left it at that.

Warda's uncles and other family members left for Israel as part of the early post-1948 waves, but she stayed behind, largely because her mother lacked agency to make the travel arrangements and because successive Yemeni governments blocked and relaxed their exit, depending on political whims. When it was Warda's turn to leave with her husband and most of her children, they had to go through London because they were instructed by the Jewish Agency, which arranged their exodus, to tell their friends and neighbours that their final destination was the United States and not Israel. Her first two daughters, both married, stayed behind for personal reasons and joined the extended family within a year.

Warda seems vague on the decisions and negotiations leading up to her departure. The Jewish Agency arranged a flight from Sana'a to London, where the family was put up in a hotel for one night before catching the next flight from Heathrow to Ben Gurion. She remembers the egg breakfast (*shakshuka*) and the weak English coffee. "Not like mine from Yemen." The agent who accompanied them to the airport in London left them after checking their luggage and instructed them not to take anything from anyone while waiting for their flight. She was "scared and shocked," but once their flight was called and ready for takeoff, everything felt right.

They were welcomed in Tel Aviv by a relative, which helped because they didn't speak Hebrew or English—just Arabic and an old form of Yemenite Hebrew, referred to as Judeo-Yemeni Arabic. (Even my friend Ayelet struggled with it when translating for me.) Although the family eventually learned modern Hebrew, Warda would periodically lapse into the old tongue in the middle of our conversations. In Yemen they spoke Arabic with their neighbours, but what Warda refers to as her "holy language" remained alive in her despite disuse. She knew she would return to it one day.

The first years in Israel were particularly difficult. Warda thought she was too old to learn a new language, and she worried about her two daughters, her mother and one sibling, all of whom stayed behind in Yemen until the next airlift operation. In her excitement while packing, she left behind some kitchen tools that she couldn't replace in Tel Aviv. She also believes some family holy books may have been stolen from her soon after she arrived in Tel Aviv. It was the first of several disappointments. "I also thought when I get to Israel, I'd have diamonds on the street," Warda says, channelling a Yemeni equivalent of the old adage about streets paved with gold. Instead, some of her children had to work to keep the family afloat.

Isolated moments of joy helped ease that rough landing. Ofra Haza, the late Israeli singer, also of Yemeni origin, welcomed families like Warda's with a concert. "It was a beautiful evening," Warda gushes. "Even three weddings wouldn't have been as good." She did remember to pack precious silver coins for each of her daughters. They in turn made necklaces of the coins and wore them on their wedding days. Once the rest of her family joined her in Tel Aviv, Warda settled in and never looked back. As long as her children are with her, she says she misses "nothing" about her old life in Yemen. "I sometimes think about it," she says, when I ask her about her views on the current war. "We had a good life. I was happy. But now there's no way I would go back . . . I have no longing for there."

At that point in our chat, one of Warda's daughters drops by with her son. Esma—a Yemeni Jewish name that connotes a determination or readiness to leave (an allusion for the return to Zion, I'm told)—was the last child to be born in Yemen and left at the age of two. Unlike her mother, she would like to go back and visit. "I tell everyone I was born in Yemen. I'm very proud of it." Esma also inadvertently explains why her father was shut out of my conversation with Warda: he misses Yemen and would love to go back. I get the sense that Warda's commitment to Zionism is so absolute that she sees her husband's return fantasy as a personal attack. "But what he misses doesn't exist anymore," she says. "He misses the way the Jews lived there. He doesn't like the way people here are secular. He would go back. Not to the Yemen of today but to the Yemen the way it was." I recognize myself in the father's return dream. Return may be about a physical relocation to an old place, but it unfolds in the mind and in that indefinable longing for former lives and bygone times.

From her experience, Ayelet says that many Yemeni Jews have an idealistic dream of what their return to Israel should look like. How can any place live up to centuries of believing in a Promised Land? For Warda's husband to even contemplate a return to Yemen is a betrayal of this idea, a rejection of such a mythologized place. I know he's twenty years older than Warda, so I calculate he's in his late eighties. Perhaps he's thinking of his final resting place; maybe he wants to be buried in the land where he was born and raised. I regret not asking him about the place of Yemen in his mind, but I also know that Warda would have been mad at me for pursuing a line of questioning she might have found offensive. As much as their place felt like home, I was a guest, welcomed as a man from the homeland of Yemen and not as an inquisitive writer from Canada.

Homeland affinities matter.

CODA

When I returned to Toronto after my trip to Israel and Egypt, I'd often show friends photos that Ayelet and I took with my phone on the veranda of Warda's house. I did so out of context and without explaining who was who. All my friends assumed the people in the pictures were the Cairo branch of my family. They could spot the physical resemblance right away, they said. I didn't have a theory about the nature of kinship to prove or a message about Arab–Israeli harmony to preach, but I took pleasure in setting them right. Ayelet and Esma could easily pass for my sisters, and Warda for my mother twenty years ago.

What I saw in the pictures transcended physical similarities, though. The poses, the way we looked at the camera, with a certain self-awareness, with longing and weary smiles—they all betrayed our search for homelands, lost, found or still elusive.

Warda found her ancestral home in Israel by leaving her

birthplace. Esma longed to revisit hers in Sana'a, a place she'd love to call home again one day. Ayelet had returned to Tel Aviv less than a year before my visit, in what started as a few months away from Toronto in the winter and might become a more permanent arrangement. And there I was, smiling for the camera but wondering if my obsession with other people's returns will lead to one of my own. As if return is a life skill I hope to pick up from them. If I hear their stories and ask them questions, do I get to join them?

A year after that trip, it dawned on me: that terraced house in a mostly working-class suburb in central Israel was the closest I got to Yemen in a journey that took me from Northern Ireland to Jamaica, Spain to Ghana, Taiwan to Israel and the West Bank, with a stop in Egypt along the way. Ayelet tells me that recent Jewish returnees from Yemen and East Africa are often settled in the same neighbourhood as they begin life in their "new" homeland. With hindsight, the thought of my quest and theirs overlapping for even one afternoon brings me comfort.

And some trepidation.

When I held Esma's son in my arms, Warda asked me how many children I had back in Canada. I dodged the question with an old Arabic proverb about how some things weren't meant to be—*mafish naseeb*. I had not forgotten that my sexuality would get in the way of the return scenario I had been scribbling in my head for years. I hadn't prepared myself for it enough. Even in Aden, where traces of cosmopolitan life have lingered long after British rule came to an end in 1967, a childless single man in his fifties would draw unwelcome attention. Warda's question pre-

viewed the conversations I could expect when I return. It forced
me to rethink how best to reconcile my own expectations of a
free and honest life with Yemen's view of the family unit as the
cornerstone of what the home and the homeland represent.

I had to shelve my plans to go back to Aden and Sana'a in
the spring and summer of 2020, when the coronavirus not only
made travel difficult but also spread unchecked through Yemen.
Until then, I'd thought I could sidestep the worst of the war
and fly to Aden, but by late summer, I realized that such a plan
would be reckless. Deaths from COVID in Yemen were five
times the global average, and the mortality rate of 27 percent
was one of the highest in the world. Inconsistency in testing and
reporting cases suggested that these dismal figures were likely
an understatement. Add in the crumbling healthcare system and
you have the makings of a disaster within a disaster. A vaccine
program for healthcare workers and priority groups began in
the spring of 2021 with an initial delivery of 360,000 doses out
of a promised 1.9 million this year. (Yemen's population is close
to 30 million.)

The world may have come to a standstill in 2020 and again
in 2021, as lockdowns, like the virus itself, mutated and became
more severe during the pandemic's second and third waves,
but my resolve to return has only gained momentum. Earlier
in the book, I wrote that returns exhibit rational and irrational
sides (or at the very least are emotionally convoluted). My new
resolve has something to do with thinking more seriously about
end-of-life matters as the numbers of cases and deaths climb in
Toronto and Canada. More likely, the longing has graduated to

an obsession, taking over how I think about and budget for my future. The more I look into academic studies of return, the less academic the matter becomes.

Delaying return will buy me more time to stem the tide of my first language loss. I vacillate between thinking that regaining my command of Arabic can still happen and accepting that my relationship with it is irreparable. I impress myself by watching an Egyptian contemporary drama on Netflix and absorbing 90 percent of it without turning on the subtitles. For period dramas, my absorption rate is closer to 60 percent, given the classical Arabic and the complex grammar in the dialogue. Then I dare to read a book in Arabic and feel discouraged after only a few pages. While the reading part is hard, writing in Arabic remains my biggest challenge. It took me more than three decades to unlearn Arabic, so perhaps I shouldn't be surprised that regaining it will require more time and effort than I'd anticipated.

In this pandemic life, time is on my side.

Living through one lockdown after another gave me the luxury of playing back the conversations I had with the many people I met on my travels to see which of their return stories I'd like to replicate. I dream of the peace and tranquility of José Ramón's life as a retiree in the Basque Country after decades in the United States. But it's too static for me. I applaud the purpose-driven life of Steve, who left California to start a new business in his hometown of Belfast. But there's something too messianic for my liking in his version of city-building around technology. I admire the courage and resilience of Jen in Taipei, who forged a new life for herself in her birthplace despite decades away, struggles with language and one emotional setback after another. But will I show the same fortitude? I have respect for Mohanad in Bethlehem and Eden in Modi'in for connecting their homeland return stories to larger narratives about the future of Palestinians or the survival of Israel. But without narrowing the gap between their stories and their political aspirations, I don't see how these versions of return can continue without more suffering and violence. I envy Kwame's serenity and rebirth as a Black man in Ghana. I don't share his history, but I love his optimism and how his return story is part of a self-fulfilling prophecy. At sixty-three, he's closer to my age than I am to Mohanad's or Eden's.

They've all influenced how I think about returns, and I plan to borrow threads from their stories to stitch my own. Just as I intend to borrow the key to the mountain house in Aden from my siblings and make my way there. When? I don't know just yet. For how long? Too soon to say. A few months, a few years or until the end of my days.

I realize that my longing for Aden may be not a new act but the start of a final one. Beginnings and endings overlap when we go back to where we come from. I'm open to all the possibilities, contradictions and mixed blessings of return.

ACKNOWLEDGEMENTS

My thanks and gratitude to the incredible people who shared their return stories, joys and heartbreaks with me. I'm grateful that you opened your homes and your workplaces to me, and responded to my questions (and pestering) with grace and generosity. I couldn't include them all in this book, but it was an honour to listen to and reflect on each one.

Jim Gifford, my editor at HarperCollins Canada, has stood by me and supported my writing over three books now. I love, and have learned so much from, his calm, insightful editorial voice. I can't thank him enough. My agent, John Pearce, championed this book from an idea to a proposal to a manuscript, and he will continue to do so after publication. His comments and encouragement kept me going, especially in the final stages of writing. Gratitude and respect to Janice Weaver, my copyeditor, whose handling of the manuscript was a masterclass in rigour and patience with, well, let's just call it my idiosyncratic writing. I'm fortunate to lean on the support of the wonderful team at HarperCollins Canada, including Noelle Zitzer, Lisa Rundle, Jennifer Lambert, Michael Millar and Iris Tupholme.

My dear friend Laurie Lynd, film and TV director extraordinaire, read an early draft and provided feedback and some great ideas that made their way into the final book. Thanks go to the lovely Shane Smith for supporting my work and being part of my Toronto family. Speaking of family, my love and gratitude to Suanne Kelman and Allan Fox for making me part of theirs. My friend Liz Millward in Winnipeg has been and will continue to be my inspiration.

For the Basque chapter, I'm indebted to Guillermo Barrutieta Anduiza for guiding me through his beautiful country's landscape and politics. Thanks for suggesting names and opening doors, Guillermo. The Jamaica trip and chapter couldn't have happened without the support of Rachel Manley and the generosity and hospitality of Julie Meeks. Thanks also to Ashante Infantry for sharing her knowledge of the island. In Northern Ireland, thanks to everyone at the Belfast Homecoming Conference for making me feel welcome, and to Brendan J. Byrne for additional contacts. In Taiwan, I'm indebted to Adam Chen and his extraordinary circle of friends. My dear friend Mike Vokins in Taipei made a city I already love feel like home. In Ghana, my thanks go to Nana Aba Duncan and Sunshine Duncan, two generous and powerhouse sisters who helped me identify people to talk to before and after landing in Accra. For the chapter set in Israel, I'm indebted to the wonderfully talented Ayelet Tsabari for conversations and suggestions—and a homemade meal with Noa and Sean. Thanks also to Bob and Melanie Sagman and Ruty Korotaiev in Toronto, Daniela Birman and Jonathan Hadad in Tel Aviv, and my dear friend Michael Bruck in Hong Kong. For the West Bank, I'm grateful to Jehad Aliweiwi in Toronto and his family in Hebron, especially Mo'ammer and As'ad.

Reporting for the Northern Ireland and Basque chapters was, in part, completed with the support of a research grant from Ryerson University's Faculty of Communication & Design. Thanks to Dean Charles Falzon and Associate Dean Charles Davis for their continuous support.

Finally, this book, like the previous two, is a tribute to the unconditional love and resilience of my family in Sana'a, Aden and Cairo. When I think return, I think of them. When I write homeland, I mean them.

NOTES

In these notes, I reference books, reports, peer-review research and major news and feature stories that are quoted directly in the text or have informed my thinking on issues covered in this book. The notes are by no means exhaustive and omit heavily reported news items or basic facts that are one database or Google search away.

Introduction The Language of Home

On belonging, see Adrienne Clarkson, *Belonging: The Paradox of Citizenship* (Toronto: Anansi, 2014).

For more on the Great Replacement theory, see Thomas Chatterton Williams's "The French Origins of 'You Will Not Replace Us'" in the December 4, 2017, issue of the *New Yorker*, https://www.newyorker.com/magazine/2017/12/04/the-french-origins-of-you-will-not-replace-us.

The death toll from Yemen's war is contested among the different factions, but the figures I use in this book rely on a December 2020 estimate by the United Nations Office for the Coordination of Humanitarian Affairs (OCHA), accessible online at https://gho.unocha.org/yemen.

For more on the narrative tropes and metaphors of certain South Asian fiction, see Naben Ruthnum, *Curry: Eating, Reading, and Race* (Toronto: Coach House, 2017).

On language as home, see Jessica J. Lee, *Two Trees Make a Forest: In Search of My Family's Past Among Taiwan's Mountains and Coasts* (Toronto: Hamish Hamilton, 2020).

There have been several studies on the loss of first languages, but I found the following two most helpful: Herbert W. Seliger and Robert M. Vago, eds., *First Language Attrition* (Cambridge: Cambridge University Press, 1991), and Monika S. Schmid and Barbara Köpke, eds., *The Oxford Handbook of Language Attrition* (Oxford: University of Oxford, 2019).

Stuart Hall's quote comes from his essay "Cultural Identity and Diaspora," first published in the journal *Framework* and reprinted in Jonathan Rutherford, ed., *Identity: Community, Culture and Difference* (London: Lawrence Wishart, 2003).

CHAPTER 1 The Age of Return. Maybe

The repatriation of Canadians abroad was covered extensively by the media in this country. Quotes in the text are from articles on the CBC website and in the *Toronto Star*, including Kathleen Harris, "Government Has Helped Bring Home 20,000 Canadians," CBC News, April 22, 2020, https://www.cbc.ca/news/politics/stranded-canadians-abroad-foreign-affairs-1.5541682, and Nicholas Keung, "Justin Trudeau Called Canadians Home," *Toronto Star*, March 23, 2020, https://www.thestar.com/news/canada/2020/03/23/justin-trudeau-called-canadians-home-and-theyre-coming-by-the-hundreds-of-thousands.html.

For more on India's Shramik Specials and the spread of the virus among workers aboard these trains, see Jeffrey Gettleman, Suhasini Raj, Sameer Yasir and Karan Deep Singh, "The Virus Trains: How Lockdown Chaos Spread Covid-19 Across India," *New York Times*, December 15, 2020, https://www.nytimes.com/2020/12/15/world/asia/india-coronavirus-shramik-specials.html.

Elif Shafak discusses motherlands and multiple belongings in a short book titled *How to Stay Sane in an Age of Division* (not available in Canada at the time of writing). The quotes given are from "Elif Shafak on What It Means to Belong in Many Places at Once," *Literary Hub*, October 9, 2020, https://lithub.com/elif-shafak-on-what-it-means-to-belong-in-many-places-at-once/.

For return as part of forming a diaspora community, see the revised edition of Robin Cohen, *Global Diasporas: An Introduction*, 2nd ed. (New York: Routledge, 2008).

For the discussion on the evolution of return as a subject of academic interest and other definitions of the return movement within migration studies, the two most informative anthologies are Fran Markowitz and Anders H. Stefansson, eds., *Homecomings: Unsettling Paths of Return* (Lanham, MD: Lexington Books, 2004), and Marianne Hirsch and Nancy K. Miller, eds., *Rites of Return: Diaspora Poetics and the Politics of Memory* (New York: Columbia University Press, 2011). The quote from Russell King appears in *Homecomings*.

For more on the intersection of race and science, see Angela Saini, *Superior: The Return of Race Science* (Boston: Beacon Press, 2019). The analysis of posts on the Stormfront forum appears in Aaron Panofsky and Joan Donovan, "Genetic Ancestry Testing Among White Nationalists: From Identity Repair to Citizen Science," *Social Studies of Science* 49, no. 5 (July 2, 2019), https://journals.sagepub.com/doi/full/10.1177/0306312719861434.

For information on natal homing in marine animals and the return journey of salmon, see the US Geological Survey at https://www.usgs.gov/ centers/wfrc/science/questions-and-answers-about-salmon?qt-science_ center_objects=0#qt-science_center_objects and the website for Vancouver Island, BC, at http://vancouverisland.com/things-to-do-and-see/ wildlife-viewing/pacific-salmon-spawning/.

For the return of artifacts from European and American museums, see Alice Procter, *The Whole Picture: The Colonial Story of the Art in Our Museums & Why We Need to Talk About It* (London: Cassell, 2020). See also Tristam Hunt, "Should Museums Return Their Colonial Artefacts?" *Guardian*, June 29, 2019, https://www.theguardian.com/culture/2019/ jun/29/should-museums-return-their-colonial-artefacts, and Tarisai Ngangura, "The Colonized World Wants Its Artifacts Back," *Vice*, December 7, 2020, https://www.vice.com/en/article/5dpd9x/the-colonized-world-wants-its-artifacts-back-from-museums-v27n4.

For the colonial history of Egyptology, see Toby Wilkinson, *A World Beneath the Sands: The Golden Age of Egyptology* (New York: W.W. Norton, 2020).

Chapter 2 The Basque Country: A Homeland for the Basques. A Homeland for Everyone?

On the differences between the Basque people in Spain and France, see Jan Mansvelt Beck, *Territory and Terror: Conflicting Nationalisms in the Basque Country* (New York: Routledge, 2005).

For a popular (and affectionate) but detailed introduction to the history and mythology of the Basque region, see Paddy Woodworth, *The Basque Country: A Cultural History* (Oxford: Signal Books, 2007).

For the genome study from Uppsala University, see Torsten Günther et al., "Ancient Genomes Link Early Farmers from Atapuerca in Spain to

Modern-Day Basques," *Proceedings of the National Academy of Sciences of the United States of America* 112, no. 38 (September 8, 2015), https://www.pnas.org/content/112/38/11917.

On the significance of language in shaping the Basque identity, I recommend Jacqueline Urla, *Reclaiming Basque: Language, Nation, and Cultural Activism* (Reno: University of Nevada Press, 2012). See also Richard Gillespie and Caroline Gray, eds., *Contesting Spain? The Dynamics of Nationalist Movements in Catalonia and the Basque Country* (New York: Routledge, 2015).

In understanding the history of ETA and its campaign of terror, I relied on the above-named sources, as well as Imanol Murua, *Ending ETA's Armed Campaign: How and Why the Basque Armed Group Abandoned Violence* (New York: Routledge, 2017). See also Raphael Tsavkko Garcia, "After ETA, the Dream of a Basque State Lives On," *World Politics Review*, July 17, 2018, https://www.worldpoliticsreview.com/insights/25106/after-eta-the-basque-separatist-dream-lives-on.

For the role of the Euskal Etxea in maintaining ethnic ties to the Basque region, see Gloria Pilar Totoricagüena, *Identity, Culture, and Politics in the Basque Diaspora* (Reno: University of Nevada Press, 2004).

To read the opinion piece I shared with Aitzbea on Maduro's handling of the situation in Venezuela, see Javier Corrales, "The Venezuelan Crisis Is Part of Maduro's Plan," *New York Times*, September 25, 2018, https://www.nytimes.com/2018/09/25/opinion/-crisis-venezuela-maduro.html.

For more on the architecture and cultural effect of the Guggenheim Museum, see Rowan Moore, "The Bilbao Effect: How Frank Gehry's Guggenheim Started a Global Craze," *Guardian*, October 1, 2017, https://www.theguardian.com/artanddesign/2017/oct/01/bilbao-effect-frank-gehry-guggenheim-global-craze.

For Santiago Abascal's use of his personal Instagram account in fostering his image as a nationalist, see Agnese Sampietro and Sebastián Sánchez-Castillo, "Building a Political Image on Instagram: A Study of the Personal Profile of Santiago Abascal (Vox) in 2018," *Communication & Society* 33, no. 1 (January 2020), https://revistas.unav.edu/index.php/communication-and-society/article/view/37241.

Chapter 3 Jamaica: Come from Foreign

For an analysis of the number of British, American and Canadian returnees killed in Jamaica between 2012 and 2018, see Diane Taylor and Josh Halliday, "UK Relatives of Murdered Jamaica Returnees Fight for Justice," *Guardian*, July 10, 2018, https://www.theguardian.com/world/2018/jul/10/uk-relatives-of-murdered-jamaica-returnees-fight-for-justice.

For the language of the Jamaica Independence Act 1962, see https://www.legislation.gov.uk/ukpga/Eliz2/10-11/40/introduction.

On the political origins of Jamaica's gang wars, see the report by Glaister Leslie, *Confronting the Don: The Political Economy of Gang Violence in Jamaica*, September 2010, https://www.jstor.org/stable/resrep10745. Further information can be found at https://www.insightcrime.org/tag/jamaica/.

For a more accurate estimate of homicides committed by deportees in Jamaica, see Zagros Madjd-Sadjadi and Dillon Alleyne, "The Potential Jamaican Impact of Criminal Deportees from the U.S.," *Journal of Ethnicity in Criminal Justice* 5, no. 2–3 (2007), https://www.tandfonline.com/doi/abs/10.1300/J222v05n02_02.

The Windrush scandal has been covered extensively by British and international news outlets, but the dedicated portal on the *Guardian* remains unparalleled, https://www.theguardian.com/uk-news/windrush-scandal.

For information on work programs in the United States for Jamaican citizens, see Cindy Hahamovitch, *No Man's Land: Jamaican Guestwork-*

ers in America and the Global History of Deportable Labor (Princeton and Oxford: Princeton University Press, 2011).

For the UK government's official guide to living and working in Jamaica, see https://www.gov.uk/world/jamaica. For coverage of the guide's recommendation to deportees, see Kevin Rawlinson, "British Residents Deported to Jamaica Told to 'Put on Accent,'" *Guardian*, April 17, 2018, https://www.theguardian.com/uk-news/2018/apr/17/outrage-over-guide-for-british-residents-being-deported-to-jamaica, and Jasmin Gray, "Fury over Government Guide That Tells Deportees to Put on Jamaican Accent," *Huffington Post*, April 17, 2018, https://www.huffingtonpost.co.uk/entry/government-guide-jamaica-deportation_uk_5ad4a8b1e4b016a07e9ecaae.

For a detailed look at the operations of Open Arms, see Luke de Noronha, *Deporting Black Britons: Portraits of Deportation to Jamaica* (Manchester: Manchester University Press, 2020).

Chapter 4 There's No Business Like Return Business

For the return of expats to New Zealand during the pandemic, see Duncan Greive, "The 'Staggering' Potential of New Zealand's Returning Diaspora," *New Zealand Herald*, August 30, 2020, https://www.nzherald.co.nz/business/the-staggering-potential-of-new-zealands-returning-diaspora/3EFJZQLU7M4AYXBJUYQHTLFKJE/. See also Natasha Frost, "New Zealand's 'Brain Gain' Boost," BBC Worklife, September 6, 2020, https://www.bbc.com/worklife/article/20200827-new-zealands-brain-gain-boost.

For Taiwan's COVID-fuelled return migration, see Amy Qin and Amy Chang Chien, "Covid? What Covid? Taiwan Thrives as a Bubble of Normality," *New York Times*, March 13, 2021, https://www.nytimes.com/2021/03/13/world/asia/taiwan-covid.html.

For more on the number and potential influence of Canadian expats, see John Stackhouse, *Planet Canada: How Our Expats Are Shaping Our Future* (Toronto: Random House, 2020).

For challenges in measuring the economic benefits of return migration, see Jackline Wahba, "Who Benefits from Return Migration to Developing Countries?" *IZA World of Labor*, February 2015, https://wol.iza.org/uploads/articles/123/pdfs/who-benefits-from-return-migration-to-developing-countries.pdf, and "Return Migration and Economic Development" in Robert E.B. Lucas, ed., *International Handbook on Migration and Economic Development* (Cheltenham, UK: Edward Elgar Publishing, 2014).

For the transnational ties of return migrants, see Giulia Sinatti, "Return Migration, Entrepreneurship and Development: Contrasting the Economic Growth Perspective of Senegal's Diaspora Policy through a Migrant-Centred Approach," *African Studies* 78, no. 4 (2019), https://www.tandfonline.com/doi/full/10.1080/00020184.2018.1555310.

On engagement with the diaspora on the governmental level, see Oleg Chirita, "Diaspora Engagement: An Unfinished Business," International Centre for Migration Policy Development, October 11, 2019, https://www.icmpd.org/news-centre/news-detail/expert-voice-diaspora-engagement-an-unfinished-business/.

On balancing the needs of homelands with the skill set of return migrants, see the workshop "Enhancing the Role of Return Migration," International Organization for Migration, 2008, https://www.iom.int/jahia/webdav/shared/shared/mainsite/microsites/IDM/workshops/return_migration_development_070708/enhancing_benefits_return_migration.pdf. See also Dovelyn Rannveig Agunias and Kathleen Newland, *Developing a Road Map for Engaging Diasporas in Development: A Handbook for Policymakers and Practitioners in Home and Host Countries* (Geneva and Washington: International Organization for Migration and Migration Policy Institute, 2012).

For more on recruiting African executives, see https://homecoming revolution.com. See also the report "Brain Gain: Skilled Diaspora Return to Africa," *Polity*, September 17, 2010, https://www.polity.org.za/ print-version/brain-gain-skilled-diaspora-return-to-africa-2010-09-17, as well as Dilip Ratha and Sonia Plaza, "Harnessing Diasporas: Africa Can Tap Some of Its Millions of Emigrants to Help Development Efforts," International Monetary Fund, Finance & Development, September 2011, https://www.imf.org/external/pubs/ft/fandd/2011/09/pdf/ratha.pdf.

For the management of return in the EU, see Anna Triandafyllidou and Alexandra Ricard-Guay, "Governing Irregular and Return Migration in the 2020s: European Challenges and Asian Pacific Perspectives," *Journal of Immigrant & Refugee Studies* 17, no. 2 (2019), https://www.tandfonline. com/doi/full/10.1080/15562948.2018.1503383?src=recsys.

The information about the number of students studying abroad and the percentage of returnees among them is derived from figures released by the Chinese Ministry of Education and reported in *China Daily* and other media outlets.

On the economic case for the China–Taiwan relationship, see Jean-Marc F. Blanchard and Dennis V. Hickey, eds., *New Thinking About the Taiwan Issue: Theoretical Insights into Its Origins, Dynamics, and Prospects* (New York: Routledge, 2012).

For rural reverse migration in China, see Coco Liu, "Returning Migrants: The Chinese Economy's Next Great Hope?" *South China Morning Post*, March 18, 2018, https://www.scmp.com/week-asia/business/ article/2137034/returning-migrants-chinese-economys-next-great-hope.

On China's talent programs and the role of the return migration of its highly skilled diaspora, see Huiyao Wang, "China's Return Migration and Its Impact on Home Development," United Nations Department of Global Communications, *UN Chronicle*, October 1, 2013, https://www.

un.org/en/chronicle/article/chinas-return-migration-and-its-impact-home-development.

For the impact of non-resident Indians on the homeland economy, see "India Calling: NRI Entrepreneurs Flocking Back to Homeland," *Franchise India*, January 21, 2015, https://www.franchiseindia.com/entrepreneur/article/starting-up/business-opportunity/India-calling-NRI-entrepreneurs-flocking-back-to-homeland-574, and Archana Rai, "Thriving Economy Lures NRIs Back to India," *Economic Times*, May 3, 2011, https://m.economictimes.com/nri/returning-to-india/thriving-economy-lures-nris-back-to-india/articleshow/8112599.cms?from=desktop.

CHAPTER 5 Northern Ireland: Call My Brother Back

For the history of the Troubles in Northern Ireland, I drew heavily on David McKittrick and David McVea, *Making Sense of the Troubles: A History of the Northern Ireland Conflict* (London: Viking, 2012), and Marc Mulholland, *Northern Ireland: A Very Short Introduction* (Oxford: Oxford University Press, 2003). Additional sources include Patrick Radden Keefe, *Say Nothing: A True Story of Murder and Memory in Northern Ireland* (New York: Doubleday, 2019), and Alan Cowell, "50 Years Later, Troubles Still Cast 'Huge Shadow' Over Northern Ireland," *New York Times*, October 4, 2018, https://www.nytimes.com/2018/10/04/world/europe/northern-ireland-troubles.html.

For the effects of the financial crisis on the Republic of Ireland's economy, see Fintan O'Toole, *Ship of Fools: How Stupidity and Corruption Sank the Celtic Tiger* (London: Faber and Faber, 2009).

On the origins of the Homecoming Conference, see Máirtín Ó Muilleoir, "Calling all Americans: A Homecoming to Belfast," *Irish Central*, September 6, 2017, https://www.irishcentral.com/news/community/calling-all-americans-a-homecoming-to-belfast.

For more on the operations of Northern Irish Connections and the stories highlighted on its website, see https://www.niconnections.com. The information on charitable contributions in Northern Ireland is drawn from data collected by the Northern Ireland Council for Voluntary Action, https://www.nicva.org/stateofthesector/giving.

CHAPTER 6 Taiwan: The ABCs of Return

On how China and Taiwan view national identity, see Lowell Dittmer, ed., *Taiwan and China: Fitful Embrace* (Oakland: University of California Press, 2017).

Xi Jinping's speech in Singapore was reported by several media outlets. See, for example, Neil Connor, "'No Force Can Pull Us Apart': China's Xi Says in Historic China-Taiwan Summit," *Daily Telegraph*, November 7, 2015, https://www.telegraph.co.uk/news/worldnews/asia/china/11981225/No-force-can-pull-us-apart-Chinas-Xi-says-in-historic-China-Taiwan-summit.html.

For the history of Taiwan, especially its relationship with China and the United States, I relied on multiple sources. These included a backgrounder by Eleanor Albert, "China–Taiwan Relations," Council on Foreign Relations, January 22, 2020, https://www.cfr.org/backgrounder/china-taiwan-relations; a report by Richard N. Haass, "The Looming Taiwan Crisis," Council on Foreign Relations, February 15, 2019, https://www.cfr.org/article/looming-taiwan-crisis; Denny Roy, *Taiwan: A Political History* (Ithaca, NY: Cornell University Press, 2003); and the aforementioned Blanchard and Hickey, *New Thinking About the Taiwan Issue*.

On return migration to China and Taiwan, see Robyn Iredale, Fei Guo, Santi Rozario, eds., *Return Migration in the Asia Pacific* (Cheltenham, UK: Edward Elgar Publishing, 2003).

For a detailed narrative of one author's return to her ancestral homeland of Taiwan, see Jessica J. Lee's *Two Trees Make a Forest*, cited in the introduction.

For more information on the Study Tour Program for Overseas Youth (the so-called love boat program), see the Overseas Community Affairs Council, Republic of China, https://www.ocac.gov.tw/OCAC/Eng/Pages/List.aspx?nodeid=4280.

For a window into the personal experiences of Asians and other people of colour as teachers of English in Taiwan, see Lianne Lin, "Reverse Racism in Taiwan," *8Asians*, October 23, 2013, https://www.8asians.com/2013/10/23/reverse-racism-in-taiwan/, and Brian Hioe, "Outrage Following Discrimination Against Non-White English Teachers at Kindergarten," *New Bloom: Radical Perspectives on Taiwan and the Asia Pacific*, June 23, 2018, https://newbloommag.net/2018/06/23/kang-chiao-racism/.

Chapter 7 Ancestral Homelands

For Larry Mitchell's GoFundMe campaign, see Cleve R. Wootson, Jr., "'Go Back to Africa'? This Man Will—If Racists Pay His Way," *Washington Post*, July 19, 2016, https://www.washingtonpost.com/news/morning-mix/wp/2016/07/19/go-back-to-africa-this-man-will-if-racists-pays-his-way/. See also BBC Trending, "'Send Me Back to Africa': A Unique Response to Racism," BBC News, https://www.bbc.com/news/blogs-trending-36845948.

On Paul Cuffee, see Henry Louis Gates, Jr., "Who Led the First Back-to-Africa Effort?" PBS, n.d., https://www.pbs.org/wnet/african-americans-many-rivers-to-cross/history/who-led-the-1st-back-to-africa-effort/.

For the history of the Back to Africa movement and the American Colonization Society, see Haroon Kharem, "The American Colonization Society," *Counterpoints* 208 (2006), https://www.jstor.org/stable/i40115862; Morgan Robinson, "The American Colonization Society," White House

Historical Association, June 22, 2020, https://www.whitehousehistory.org/ the-american-colonization-society; and Clair MacDougall, "These Abandoned Buildings Are the Last Remnants of Liberia's Founding History," *Smithsonian Magazine*, July/August 2016, https://www.smithsonianmag. com/history/liberia-created-former-slaves-fading-into-history-180959503/.

On the legacy of Marcus Garvey's Universal Negro Improvement Association, see John Henrik Clarke and Amy Jacques Garvey, eds., *Marcus Garvey and the Vision of Africa*, rev. ed. (Baltimore: Black Classic Books, 2011), and Raymond Gavins, *The Cambridge Guide to African American History* (Cambridge: Cambridge University Press, 2016).

On Alex Haley's book, the TV adaptation, and the performance of roots seeking, see the aforementioned Hirsch and Miller, *Rites of Return*.

For the influence of a return to Africa on images of royalty in popular culture, see Takondwa Semphere, "Beyond African Royalty," *Africa Is a Country*, September 25, 2020, https://africasacountry.com/2020/09/ beyond-african-royalty.

For the great reverse migration, see Charles M. Blow, "We Need a Second Great Migration," *New York Times*, January 8, 2021, https:// www.nytimes.com/2021/01/08/opinion/georgia-black-political-power. html, and Alana Semuels, "Reverse Migration Might Turn Georgia Blue," *Atlantic*, May 23, 2018, https://www.theatlantic.com/politics/ archive/2018/05/reverse-migration-might-turn-georgia-blue/560996/.

The most thorough discussions of ethnic return migration, including those of ethnic Germans, appear in Takeyuki Tsuda, ed., *Diasporic Homecomings: Ethnic Return Migration in Comparative Perspective* (Stanford, CA: Stanford University Press, 2009). For more on ethnic German expellees, see Anil Menon, "Postwar Forced Resettlement of Germans Echoes Through the Decades," *The Conversation*, May 7, 2020, https:// theconversation.com/postwar-forced-resettlement-of-germans-echoes-through-the-decades-137219, and Henning Süssner, "Still Yearning for the Lost *Heimat*? Ethnic German Expellees and the Politics of Belonging," *German Politics & Society* 22, no. 2 (Summer 2004), https://www.jstor.org/stable/23740553.

For reports on recent immigrants from France to Quebec, see Fannie Olivier, "The Failures of French Immigration in Quebec: A One-Way Ticket to Problems?" *Wall Street Journal*, August 13, 2007, https://www.wsj.com/articles/SB118680079272894989; Benjamin Shingler, "Montreal's French Invasion: Why Immigrants from France Are Moving In En Masse," *Globe and Mail*, October 14, 2014, https://www.theglobeandmail.com/news/national/montreals-french-invasion-why-immigrants-from-france-are-moving-in-en-masse/article21085397/; and Sarah Treleaven, "In Montreal, French Expats Find Language Doesn't Translate to Community," Bloomberg CityLab, October 23, 2017, https://www.bloomberg.com/news/articles/2017-10-23/montreal-s-influx-of-french-immigrants-brings-new-tensions.

Much has been written about the Arab-Israeli conflict, but for a detailed and balanced overview, see Ian Black, *Enemies and Neighbours: Arabs and Jews in Palestine and Israel, 1917–2017* (London: Penguin Books, 2017). See also the eighth revised edition of Walter Laqueur and Dan Schueftan, eds., *The Israel-Arab Reader: A Documentary History of the Middle East Conflict* (New York: Penguin Books, 2016).

For a report on the legal and historical merits of the Palestinian right of return, see Dahlia Scheindlin, "Neither Intractable nor Unique: A Practical Solution for Palestinian Right of Return," Century Foundation, April 28, 2020, https://tcf.org/content/report/neither-intractable-unique-practical-solution-palestinian-right-return/. See also Adi Schwartz and Einat Wilf, *The War of Return: How Western Indulgence of the Pales-*

tinian Dream Has Obstructed the Path to Peace, trans. Eylon Levy (New York: All Points Books, 2020).

CHAPTER 8 Ghana: The Year of Return

Dionne Brand, *A Map to the Door of No Return: Notes to Belonging* (Toronto: Vintage Canada, 2002).

For general information on the Year of Return, see https://visitghana. com/year-of-return-ghana-2019/.

On visitors, tourism and revenues, see Reality Check Team, "African Diaspora: Did Ghana's Year of Return Attract Foreign Visitors?" BBC News, January 30, 2020, https://www.bbc.com/news/world-africa-51191409, and Heather Greenwood Davis and Starlight Williams, "How Ghana Became the Hottest Destination for African-American Travelers," *National Geographic*, February 14, 2020, https://www.national-geographic.com/travel/destinations/africa/black-americans-are-going-to-west-africa-in-search-of-roots.

For a critique of the Year of Return, see Frederick Dayour and Albert N. Kimbu, "The Problem with Ghana's Year of Return Diaspora Campaign to Boost Tourism," *Quartz (Africa)*, August 8, 2019, https://qz.com/africa/1684130/ghanas-year-of-return-campaign-for-diaspora-tourism/.

For more on the Joseph Project in Ghana, see https://www.africa-ata. org/gh9.htm.

Ivy Prosper's book *Your Essential Guide on Moving to Ghana* is self-published but can be bought in either a paperback or ebook edition from most online book retailers.

For the activities of the African-American Association of Ghana, see https://aaaghana.org.

For Kwame Nkrumah's policies and legacy, see David Birmingham,

Kwame Nkrumah: The Father of African Nationalism (Athens: Ohio University Press, 1998).

For the breakfast club program, see Arielle Milkman, "The Radical Origins of Free Breakfast for Children: How the Black Panther Party and Women's Organizations Fueled American Food Policy," *Eater*, February 16, 2016, https://www.eater.com/2016/2/16/11002842/free-breakfast-schools-black-panthers. See also Ruth Gebreyesus, "'One of the Biggest, Baddest things We Did': Black Panthers' Free Breakfasts, 50 Years On," *Guardian*, October 18, 2019, https://www.theguardian.com/us-news/2019/oct/17/black-panther-party-oakland-free-breakfast-50th-anniversary.

CHAPTER 9 Israel and the Palestinian Territories: Competing Returns

For the language of the Law of Return, see https://www.knesset.gov.il/laws/special/eng/return.htm. Further details come from Martin Gilbert, *Israel: A History* (Toronto: Key Porter, 2008). This is the revised edition of a book first published in 1998.

For some basic information on Birthright Israel, see https://www.birthrightisrael.com/faq, and for Nefesh B'Nefesh, check out https://www.nbn.org.il. More information on the Olive Tree Campaign's Keep Hope Alive initiative can be found at https://www.facebook.com/OliveTreeCampaign/.

There are literally thousands of reports on the supposed deal of the century. The quote in this chapter is from Jeremy Bowen, "Trump's Middle East Peace Plan: 'Deal of the Century' Is Huge Gamble," BBC News, January 29, 2020, https://www.bbc.com/news/world-middle-east-51263815. See also Abeer Alnajjar, "'The Deal of the Century': How Global Media Silenced the Palestinians," Open Democracy, February 20, 2020, https://www.opendemocracy.net/en/north-africa-west-asia/ the-deal-of-the-century-how-global-media-silenced-the-palestinians/.

For a fuller picture of initiatives undertaken and research papers published by BADIL Resource Center, see https://www.badil.org/en.

For the influence of Russian-speaking immigrants on Israeli society, see a report by Lily Galili, "The Other Tribe: Israel's Russian-Speaking Community and How It Is Changing the Country," Brookings Institution, September 21, 2020, https://www.brookings.edu/research/the-other-tribe-israels-russian-speaking-community-and-how-it-is-changing-the-country/.

The numbers of Yemeni Jews who returned to Israel tend to vary among sources, but to me, the most reliable one is the Jewish Virtual Library at https://www.jewishvirtuallibrary.org/jews-of-yemen. See also Kyilah Terry, "Yemeni Identity in Israel," UCLA International Institute, February 1, 2019, https://www.international.ucla.edu/Institute/article/199844.

Coda

Reliable data on COVID in Yemen is hard to come by, given the political instability and the tendency of all sides of the conflict to underplay or suppress numbers. I relied on figures from the WHO, https://www.who.int/emergencies/crises/yem/en/ and UN News, https://news.un.org/en/.

See Mun-Keat Looi, "Covid-19: Deaths in Yemen Are Five Times Global Average as Healthcare Collapses," *BMJ* (*British Medical Journal*), July 27, 2020, https://www.bmj.com/content/370/bmj.m2997. Another source of coronavirus data in Yemen is https://www.worldometers.info/coronavirus/country/yemen/.